D0494863

1088

stamp

ILLUSTRATED HISTORY OF ENGLISH LITERATURE

VOLUME ONE

ILLUSTRATED HISTORY
OF ENGLISH LITERATURE

VOLUME ONE

CHAUCER TO SHAKESPEARE

by

A. C. WARD

ILLUSTRATIONS COLLECTED BY
ELIZABETH WILLIAMS

LONGMANS GREEN AND CO
LONDON . NEW YORK . TORONTO

LONGMANS, GREEN AND CO LTD
6 & 7 CLIFFORD STREET LONDON W I
ALSO AT MELBOURNE AND CAPE TOWN

LONGMANS, GREEN AND CO INC
55 FIFTH AVENUE NEW YORK 3

LONGMANS, GREEN AND CO
215 VICTORIA STREET TORONTO I

ORIENT LONGMANS LTD
BOMBAY CALCUTTA MADRAS

First Published 1953

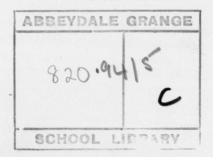
PRINTED IN GREAT BRITAIN BY
SPOTTISWOODE, BALLANTYNE AND CO. LIMITED
LONDON AND COLCHESTER

THE AUTHOR TO THE READER

THE formal needs of literature students are amply met in a wide range of manuals and specialist works. The present volume and the two planned to follow it are designed to provide the general reader with a small-scale survey of the extensive territory of mind and imagination with which English literature has been concerned through the centuries up to 1950.

For the great majority of English readers the literature of their nation begins, still, with Chaucer—a view which, however unhistorical, is understandable when the language difficulties of the earlier writings are taken into account. The first chapter in this book glances at the Anglo-Saxon and early medieval works with the sole intention of recording that other voices preceded Chaucer's. The æsthetic qualities of the poetry and prose of those times can be appreciated only by those who master the dialects, and readers at that stage of linguistic attainment will turn to other books than this.

The standard exhaustive histories of English literature (for example, the long-ago completed Cambridge history and the Oxford history now in progress) fill a dozen or more lengthy volumes and are by many hands. A compact history by a single author, who has the advantage of a consistent vision, must needs be selective if it is to be more than a catalogue. Readers will not find and few will expect to find here mentioned every piece of English literature. But little that is of general interest and high merit is knowingly omitted. I have frankly exposed my own likings and some of my dislikings, for enthusiasm can only be made infectious through the reader's trust in his author's honesty of intention and performance. It is not in my nature to strain after a flat, artificial objectivity; but nor do I consciously grind any partisan axe, though I am unable to assess the degree in which the blood of my ancestors may at times direct me unawares.

If here and there in the following pages a rude cheerfulness

Page

VII ELIZABETHAN PROSE 144

Pamphleteers (Fish, Knox, Marprelate Tracts, Greene)
(146)—Novelists (Lyly, Greene, Lodge, Sidney, Nashe,
Deloney) (153)—Critics and Essayists (Wilson, Puttenham, Gosson, Sidney, Ascham, etc.) (162)—Other
Prose Writings (Painter, Hooker, Hakluyt, etc.) (169)

VIII TUDOR DRAMA 172

Conditions of Performance (173)—The Intermediate
Drama (Heywood, *Gorboduc, Ralph Roister Doister, Gammer
Gurton's Needle*, Preston, Gascoigne, Lyly) (175)—The
Professional Stage (London Theatres, etc.) (184)—
Marlowe and Kyd (186)

IX SHAKESPEARE 195

DESCRIPTIVE NOTES TO THE ILLUSTRA-
TIONS. By Elizabeth Williams 217

INDEX 233

ILLUSTRATIONS

PLATES

1–14	*Between pp.* 16–17
15–23	,, 48–49
24–39	,, 96–97
40–49	,, 128–129
50–62	,, 160–161

Illustrations in the text on pp. 27, 57, 67, 78, 83, 90, 124, 140, 151, 176, 181, 188, 194, 216

INTRODUCTION

THE natural desire of an orderly mind to begin at the beginning is thwarted in the approach to literature by the fact that no beginning is discoverable. We find ourselves in the situation of spectators entering a theatre where the play is already proceeding, neither we nor any others in the audience knowing when it started or what had transpired before we came in.

The earliest surviving English works do show, however, that the poets (for poetry always precedes prose) had behind them a developed æsthetic tradition, an inheritance of skill in the choice and control of words. They are not merely saying something, they are also saying that something in memorable language; and memorable language does not arrange itself haphazardly—it requires an arranger. In short, these early poets, like all their notable successors, were artists.

Since the writing of a brief account of English literature lays upon the writer the task of choosing, as the significant landmarks, comparatively few from among the multitude of works accumulated during some thirteen centuries, it is well to indicate the principles which govern the selection; and that leads back to the primary question, *What is literature?* That is to say, *What is literature in its own nature?* and not in any limited sense as the vehicle of communication of a particular body of information or belief or ideas.

If the history of literature demonstrates one thing above all else, it is that literature, if it is to last, must serve first for delight and not first for any didactic purpose, however important or noble. Countless volumes on religion and politics would have survived in English literature if learning, spiritual fervour, and zeal for reform and general human welfare were enough to give permanent life to books. As it is, however, accepted classics of religion and politics are extremely rare. The innumerable works on these subjects that have perished, perished for want of art; the handful that have survived commend themselves to one generation after another, of the converted and the unconverted alike, through their verbal dexterity and grace—by the quality called literary style which arises from each individual writer's taste and skill as a chooser and arranger of words. There is no other reason for the impressive fact that the writings of one relatively uneducated godly tinsmith have outlasted those of a multitude of godly scholars and learned theologians who were not less passionately devout than John Bunyan.

Although Bunyan was a matchless literary artist, in our present sense as a chooser and arranger of words, it is impossible to suppose him a self-conscious artist juggling words by trial and error into harmonious collocations. However little the modern critical mind may allow to inspiration, Bunyan surely owed everything to divine favour. His least effects compel admiration, and even if we could detect the mechanics behind the effects we could not hold that they result from deliberate contrivance. 'So he passed over, and all the trumpets sounded for him on the other side.' When we examine this moving and tremendous sentence, asking why it moves us and why at a hundredth reading its tremendousness is still unlessened by familiarity, there seems a gross inadequacy in suggesting that it all comes from a particular grouping of broad and deep-toned vowels in harmony with particular consonants; or, even, that it comes from certain spiritual and emotional overtones that pervade *The Pilgrim's Progress* throughout, affecting readers who lack sympathy with Bunyan's evangelical Christianity no less than those who share his convictions.

Bunyan represents almost at its best one of the two main types of English writers: the type in which instinctive artistry and instinctive knowledge predominate. Among such, Shakespeare is supreme. Those who are perplexed by the apparent gulf between Shakespeare's limited schooling and his unlimited knowledge and comprehension fail to take account of the phenomenon which alone makes sense of a great deal of literary history: namely, that every great writer knows far more than he can be taught through the common channels of learning. But for this innate or instinctive knowledge and understanding there could hardly be poets at all, for the whole value of poetry consists in its power to give the world more than the world gives the poet. Only at a time when genius—both the word and all that the word implies—is suspect and out oi favour would so much ingenuity be directed, as in the present century, to attempts to find a pseudo-Shakespeare deemed fit to be the author of *Hamlet* and the other works of Shakespeare himself. Whether or not Francis Bacon had the learning to write them is irrelevant, or relevant only in that the plays if written by Bacon would have displayed a pedantic correctness which in truth they conspicuously and gloriously lack. Bacon and the Earl of Oxford and other assignees of the anti-Shakespearians, even if they could have written the best of Shakespeare, would certainly have scorned and been at pains to avoid the blunders which were a consequence of Shakespeare's deficiencies in formal and academic education. Natural genius, however, sets at naught the finicking nicenesses of pedagogues and peers.

The case of Shakespeare of Stratford and his modern detractors has significance in relation to the history of English literature as a whole. There has been a continuing struggle, since criticism began, between the academic literary lawgivers and the men of genius who create according to the internal law of their own powers. The progress of one such struggle can be observed in the sixteenth-century correspondence between Edmund Spenser and his friend Gabriel Harvey, whose irate passion for classical correctness was fortunately unheeded in practice by the author of *The Faerie Queene*. Criticism may serve as a check on licence and anarchy; but almost of necessity, for it must codify its rules, criticism is bound by the letter, and the free-ranging spirit of the creative artist is rarely understood or approved by formalist critics.

In the twentieth century, when the critical intelligence is disposed to feed upon itself and to become desperately more self-conscious rather than more penetrating or more subtle, the tendency is to reject simple values and to set up complex or contorted ones. This tendency has given a twist to literary criticism and in some measure to literary history also. When far-fetched interpretations are preferred to plain, there is a corresponding desire to resurrect minor 'difficult' writers and to raise them above their proper station. All this is an aspect of fluctuating literary fashion, for fashion operates as much and is almost as fickle in literature as in women's dress, and a proper function of literary history is to hold a steady course amid the cross-currents of fashion, though without overlooking that the special needs of one generation may be best served by

a Spenser or a Tennyson, while those of another are better
satisfied by a Milton or a Donne.

Bunyan and Shakespeare have here been singled out as belonging to the type of instinctive genius that works by innate
ability. But literature also owes much to the complementary
type which operates mainly through acquired knowledge and
conscious artistry. The difference is as that between nature
and culture, between power and contrivance; the difference,
say, between Shakespeare and Congreve, between Bunyan and
Sir Thomas Browne, between Dickens and Henry James.

The effect of Bunyan's '. . . and all the trumpets sounded
for him on the other side' depends upon something imponder-
able, something beyond the mere arrangement of words in a
particular order. A phrase which does depend almost wholly
upon word-order and which might well have been (whether
in fact it was or not) the product of conscious skill in versification rather than of spontaneous composition is Walter de la
Mare's 'Very old are the woods'. There could scarcely be a
plainer instance of how a prose phrase ('the woods are very
old') can become transformed into fine poetry. It is of course
possible to be tone-deaf to poetry as to music, and to find no
difference between 'The woods are very old' and 'Very old
are the woods'; but the sensitive ear [1] will detect that the in-
version (the poetic device of transposition) compels the voice
to give 'very old' a fuller time-value when the words are set
at the beginning of the line: and that the vocal extension in
time supports the notion of antiquity which it is the poet's aim
to suggest by sound. By no other means than sound can he
suggest it, indeed, since the reading eye translates almost in-
stantaneously. Thus, being addressed to the ear, not to the eye,
poetry loses much of its beauty and value unless it is spoken.

Literature was defined as 'the best words in the best order'
in an earlier generation when a select literary vocabulary was
in vogue. The aim of many writers during the second quarter
of the twentieth century, however, was to abolish any distinction
between the vocabulary of literature and the common everyday
vocabulary. No longer therefore, until the fashion changes, are
there best words and other words. Denied a literary language

---

[1] It will be assumed throughout this book that the reader *hears* mentally
all printed words, not only sees them with his eyes.

or a poetic diction—which customarily employs picturesque, colourful, and sometimes pompous and polysyllabic words rarely used in ordinary speech—mid-twentieth-century writers find themselves with either a more difficult æsthetic problem than faced their predecessors or with no problem at all. Either they seek beauty and power in everyday verbal material; or they accept the doctrine that the single purpose of literature is to instruct and to convince—that writing has an immediate practical purpose but no (or only a subsidiary) æsthetic one. As has already been suggested, literary history shows that the exclusively purposive view of literature is fallacious. Theological and political writings die multitudinously, leaving no trace; only those survive which have æsthetic value in addition to their hortatory aim. It is true that certain writers have been great literary artists because a dynamic spiritual or social purpose provided the passionate energy necessary to give power and beauty to their words: but it is also true that most of those continue to be read because they created works of literary art, rather than for any non-æsthetic virtue. John Donne's sermons, Bunyan's writings in general, Burton's *Anatomy of Melancholy*, Burke's essays and speeches are still read because their magnificent prose gives æsthetic pleasure. If that pleasure were not available they would long ago have joined the legion of the forgotten.

The present history of English literature is, therefore, concerned principally with those writings which live as works of literary art, though it also attempts to bring into perspective such lesser works as provided a causeway in the flat lands between one masterpiece and another. We may no longer be impelled to read Lydgate's *Falls of Princes* for pleasure, nor Lyly's *Euphues*, nor Macpherson's *Ossian*, nor Godwin's *Political Justice*, but it would be foolish to overlook them entirely or to ignore their influence upon writers who have greater importance for us. Literature, properly so called, has a long-term value: yet among the men and women who write for their own generation alone are some at least whose words fertilize other men's minds and, through them, live again more potently.

CHAPTER I

UNTIL CHAUCER

Early English Literature

BRITAIN has no ancient indigenous literature, though a few legends were preserved in those western parts of the island where the Celts found refuge from the successive waves of continental invaders, and of these the Arthurian stories have taken an un-shakable hold upon the imagination of English writers down to the present century.

The earliest of the English poems now extant were, in part at least, importations from their north European homelands (Jutland, Schleswig, and Holstein) by those who overran England from the middle of the fifth century A.D. Not until about 660–80 is there any record of a literary work certainly composed in this country—by Cædmon and as described by Bede in the *Historia Ecclesiastica Gentis Anglorum* (Ecclesiastical History of England), completed in 731. Bede tells how Cædmon —until late in life an inarticulate herdsman—was endowed through visionary inspiration with the ability to compose religious verse. He was thereupon taken by the abbess Hilda into the service of the monastery at Whitby, where as a lay brother he 'sang first of the earth's creation and the beginning of man and all the story of Genesis . . . and afterwards about the departure of the people of Israel from the land of Egypt and their entry into the land of promise . . . and about Christ's incarnation and His passion and His ascension . . . and about the coming of the Holy Ghost, and the teaching of the apostles: and again about the day of judgement to come, and about the terror of hell torment, and about the kingdom of heaven'. Except the brief fragment known as *Cædmon's Hymn* (inserted in the original Northumbrian dialect in four manuscripts of Bede's *History*, nothing certainly by Cædmon has been preserved (*see below*, p. 5). But a manuscript once believed to contain Cædmon's works was brought to Milton's notice and is thought to have had some direct influence on *Paradise Lost*.

What remains of early English (Anglo-Saxon) poetry, apart

from a few fragmentary pieces, is preserved in four manuscript books: (1) the *Beowulf* MS. in the British Museum; (2) the Exeter Book in the cathedral library at Exeter, including *Widsith, The Ruin* (possibly referring to the destruction of the city of Bath in A.D. 577), *The Wanderer, The Seafarer,* with other short pieces, and important poems by Cynewulf; (3) the Vercelli Book, acquired by unrecorded means by the Chapter library at Vercelli, northern Italy, where it was discovered in 1833, containing Cynewulf's other poems, besides some sermons in prose; and (4) the formerly called Cædmon MS. in the Bodleian Library at Oxford, containing verse paraphrases of Genesis, Exodus, Daniel, and other poems, all at one time attributed to Cædmon, an attribution now abandoned.

These manuscripts, dating severally from about the tenth to about the twelfth centuries, are translations into the West Saxon dialect of works which were in all probability first put into writing in the dialect of Northumbria (a region comprising the present eastern lowlands of Scotland below the Firth of Forth, and the English counties of Northumberland, Durham, Yorkshire, and Lancashire south of Morecambe Bay to the river Ribble) where a school of poets flourished in the seventh to eighth centuries. But early English poetry, like early poetry elsewhere, was oral in origin, and the poets must be thought of as singers (bards or minstrels) not as scribes. Not until later times did a poet become his own amanuensis or, indeed, regard his verses at all as material to be transmitted by any means other than speech.

While Anglo-Saxon is a language as foreign to the modern English reader as German or Norwegian, it is nevertheless the language from which modern English developed by processes of evolution and adaptation and by absorption of new elements from other tongues, and also by the rejection of native words and forms when these were no longer serviceable. Though the English have been ungrudgingly hospitable to words from other languages, they have always assimilated the alien elements and made them part of their own tongue. Even the Norman Conquest, which established Norman-French for a long time as the language of the Court and the learned professions, became at length a source of enrichment to English instead of its destroyer. The eventual adoption of the East Midland dialect as the national language was due to its use in London, at Court, and in the universities; and, especially, its use by Chaucer cleared the way for its gradually widening acceptance as the standard for literature and cultured speech, whereby it became the immediate ancestor of modern English. It is certainly an academic affectation to declare that Chaucer's English presents little or no difficulty to the common reader to-day, yet it does not baffle him entirely nor make it impossible for him to read, however haltingly, *The Canterbury Tales* unmodernized; and possibly Chaucer could have read *Beowulf* with no greater difficulty than we read Chaucer. The continuity of development in the English language is beyond doubt, and even in recent times when it has been thought desirable to clear modern English speech and writing of prettifying and enfeebling mannerisms, a reinfusion from Anglo-Saxon sources has usually been advised and tried experimentally, as it was by William Morris in the late nineteenth century.

But it is not only the language link which makes it necessary to look back beyond Chaucer for the roots and soil of English literature. English writers have expressed themselves in many moods: in humour, in wit, in irony; in delicacy of manner; in full-blooded boisterous comedy; in exquisite sensibility, intellectual refinement and subtlety. As a persistent undertone, however, there is 'the still, sad music of humanity', the conviction that life is to be endured rather than enjoyed; that there is a dark ever-impending fatefulness to be placated by unremitting self-mortification. This could be summed up in one word as *puritanism*. Puritanism is not a state of soul or attitude of mind first called up by those who named themselves Puritans in the seventeenth century. It is endemic, a dour quality embedded in the English temperament ages back: a quality plainly evident in the earliest English poetry. *Deor's Complaint*, belonging, it is thought, to about the sixth century, rehearses the sorrows which others have endured, reaching in the final stanza the general reflection that

> As a man sits, cut off from pleasure's view,
> It seems to him as though the stretch of ill
> Which lies before him, mounting like a hill,
> Is endless.[1]

[1] From the modern verse rendering in *Anglo-Saxon Poetry* by Gavin Bone (Clarendon Press, Oxford, 1943).

And each of the stanzas ends with a refrain which might
be rendered 'He overcame *that*, so can I *this*', a conclusion
reminiscent of the idea behind Greek tragedy that the contemplation of others' misfortunes can steel us to endure our
own.

In the Anglo-Saxon epic poem, *Beowulf* (*c.* 7th–8th century),
life is hard and difficult indeed, in spite of the feastings which
are common to northern heroic poetry. Beowulf overcomes the
death-dealing monster Grendel, and afterwards dives to a cave
at the bottom of a grim mere where, after great peril, he kills
Grendel's mother also. At length he is himself destroyed in
combat with a poisonous fire-breathing dragon. Deep fatalism
overhangs the whole poem (even though some Christian tone
appears to have been given to the pagan original here and
there by a later monastic transcriber), and its prevailing mood
is condensed by Beowulf's friend Wiglaf into the words 'Death
is better than ignominious life'—a summation virtually identical
with that expressed some twelve or thirteen centuries later
in T. S. Eliot's *The Cocktail Party*, after the story of Celia's
martyrdom has been told.

Anglo-Saxon poetry has therefore more than an antiquarian
interest and importance for modern readers. Among the poetry
with a positive literary quality that of Cynewulf is outstanding.
Who Cynewulf was is unknown, as his name would be also if
he had not 'signed' four poems (*The Ascension of Christ*, *The
Legend of St. Juliana*, *Elene*, and *The Fates of the Apostles*) by in-
corporating in the lines runic characters which make up the
name, while each of these characters is also a word in the text
of the poem.[1] His return for this purpose to the pre-Roman
alphabet and his rich almost Celtically colourful language,
suggest that his pagan ancestry was still in ferment below
the profound Christian temper pervading Cynewulf's writings,
which some scholars would extend beyond the four that bear
his name.

From Anglo-Saxon sources have been inherited certain
characteristic features of English versification which have
assumed a renewed importance in the present century. Much
has been said and written about 'the breakdown of traditional

[1] For the characters and their meanings see Sweet's *Anglo-Saxon Reader*
(Clarendon Press, 11th edn., 1948).

verse-forms' since Whitman in the 1850s found free verse ideally suited to the rhythmic flow of his poetry. Though free verse was to encounter much opposition and derision, by 1950 it had become established as a vehicle well fitted to the purposes of contemporary poets who aimed to bring verse into closer relationship with natural speech. As its name suggests, free verse cannot be defined or analysed with precision; the term embraces all unrhymed verse which eschews regular metre and employs rhythm as the sole controlling factor. Its virtue is in its flexibility. No limit is set to the number of unstressed syllables which a line may be made to carry, except the limits of its rhythmical capacity. Since free verse has no prosodic laws, no written constitution, it is controlled by nothing but the poet's ear and the inner necessity of the poem. This is less anarchic than might appear, for later Shakespearian and Miltonic blank verse departs at will from the metrical norm and assimilates additional unstressed syllables, or has recourse to shortened lines when the nature of the poetry demands, as it were, more elbow room.

The freedom of versification thus gained is, in part at least, a return to Anglo-Saxon practice, which was based upon a line with four stresses but an unspecified and variable number of unstressed syllables. Anglo-Saxon verse, however, except for this valuable flexibility of movement, was in set form. It was alliterated, and each line was divided by a natural voice-pause into two half lines with, usually, two alliterative consonants or vowels beginning the accented words in the first half-line and a third alliterative initial in the second half-line. Here is *Cædmon's Hymn* in (1) the Northumbrian dialect (*c.* late seventh century) and (2) the West Saxon (9th–10th century):

(1) Nū scylun hergan hefænrīcæs Uard,
  Metudæs mæcti end his mōdgidanc,
  uerc uuldurfadur, suē hē uundra gihuæs,
  ēci Dryctin, ōr āstelidæ.
  Hē ærist scōp ælda barnum
  heben til hrōfe, hāleg Scepen.
  Thā middungeard moncynnæs Uard,
  ēci Dryctin, æfter tīadæ
  fīrum foldu, Frēa allmectig.

(2) Nū wē sculan herian   heofonrīces Weard,
Metodes mihte   and his mōdgeþonc,
weorc Wuldorfæder;   swā hē wundra gehwæs,
ēce Dryhten,   ord onstealde.
Hē ǣrest gesceōp   eorðan bearnum
heofon tō hrōfe,   hālig Scyppend;
ðā middangeard,   moncynnes Weard,
ēce Dryhten,   æfter tēode
fīrum foldan,   Frēa ælmihtig.

(Now let us praise the heavenly Guardian, the might of the Maker, the thought of his mind, the works of the Father of glory; how He, the everlasting Lord, established every wonder. He, the holy Creator, first made heaven as a roof for mankind, then made the earth as a floor for them; He, the Lord everlasting, the Almighty God.)

Alliteration (or head-rhyme) has never lost its attraction, though in modern times it has been more misused for facetious or other trivial ends than employed legitimately. Swinburne was fascinated by alliteration and frequently used it with striking poetic effect, as in passages of *Atalanta in Calydon*:

Maiden, and mistress of the months and stars
Now folded in the flowerless fields of heaven . . .

But Swinburne was also aware of his over-fondness for alliteration and parodied himself in *Nephelidia*:

From the depth of the dreamy decline of the dawn
through a notable nimbus of nebulous noonshine,
Pallid and pink as the palm of the flag-flower that
flickers with fear of the flies as they float . . .

The alliterative school of poetry flourished, as has been said, in Northumbria, but the Viking attacks on the north-eastern coast of Britain which began at the end of the eighth century destroyed the great Northumbrian centres of learning and literary culture. The seat of scholarship then passed to Wessex, where King Alfred (849–901) took a leading part in the establishment of a fruitful period of prose-writing and translation, during which a great deal of the northern poetry was rendered into the West Saxon dialect in which it has come down to us in the manuscripts. Alfred caused part of Bede's *Ecclesiastical*

History to be turned from Latin into English, as well as Boethius's *Consolation of Philosophy* (of which Chaucer was subsequently to undertake a new translation into Middle English). Above all, Alfred was responsible for the compilation of *The Anglo-Saxon Chronicle*, the first masterpiece of English prose and the first historical work produced in this country. Continued in later reigns, the *Chronicle* ultimately carried the record down to the middle of the twelfth century.

Meanwhile, Aelfric (tenth to eleventh centuries), whose homilies and other works made him the foremost prose-writer of the age, took some part in the translation of a substantial portion of the Bible. In the same period, which was one of distress due to the turmoil of the Danish invasion and persecutions, patriotic literature found a place among the homilies of Wulfstan, Archbishop of York, who wrote in English (though the MS. in the Bodleian Library has a Latin title, *Sermo Lupi ad Anglos*) a scarifying discourse to convince his countrymen that their powerlessness against the Danish terror was the consequence of their sinfulness and that only through repentance could they hope for succour. This work by Wulfstan could be regarded as an early forerunner of homilies addressed by Frenchmen to the French during the German occupation of their country in the 1940s.

After the Norman Conquest

The Norman Conquest accelerated that flow of French literature into England which had begun a generation before in the reign of Edward the Confessor, whose youthful period of exile in Normandy made him receptive to the Romance literature which, from about A.D. 1100, was to dominate western Europe. It was also to be a source of inspiration to English writers and an important influence in the transition of their language from a medieval to a modern tongue. What are almost the first fruits of the new age appear in Layamon's *Brut*, a largely fictitious 'history' of Britain written mainly in alliterative verse, but diverging frequently into other prosodic forms, including rhymed verse. *Brut* is in fact a curious patchwork of old style and new style, and is of mixed descent, being derived in part from Wace's *Geste des Bretons*, a French translation of the Welsh priest Geoffrey of Monmouth's Latin *Historia Regum Britanniæ*.

Geoffrey, himself drawing from a variety of sources including Nennius (the eighth-century chronicler of the alleged 'historical' King Arthur), was the originator of the romantic cult of Arthur. From the *Historia* Layamon got the Arthur story which is presented for the first time in English in the *Brut*, in which are also (and again in their first English dress) the stories of Lear and Cymbeline.

The *Ormulum*, an inordinately long and tedious poem paraphrasing and commenting on the Gospels and written in the earlier part of the thirteenth century by an Augustinian named Orm or Ormin, is valuable to language students, for the author devised a system of spelling which serves as a guide to contemporary pronunciation. The *Ancren Riwle* (The Anchoresses' Rule, or Guide), written about 1200 for 'three young maidens of gentle birth who had withdrawn from the world to cells by the wall of a church',[1] is charming though not unmixed with intellectual subtlety, and in the excellence of its style, in the original, it is the most distinguished prose work of the period.

> All that I have said concerning the mortification of the flesh is not for you, my dear sisters, who, upon some occasions, suffer more than I could wish, but it is for some one who will give this advice readily enough, who nevertheless handleth herself too softly. Men fence round with thorns young trees, lest beasts should gnaw them while they are tender. Ye are young trees planted in God's orchard. Thorns are the hardships which I have spoken of, and it is necessary for you that ye be fenced around with them, that the beast of hell, when he comes sneaking towards you to bite you, may hurt himself upon the hardness, and slink away from you.[2]

Although the Norman Conquest was but one in a succession of conquests to which the island had been subjected for more than a thousand years, it was a conquest with a difference. To literature it ultimately brought liberation. As we have seen, Anglo-Saxon poetry was dominated by a fatalistic outlook, pagan in origin, which continued to loom darkly even through

[1] See R. W. Chambers: *On the Continuity of English Prose* (Early English Text Society, 1932), p. xcvi.

[2] Part VI 'Of Penance'. From *The Nun's Rule*. Being the Ancren Riwle modernized by James Morton (Chatto, London, 1926). For the original text of this passage see the Early English Text Society edition, 1952, p. 172, ll. 23–33.

superimposed Christian emendations. It was still felt that Death had claims upon Life which were in one way or another stronger than the claims of Life itself. But the coming of the French brought in a sensation of brightness and joy, an abounding delight in pageantry, and a colourful ritual of love. While it is true that this ritual of Courtly Love had its own restraints and semi-religious observances and austerities, it is also true that it was in essence youthful and ardent, however chastened by the formalities of chivalry and the complexities of moral allegory. Its conventional setting entailed much resort to gardens in which flowers gave scent and colour and birds made music, and the actors in this pretty drama were handsomely and often extravagantly costumed. It might be no more than a game of make-believe, but at least it was a game in the sunshine, whereas the only games of which much is heard in Anglo-Saxon poetry are indoor drinking in torchlit halls while gleemen sing of war or of combats to the death against monsters and dragons. The Arthurian stories are battle-haunted also, and there is evil and treachery and horror and death in them; yet the climate and atmosphere are far less dejecting than in *Beowulf*, and over all is the spirit of Christian hope, the ideal of purity of heart, the radiance of the Holy Grail.

Moreover, the Arthurian stories with their many ramifications were only one of several cycles of stories which a French epic poet of the time divided into three categories as 'the matter of France', 'the matter of Britain', and 'the matter of Rome': the first comprising the *Song of Roland* and other less widely reputed French epics; the second, the whole of the Arthurian legends and the 'Breton lays', i.e. stories such as *Sir Orfeo* (Orpheus) and *Sir Launfal*, of Celtic origin or transmission. 'The matter of Rome the Great' embraced all the stories of classical antiquity, including the stories of Troy and Thebes and those associated with Alexander the Great: 'the matter of Rome' gave us Troilus and Cressida and Palamon and Arcite, both used by Chaucer (the latter in *The Knight's Tale*), by Dryden, and in John Fletcher's play *The Two Noble Kinsmen*.

But of all the story material circulating in the thirteenth to fourteenth centuries, the French poetical romance *Le Roman de la Rose* (started romantically by Guillaume de Loris and

completed satirically by Jean de Meung) left the deepest immediate influence on English poetry. The first part, a fragment
of which was afterwards translated by Chaucer, stands as the
pattern for Courtly Love, which imposed upon the lover un-
conditional service to his lady without claim to reward, least
of all the reward of marriage: if he suffered the pangs of
unrequited love he must suffer in secret; he must honour not
only his own beloved but all women; his general conduct
must be above reproach; he must be cleanly in person and
seemly in dress.

Glancing back to the end of the twelfth or the early years
of the thirteenth century, reference must be made to *The Owl
and the Nightingale*, a poem of some 1,800 lines in the debate
form which fascinated the medieval mind. Written, it seems,
either by John of Guildford or by Nicholas of Guildford, the
poem has been variously interpreted in terms of allegory, one
of the most attractive suggestions [1] being that the dour owl
speaks in defence of the established didactic poetry and the
nightingale in commendation of the newer love poetry. But for
the difficulty of the (mainly Surrey) dialect, *The Owl and
Nightingale* would be generally valued as among the finest contemporary achievements, both for skill in argument and for
poetic beauty.

The Alliterative Revival

Nothing in Middle English poetry before Chaucer equals in
merit and attraction the works attributed to the anonymous
author of *Pearl*, an elegy written (*c.* 1375) in octosyllabic
alliterative verse of twelve-line stanzas with an elaborate rhyme-
scheme. The poem tells how in a dream the narrator sees his
dead two-year-old daughter Marguerite (i.e. Pearl) on the far
side of a river. Now a mature maiden, she rebukes his grief
by making him understand that she is among the blessed in
Paradise. He has the impulse to swim across to her, but wakes
and is thereafter comforted by the assurance of her immortality.

---

[1] See J. W. H. Atkin's Introduction to his edition, containing the two
extant versions and a modern prose translation (*The Owl and the Nightingale*,
Cambridge, 1922); also the Early English Text Society edition by J. H. G.
Grattan and G. F. H. Sykes, 1935.

The poem is exceptionally beautiful and impressive in its depth of feeling and rich imagery, while in structure it is as masterly as it is ambitious. Its 101 stanzas (rhyming *ababababbcbc*) are grouped into twenty sections. The stanzas in each section have an identical refrain, and either the last word of each stanza or some more important word of the refrain recurs in the opening line of the stanza following. The pattern was completed by making the final line of the whole poem echo the first line.

> More mervayle con my dom adaunt;
> I segh byyonde that myry mere
> A crystal clyffe ful relusaunt;
> Mony ryal ray con fro hit rere.
> At the fote therof ther sete a faunt,
> A mayden of menske, ful debonere;
> Blysnande whyt was hyr bleaunt;
> I knew hyr wel, I hade sen hyr ere.
> As glysnande golde that man con schere,
> So schon that schene an-under schore;
> On lenghe I loked to hyr there;
> The lenger, I knew hyr more and more.[1]

> More marvels now my soul beguiled;
> I saw, beyond that merry mere,
> Bright crystal cliffs on bright cliffs piled,
> Radiant with rays that have no peer:
> At which cliff's foot there sat a child,
> A gracious maid, full debonair:
> Her dazzling robe was undefiled;
> I knew her well, I had seen her ere.
> As glistening gold, pure and sincere,
> So shone she on that shining shore:
> Long gazed I eagerly on her there:
> The longer, I knew her more and more.[2]

The unique manuscript (in the British Museum) containing *Pearl* dates from the late fourteenth or early fifteenth century and includes three other poems: *Cleanness* (or *Purity*), *Patience*, and *Sir Gawayne and the Grene Knight*. All are in the West Midland dialect, and appear to belong to Lancashire or Cheshire.

[1] Part III, stanza 4. The old English characters for th, y, etc., have been modernized here.

[2] From G. G. Coulton's modernization: *Pearl* (Nutt, London, 1906).

Cleanness, epic in character and in alliterative unrhymed verse, describes the Flood, the destruction of Sodom and Gomorrah, and the fate of Belshazzar. *Patience* retells the story of Jonah in verse similar to that of *Cleanness*. Likeness in imagery, style, and descriptive power gives ground for attributing both these poems to the author of *Pearl*, while stylistic and prosodic features of all three appear in the last poem in the manuscript. This is an exciting adventure story about a knight with green skin, green hair, and green armour who rode on New Year's Day into the hall at Camelot where Arthur and his knights were about to feast. The stranger issued a challenge to the company, specifying that the acceptor of the challenge must swear that after striking a blow with the axe carried by the Green Knight he will a year hence submit to a return blow. Gawain accepts, takes up the weapon and severs the Knight's head. The Green Knight rides away bearing his head, after charging Gawain to meet him at the Green Chapel on the next New Year's Day. On his journey at the end of the year to fulfil his pledge Gawain spends the night of Christmas eve at a castle, where he is invited to stay on for the feast. The host goes hunting on the following three days, leaving his guest behind. Gawain is tempted by the lady of the castle, who on each day kisses him and on the third day gives him also a green girdle which she says will protect him from harm. He and the host have bargained to exchange each day whatever they win, but though Gawain gives the kisses and receives the product of the hunt he conceals the 'magic' girdle. On New Year's Day he reaches a cave which is the Green Chapel and discovers that his host at the castle is the strange visitor of the year before. The Green Knight now bears a greater axe with which to deliver the return blow. He makes two mock attempts to strike, and then, the third time, wounds Gawain slightly in the neck, saying that he would have escaped injury altogether if he had not concealed the girdle, that and the wife's kisses having been bestowed to test his integrity.

Sir Gawayne and the Grene Knight is the finest of the medieval English alliterative romances, a genuinely gripping story which avoids the long-windedness and tedium common to much of the literature of the period. It is rich in colour and in effective descriptions of natural scenery and medieval life. Though written mainly in unrhymed alliterative verse, at irregular intervals throughout quatrains (rhyming *abab*) are introduced. With these works the alliterative tradition of the older English poetry underwent an impressive revival due to the skill of a writer who showed that it could be put to new uses and be made to carry fresh matter suited to the taste of a new age. It is tempting to speculate upon how English poetry might have developed along such lines if the genius of Chaucer had not found a more fruitful way which led into a sunnier poetic climate. But just as Chaucer was beginning, the old mode produced in *Piers Plowman* its own most impressive memorial.

CHAPTER II

CHAUCER, HIS CONTEMPORARIES, AND HIS SUCCESSORS

William Langland

THE composite poem known as *The Vision concerning Piers Plowman* exists in a number of manuscripts embodying three principal versions, the first written probably about 1360, the second about 1380, and the latest and fullest shortly before 1400. The text contains references to 'long Will', who is presumed to be one William Langland and the author of *Piers Plowman*. But scholars have reached no final conclusion upon the problem of its authorship, and uncertainty remains concerning whether the work is a composite production to which several authors contributed. For general purposes, however, it is enough to accept it as the work of Langland and to approach it as what it is: one of the truly great English poems. It is particularly necessary to stress the poetic worth of *Piers Plowman*, for the difficulty of the language has encouraged the production of modernized versions which concentrate upon its subject-matter and tend to foster the impression that it should be read as a propagandist tract against social abuses and ecclesiastical corruption.

William Langland appears to have been born about 1330 near Malvern (Cleobury Mortimer in Shropshire has been suggested as his birthplace) and to have been educated in the monastery at Great Malvern. He probably held some minor and unbeneficed priestly office, for he says (Passus VI of the third version) in a passage concerned with a time when he was in London:

> And ich lyue in Londone and on London bothe;
> The lomes þat ich laboure with and lyflode deserue
> Ys *Paternoster*, and my Prymer, *Placebo* and *Dirige*,
> And my Sauter som tyme, and my Seuene Psalmes.
> Thus I synge for hure soules of suche as me helpen,
> And þo þat fynden me my fode vochen saf, ich trowe,
> To be wolcome wanne ich come oþerwyle in a month,
> Now with hym and now with hure; and þusgate ich begge
> Withoute bagge oþer botel bote my wombe one.

(I live in London and on London; the tools I work with and earn my living by are the Lord's Prayer, my manual of devotion, vespers and matins for the departed, and sometimes my Psalter and the Seven Psalms. I sing for the souls of those that help me; and those that provide me with my food make me welcome once a month or so in their houses; I beg thus, since I have no wallet for food, no bottle for drink, but my own belly.)

Langland was evidently well acquainted with poverty, and this in conjunction with his Christian compassion made him as sensitive as *Piers Plowman* shows him to have been to the sufferings of all ill-used people. In line with the fashion of medieval literature he used the dream-vision device, telling that he fell asleep on a sunny May morning on the Malvern hills and saw 'a field full of folk'—many sorts and conditions, rich and poor, good and bad, workers and idlers. Among the churchmen were those who fattened upon the credulous; among the lawyers those who cared nothing for just dealing and would not open their mouths to plead except for profit; among the butchers and bakers, tinkers and tailors, masons and miners, ditchers and delvers, those who shirked honest toil. But while there is no lack of bitter satire in *Piers Plowman* there is also no want of praise for well-doing. The poem proceeds to a vision of Holy Church personified as a beautiful woman. When the dreamer begs her to teach him how he may save his soul, she discourses to him on Truth and Mercy, Love and Charity. She points out amid the throng a magnificently dressed woman, Lady Meed, who is to marry Falsehood. With Simony, Flattery, Civil Law, Guile, and others the company sets off for the royal court at Westminster where Conscience, prompted by True-Talk, informs against them to the king. They are ordered to be arrested and punished, but they all escape except Meed. After the justices and clerks and a confessor have fawned upon her in prison, Meed is brought to trial before the king, who threatens to shut her up in Corfe Castle or some worse place unless she reforms and repents of her wantonness. He suggests that Conscience should marry her, but Conscience objects and catalogues at length her sins and faults. Meed speaks eloquently in her own defence but is answered by Conscience, who charges her with responsibility for most of the world's ills. At last the king interrupts and commands Conscience and Meed to kiss and be friends, but Conscience declares that he would rather die, unless Reason should instruct him to obey. Reason is summoned; Wisdom, Wit, Wrong, and Peace also appear, and an elaborate interweaving discussion proceeds before Meed is overcome by Meekness and the king invites Reason to be his Chancellor and Conscience his Chief Justice.

Langland's mastery is shown in the ease with which he marshals and deploys his large company of personified virtues and vices within the allegorical framework. The narrative is conducted with sustained verve, with much ingenuity of argument, and with many touches of wry humour and acute observation of men and manners which show that Langland had a sharp eye upon the behaviour of living men and women as he moved among them both in the country and in London. This feeling of direct contact with actual people gives *Piers Plowman* its dramatic force and raises it much above the level of abstract sermonizing. Moreover, the alliterative verse (through the more than 7,000 lines in the fullest version) avoids monotony and, as Langland employs it, is a well-tuned instrument.

The later parts of the poem, after Reason and Conscience have prevailed against Meed and her creatures, introduce other visions, including a Vision of the Seven Deadly Sins. It is not until Passus VI that Piers the Ploughman himself comes into the picture, at the point where a multitude of persons goes pouring over the hills and through the valleys in quest of Saint Truth. Piers tells them that he has been Truth's servant for more than fifty years, and when they offer him money to guide them he refuses it but describes the way. Thenceforward the poem is dominated by Piers, who is a curiously complex character, being at whiles a kind of Sanctified Common Man but also, and in the main as the narrative proceeds, a Christlike figure. Following the end of the main poem come three supplementary visions, Do-wel, Do-bet, and Do-best,[1] in which Piers loses any separable identity and becomes merged with the Divine Person.

Piers Plowman should be read with the events of contemporary

[1] A detailed examination of possible complex significances of Do-wel, Do-bet, and Do-best is given in *The Pardon of Piers Plowman*, by Nevill Coghill (*Proceedings of the British Academy*, xxxi, London, 1945).

re·hie gepunðan· peall prænċinc· up forð timbran· ac
hie ænun·lice·hǽpum to hloðon· hlǽðrum geðæcte·
pær oðcie· æghpilc poroðr mæg burh prænðe· rǽð an
mǽoo tobræð· þurh hir mihta rreð· monna rprǽce·

1. Scenes from the life of Nimrod, from the paraphrase of *Genesis*

2. Dragons fighting under Vortigern's Tower, from *Brut*

3. The building of Stonehenge, from *Brut*

4. Merlin and Vortigern from Geoffrey of Monmouth's *Prophetia Merlini*

5. The Green Knight appears headless before King Arthur, from *Gawayne and the Grene Knight*

. Pearl appears to the Poet, from *Pearl*

7. Piers Plowman dreaming

8. *A Piers Plowman* manuscript

Kyndnes wittel hem · trewely to sen þe same
What kyn of Osye · and wees kyn of Gascoigne
Of þe kyn and of þe Rochel · þe loost to drye

passus primus de visione

What þis mountaigne bymeney · and þe mirke dale
And þe feld ful of folk · y shal yow faire shewe
A louely lady of leere · in lynnen yclothed
Cam doun from a Castel · and called me faire
And seide sone slepestow · sestow þis peple
How bisie þei ben · alle aboute þe mase
The mooste partie of þis peple · þat passep on þis erþe
Haue þei worship in þis world · þei wilne no bettre
Of oþer heuene þan here · holde þei no tale

I was afeed of hire face · þeiȝ she faire weere
And seide mercy madame · What is þis to meene

The tour on þe toft quod she · truþe is þ inne
And wolde þt ye wrouȝte · as his word techeþ
ffor he is fader of feiþ · and formed yow alle
Boþe wt fel and wt face · and yaf yow fyue wittes
ffor to worshipe hym þ with · while þt ye ben here
And þfore he hiȝte þe erþe · to helpe yow echone
Of wollene of lynnen · of liflode at nede

9. The Franklin   10. The Wife of Bath

11. The Friar

from the 'Ellesmere' Chaucer

How he ý Susann was mayden marie
And kept his loue floure and fructifie

Althogh his lyfe be queynt ye resemblaunce
Of him hath in me so fressh lyflynesse
Yat to putte othir men in remembraunce
Of his psone I haue heere his lyknesse
Do make to yis ende in soothfastnesse
Yat yei yt haue of him left yought & mynde
By yis peynture may ageyn him fynde

The ymages yt in ye chirche been
Maken folk yenke on god & on his seyntes
Whan ye ymages yei be holden & seen
Were oft vnsyte of hem causith restreyntes
Of youghtes gode whan a ymg depeynt is
Or entayled if men take of it heede
Thoght of ye lyknesse it wil in hym brede

Yit some holden oppynyon and sey
Yat none ymages schuld ymaked be
Yei erren foule & goon out of ye wey
Of trouth haue yei scant sensibilite
Passe ouer yt now blessid trinite
Vpon my maistres soule mcy haue
Ffor him lady eke y mcy craue

More othir ymg wolde I fayne speke & touche
Heere in yis booke but such is my dulnesse
Ffor yt al voyde and empty is my pouche
Yat al my lust is queynt wt heuynesse
And heuy spirit comaundith stilnesse

12. Geoffrey Chaucer

13. Chaucer reading his poems to a noble company

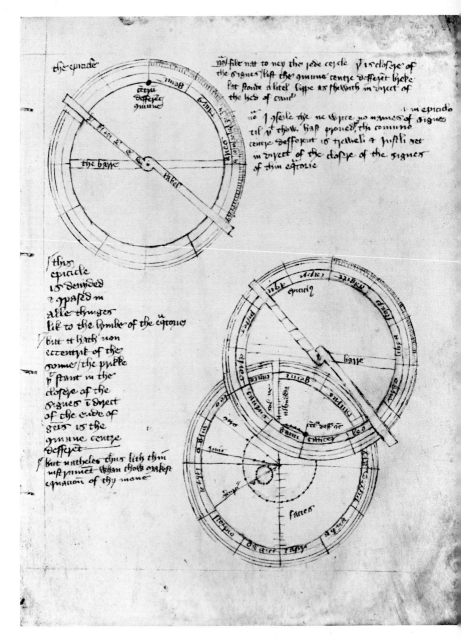

14. A page from *The Equatorie of the Planetis*, possibly by Geoffrey Chaucer

English history in mind. Within Langland's lifetime there were recurrences (1360, 1379) of the Black Death (the bubonic plague which swept England thrice in the fourteenth century) and between the writing of the first and third versions came the uprising of the peasants under Wat Tyler and John Ball (1381). Ball brought Piers Plowman's name into his letter written to the peasants of Essex during the revolt. These events, symptomatic of widespread distress and discontent among the English people, were a vital factor in *Piers Plowman*, which

> stands alone as a revelation of the ignorance and misery of the lower classes, whose multiplied grievances came to a head in the Peasant's Revolt of 1381. It must not be supposed that Langland idealized the labourers. Their indolence and improvidence are exposed as unsparingly as the vices of the rich; and Piers himself is not so much a representative of the English workman in the fourteenth century as a character drawn straight from the Gospels. . . . The poet himself rather deprecates political action. His satire is directed against the general slackening of the bonds of duty that marked the last years of an outworn system of society. For the remedy of abuses he appeals not to one class but to all: king, nobles, clergy, and workers must model their lives on the pattern of the Gospels.[1]

For us, now, *Piers Plowman* is all this and more: it is the poem in which we see not only a parade of the great Abstractions but also the English land full of such folk as Cis the shoemaker, 'Watt the gamekeeper and his wife—drunk', Tom the tinker, Hick the hackneyman, Clarice of Cock Lane, Daw the ditcher, 'a fiddler, a ratter, and a Cheapside scavenger, a ropemaker, a trooper, and Rose of the Small Shop, a watchmaker and a hermit, and the Tyburn hangman'. Even if Bunyan had no direct knowledge of Langland's *Piers Plowman* we must nevertheless look upon him as a seventeenth-century prose counterpart of the fourteenth-century poet, for no two English writers show a closer relationship in spirit and temper.

Geoffrey Chaucer

Only when Chaucer is seen against the background of earlier literature can the character and magnitude of his own achieve-

---

[1] Kenneth Sisam (ed.): *Fourteenth Century Verse and Prose* (Clarendon Press, 1937).

ment be estimated. What was that achievement? Altogether apart from the influence that his immediate and enduring literary repute had in stabilizing the language (in which the East Midland dialect adopted by the Court and the universities was taking on a national character) Chaucer was a great originator who brought into English poetry something that had not been there before: human individuality. He invented for the literature of his country the invaluable device of characterization, by means of which men and women are seen not in the mass as *people* but differentiated from one another as persons in their own right. Beowulf is not in this sense a person, he is an Epic Hero; the father in *Pearl* is not a person, he is a Sorrowing Parent; Gawain and the Green Knight are not persons, they are Romantic Figures. In *Piers Plowman* Cis and Watt and Tom and Hick and Clarice and Daw and Rose of the Small Shop are pinhead creatures in a landscape, not individualized but only known as a shoemaker, a gamekeeper, a tinker, a hackneyman, and so on. They give a swarming generalized life to the poem and mark an advance upon anything that had been done before in English poetry; but we get no stronger clue to their individual identity than if they were ants scuttering about an anthill. No exhausting trial of the imagination would be required to enable us to guess at what Rose of the Small Shop would have become as a character in a poem by Chaucer, or at how much more we should know of 'Watt the gamekeeper and his wife—drunk', though the laconic punch of that last word in Langland's phrase has its own revealing force.

With the coming of Chaucer English poetry moved from a preoccupation with types of humanity to a curiously friendly and humorous (though sometimes also sardonic) interest in Harry Bailey and (might we not say?) Cressida Brown, and Troilus Jones, and Pandarus Robinson, for these are no longer lay figures in an oft-told tale from 'the matter of Rome the Great' but persons of flesh and blood who might live up the lane or in the street round the corner. Nothing could be more fortunate than that Langland and Chaucer were near-contemporaries, writing of different halves of English life— Langland of the needy and wretched, Chaucer of the well-fed and contented; the one knowing the Church from the inside, the other with first-hand knowledge of the Court. The essential difference between them is that Langland imposes as it were a wall of glass between us and his 'field full of folk', whereas Chaucer takes us on to the highway of the world where the Southwark innkeeper and the Oxford clerk, the gentle-hearted nun and the bawdy Wife of Bath, the dandified young squire and the gross wart-nosed miller, are of one company and sisters and brothers under the skin.

We know too little of Langland's movements to be able to form any opinion of how far he had ranged from the road between Malvern and London, but of Geoffrey Chaucer's wide experience of places and people we are well informed. He was born about 1340, the son of John Chaucer a London vintner who became Deputy Butler to Edward III in 1348. John's wife had been married before to the Keeper of the King's Wardrobe, and at some time before 1357 (when his name appears in the household books as receiving articles of clothing and a Christmas allowance) Geoffrey became a page to the king's son Lionel, later Duke of Clarence. In 1359 or the next year, while on military service in France, Chaucer was taken prisoner but soon ransomed. Probably in 1366 he married Philippa (daughter of Sir Payne Roet), whose sister Katherine became the third wife of John of Gaunt. By 1367 Chaucer was a valet of the king's bedchamber and shortly after was sent abroad on the first of the several diplomatic missions with which he was entrusted over a period of years. Following another spell of military service in France he went to Genoa on a trade mission in 1372 and visited Florence also. Two years later he was appointed a Comptroller of Customs in the port of London at a yearly salary representing in present currency about £500 and with responsibility for the wool, skins, and hides passing through the port. He also received the grant of a house at Aldgate, one of the entrances through the London wall.

Further missions abroad in 1377 (the year of Richard II's accession) made it necessary for Chaucer to be allowed a deputy at the Customs; and at about this time he made a second journey to Italy, the last of his foreign visits. Another Customs appointment was given to him in 1382; in 1385 he was made a Justice of the Peace for Kent, the county of *The Canterbury Tales*; and although in 1386 he entered parliament as a knight of the shire for that county, he fell into disfavour in the same year, when the Duke of Gloucester became all-powerful at Court, displacing the John of Gaunt party. Chaucer lost his appointments and also his house; and in 1386 or 1387 his wife died. His fortunes revived in 1389 when Richard II took control of affairs on coming of age. Chaucer then became Clerk of the King's Works, receiving a substantial salary (about £1,400 in our money) and in the following years certain gifts and pensions. He was attacked and robbed in 1390, and re-signed his offices a few months later, though almost simultane-ously he was appointed Deputy Forester of the royal forest at North Petherton in Somerset. As the poem called *A Complaint to his Purse* indicates, Chaucer was for a period in difficulty, but in 1399 (Henry IV having succeeded Richard II) his pension was renewed and increased. He took a house in Westminster Abbey garden, where he died in October 1400. His burial in the Abbey was the first in that part since called Poets' Corner.

Few poets' lives and works fall into so orderly a pattern as Chaucer's. As a Court official and civil servant he divided his activities between France, Italy, and England, and in his poetry there is strong French influence, and a lesser Italian phase, while in his final period *The Canterbury Tales* made him, through the Prologue and the interlinking passages between the tales, the greatest poet of English life and character up to that time.

It was probably about 1360, at the age of twenty, that he began in earnest as a poet by undertaking an English version in octosyllabic couplets of the first part of the French *Roman de la Rose*, written more than a century earlier. On this he worked at intervals until 1368, though he is now believed to have translated only a portion of the 7,000–8,000 lines formerly credited to him. After John of Gaunt's first wife, Blanche, died in 1369 Chaucer wrote as an elegy *The Book of the Duchesse*. Allegorical in type, it employs the familiar dream device to introduce a hunting party where the poet meets a Man in Black mourning the death of his lady, upon whose virtues he descants and tells of their courtship. Though Chaucer draws in this poem mainly from French sources, Machault and Froissart, with some debt to Ovid also, he was already showing that what he took from his models was to be no more than raw material to be moulded to his own purposes; and already he was demonstrating his genius for characterization by giving through the Man in Black's description of the lost lady his own portrait of the Duchess Blanche.

In *The Hous of Fame* (*c.* 1380) the poet, again in a dream, finds himself in a building of glass which is discovered to be the temple of Venus, richly furnished with golden images and pictures telling the story of Æneas after the fall of Troy. An eagle 'that shoon with fethres as of gold' swoops upon the poet after he leaves the temple and, revealing himself as Jupiter's servant, converses during the flight towards the House of Fame, the interior of which Chaucer describes in elaborate detail. It is adorned with numerous statues of classical worthies and others, and Lady Fame is enthroned there to judge the claims of the many suppliants who approach her. Chaucer expresses to a bystander his indifference to fame, saying that he can assess his own merit, and that he would be more interested in some new tidings, of love or other gladness. He is led to a vast whirling labyrinth to which he is unable to gain entrance until the eagle assists him, whereupon he finds himself dazed by an uproar of ceaseless rumour and lies. When at last he thinks he is about to hear tidings he desires from 'a man of great authority' the poem breaks off unfinished, and what was apparently to have been a surprise revelation to end the poem is left a mystery. Strains from Dante and Boccaccio appear to have been active in Chaucer's imagination at that time, and with *The Hous of Fame* his Italian period may be said to begin, though his lifelong love of French poetry remained much the stronger influence.

Yet again dream and allegory operate in *The Parlement of Foules* (*c.* 1382). The poet is conducted into a beautiful garden by the African, Scipio (whose dream story—'Tullius of the dreme of Scipioun'—he had been reading before he went to bed), and there he finds certain classical deities and abstractions familiar to lovers, presided over by Nature 'the vicaire of th'almyghty lorde'. As it is St. Valentine's day all the birds have gathered to select their mates and a debate ensues upon which of three eagles shall win the formel (i.e. female) eagle that Nature bears upon her wrist. After the royal eagle and his competitors have spoken, various birds put forward views on love and lovers according to their kind, ranging from the cynicism and gluttony of the duck and the cuckoo to the gentleness and constancy of the turtle dove. The debate is adjourned for a year to permit the formel eagle to make up her mind whom to select from her suitors, but the other birds make their choice forthwith and their joyful clamour wakes the poet. It is likely that *The Parlement of Foules* embodies allusions to the wooing of Anne of Bohemia by Richard II, though that is of little moment beside the beauty of the poem as an æsthetic creation and as a masterpiece of natural description and gentle comedy touched with irony.

> The waker goos; the cukkow ever unkinde;
> The popinjay, full of delicasye;
> The drake, stroyer of his owne kinde;
> The stork, the wreker of avouterye;
> The hote cormeraunt of glotonye;
> The raven wys, the crow with vois of care;
> The throstle olde; the frosty feldefare.

waker] vigilant   avouterye] adultery   hote] voracious

The Parlement of Foules shows unmistakably the influence of Boccaccio, for it incorporates passages adapted from the Italian poet's *Il Teseide* (the Theseus story), used again and more fully by Chaucer for *Anelida and Arcite* and *The Knight's Tale*. There are occasional glimpses in his works of a knowledge of Dante, and in the first part of *Troilus and Criseyde* he paraphrases a sonnet by Petrarch; but of the three great Italian writers Chaucer was most in harmony with Boccaccio, whose curiosity about the doings of men and women was akin to Chaucer's own. His chief debt to Boccaccio is invested in *Troilus and Criseyde*, based upon *Il Filostrato*; yet Chaucer repaid the debt handsomely by transforming it into the greatest and most original English poem produced up to that time (*c.* 1379–83), selecting his material from rather less than half of the Italian work but making his own poem half as long again as Boccaccio's. Chaucer was taking up a story already so familiar as to have become hackneyed, though this is a handicap which has more than once been turned to advantage by genius. A writer who elects to use yet again a well-worn tale must enliven and grace it with something wholly his own. No modern reader can care greatly about the traditional Troilus-Pandarus-Cressida story merely as a story: the impatient and headstrong young lover, the go-between, the irresistible young harlot offer few surprises and little intrinsic charm in their age-old game of amorous chess. They are in truth a bore. But Chaucer's *Troilus and Criseyde* does not stale. Not only are the three characters more fascinatingly real than real persons, not only is the story given overtones of tragedy which add dignity to the elements of comedy and pathos, but the poetry itself is as fresh and various as the passing hours of a perfect April day, with the growing and later the dwindling light changing the aspect of things from moment to moment until night falls again. Chaucer works his miracle of transfiguration within the given limits; though he enlarges the mould he does not shatter it, nor make another story with alien conventions. He achieves perfect freedom within the rules, and perfect success by naturalizing the characters and bringing to bear upon them his individual poetic genius, which works through his unsurpassed imaginative insight and technical mastery of versification. Chaucer's happy ability to unify in poetry the perceptions of the seeing eye, of the hearing ear, and of acute emotive sensibility is illustrated by many passages in his works, as in this from *Troilus and Criseyde* (II, 904 ff.):

> The dayes honour, and the hevenes yë,
> The nightes fo, al this clepe I the sonne,
> Gan westren faste, and dounward for to wrye,
> As he that hadde his dayes cours y-ronne;
> And whyte thinges wexen dimme and donne
> For lak of light, and sterres for to appere,
> That she and al hir folk in wente y-fere.

> So whan it lyked hir to goon to reste,
> And voyded weren they that voyden oughte,
> She seyde, that to slepe wel hir leste.
> Hir wommen sone til hir bed hir broughte.
> Whan al was hust, than lay she stille, and thoughte
> Of al this thing the manere and the wyse.
> Reherce it nedeth nought, for ye ben wyse.

A nightingale, upon a cedre grene,
Under the chambre-wal there as she lay,
Ful loude sang ayein the mone shene,
Paraunter, in his briddes wyse, a lay
Of love, that made hir herte fresh and gay.
That herkned she so longe in good entente,
Til at the laste the dede sleep hir hente.

And, as she sleep, anoon-right tho hir mette,
How that an egle, fethered whyt as boon,
Under hir brest his longe clawes sette,
And out hir herte he rente, and that a-noon,
And dide his herte in-to hir brest to goon,
Of which she nought agroos ne no-thing smerte,
And forth he fleigh, with herte left for herte.

Now lat hir slepe, and we our tales holde . . .

yë] eye   fo] foe   clepe] call   wrye] hide   y-fere] together   voyded]
departed   hust] quiet   ayein the mone shene] towards the bright moon
paraunter] perhaps   anoon-right] immediately   mette] dreamt
agroos] was terrified   no-thing smerte] felt no pain

The Legend of Good Women (*c.* 1386) is a gathering of 'lives of
Cupid's saints' (Cleopatra, Thisbe, Dido, Medea, Lucrece, and
five others; Chaucer intended to include more, but the poem
remained unfinished), introduced by a Prologue which is more
readable and important than the somewhat tedious 'lives'.
Chaucer was never far from his best when he wrote about
himself, and in the Prologue to the *Legend* he tells enchantingly
of his love of the daisy and of the pleasure he had from
wandering in the fields (lines 36 ff.):

. . . whan that the month of May
Is comen, and that I here the foules singe,
And that the floures ginnen for to springe,
Farwel my book and my devocioun!
Now have I than swich a condicioun,
That, of alle the floures in the mede,
Than love I most these floures whyte and rede,
Swich as men callen daysies in our toun.
To hem have I so greet affeccioun,
As I seyde erst, whan comen is the May,
That in my bed ther daweth me no day
That I nam up, and walking in the mede
To seen this flour agein the sonne sprede,

Whan hit upryseth erly by the morwe;
That blisful sighte softneth al my sorwe,
So glad am I whan that I have presence
Of hit, to doon al maner reverence,
As she, that is of alle floures flour,
Fulfilled of al vertu and honour,
And ever y-lyke fair, and fresh of hewe;
And I love hit, and ever y-lyke newe,
And ever shal, til that myn herte dye; . .

After much more on the daisy, he goes on to show, later in this Prologue, that his purpose in writing *The Legend of Good Women* was to make atonement for his conviction as a heretic by the God of Love because of the slur of inconstancy he had laid against women in earlier poems. He was always adept when poking quiet fun at himself, and here he refers to and quotes from French poems, saying slyly that he was himself only a gleaner in the field of poetry, glad to pick up 'any goodly word'. Though among the most engaging of Chaucer's pieces of self-revelation is his repeated indication that he was an insatiable reader and lover of books, his time for reading must have been severely restricted both by his duties as a person of affairs and by that unflagging interest in men and women which gave him what was by far the most important first-hand material for his finest poems.

Delightful though *The Legend of Good Women* Prologue is, it is outclassed by the Prologue to *The Canterbury Tales*, which stands next in the chronology of Chaucer's works. Modern novelists have made a *cliché* of the device of assembling a heterogeneous band of men and women around some focal point (a Grand Hotel, or a Stamboul Train, or what you will) so that their peculiarities and passions can be noted in some detail. It was already a formula in the Middle Ages, but Chaucer used it with a democratic difference. In Boccaccio's *Decameron*, and in other collections of tales after that pattern, the various tellers of the stories within the common framework are on much the same social plane, and they are usually cut off accidentally and temporarily from their customary way of life—in the *Decameron* by an outbreak of plague. Consequently, in such collections, the formula imposes a virtual stasis, a closed circle, a stagnant atmosphere, and an acute consciousness of unreality. How obvious (it now seems) was the remedy for the disadvantages and limitations of the formula. All that was required was to get the group of storytellers out into the living everyday world and on the move. How obvious to us; but how unobvious until it occurred to Chaucer that a company of pilgrims was a uniquely mixed bag of humanity, and that only on the road and with an ostensibly religious end in view would such a company hold together for a period in mutual toleration.

The Canterbury Tales, like *The Legend of Good Women*, is unfinished. If the proposal made by Harry Bailey, the host of the Tabard Inn at Southwark, had been carried out—namely that each pilgrim should tell two stories on the outward way to Canterbury and two more while returning to Southwark—there would have been 120 tales (or more, for either there was an error in Chaucer's counting of twenty-nine pilgrims besides himself or some addition was made later: there are thirty-one pilgrims in all). Fragmentary works always tease the imagination, but only gourmand Chaucerians could feel certain that ninety-seven or so tales added to the existing twenty-three would not be too much of a good thing, though no one will fail to lament the loss of further interlinking passages (such as the Wife of Bath's prologue to her own tale) and, no doubt, an Epilogue to balance the general Prologue and round off the whole work. The tales that Chaucer did put into the pilgrims' mouths comprise an anthology of stories translated and adapted from a variety of sources, from Boccaccio especially, but some still unidentified. The tales told by the Knight, the Miller, the Reeve, the Man of Law, the Wife of Bath, the Friar, the Summoner, the Clerk, the Merchant, the Squire, the Franklin, the Canon's Yeoman, the Pardoner, the Prioress, and by Chaucer himself show the poet's mastery of an extraordinarily wide range of poetical material. Some are beautiful, some ugly, some innocent, some scurrilous, but each is in character with the particular teller, each furthers Chaucer's purpose of presenting every pilgrim in the true colours of life, and each declares, therefore, the poet's absolute integrity as a literary artist.

The two tales which he tells in his own person reflect two significant aspects of Chaucer's personal make-up. *The Tale of*

Sir Thopas, parodying the interminable yarns in jogtrot ballad-metre which were extremely popular in the Middle Ages, is effective as criticism of contemporary taste and is perennially attractive because it gives so excellent an impression of Chaucer's sense of fun, a characteristic often missing in those who claim

The Pilgrims at Table

a sense of humour. There is no single term to embrace Chaucer's wit, humour, fun, and capacity for both delicate comedy and indelicate belly-laughter. While it is true that he is a dramatic poet in so far as he depicts individual men and women possessing just those qualities which fit their nature precisely, it is equally true that Chaucer himself was an amalgam of a multitude of disparate qualities. We have little overt evidence concerning his interior personal life and domestic relationships, but there is no reason to suppose that he was other than a happy man or that his many-sidedness, his understanding of all sorts and conditions, arose from any conflict in his own nature. There is an overriding unity in his diversity, and that large serenity of outlook which leads a man to accept himself and the rest of humanity as God and the Devil have made them.

The other tale that Chaucer allots to himself, *The Tale of Melibeus*, illustrates what (for want of a more explicit word) may be called his *instructional* side. Though he eschewed pedantry and was not in the least afflicted with the dry cough of a pedagogue, and though he would have been unlikely to show enthusiasm for Wordsworth's determination to be 'a teacher or nothing', it is probable that he could have said of himself as of the Clerk of Oxenford that 'gladly wolde he lerne, and gladly teche'. The *Treatise on the Astrolabe*, written by Chaucer for his young son Lewis, is a piece of his glad teaching, and if we find the Melibee story more than a little dull we must remember that in the Middle Ages—and for long after—'learning without tears' was unknown and even undesired: the gladness of learning was at least in part a delight in taking pains, the joy of achievement in getting knowledge the hard way. But if Chaucer is to be considered as in some measure a teacher, what must be put first of all is the lesson he teaches mankind at large—to extend to all an unbounded human charity, not as a vague mass emotion but individually to Jack and Jill, and to greasy Joan as readily as to Madame Eglentyne.

To that human charity, rooted in a curious interest and an acute understanding, the Prologue to *The Canterbury Tales* is the lasting and finest memorial, as it is also Chaucer's masterpiece. There his genius was working directly on living material with no literary convention interposed. Since he had made Troilus and Cressida come newly alive out of their antique tomb, it was to be expected that the Canterbury pilgrims would have a still more abundant life at Chaucer's calling. Yet *was* it to be expected? Word-portraits from living models are sometimes much inferior to those that come wholly from a writer's imagination. We know now, of course, that Chaucer was even more skilled at drawing from the life than from library models; that he was more greatly gifted as a creator than as a re-creator.

If the Host's miniature verbal sketch of Chaucer were to be

taken as an authentic portrait-in-little we should suppose that
the poet was shy and reserved:

> . . . 'what man artow?' quod he;
> 'Thou lokest as thou woldest finde an hare,
> For ever up-on the ground I see thee stare. . . .'

but the poet has already in the early lines of the Prologue
enabled us to judge of his readiness to fit in with a motley
gathering:

> At night was come in-to that hostelrye
> Wel nyne and twenty in a companye,
> Of sondry folk, . . .
>
> . . . . . .
>
> And shortly, whan the sonne was to reste,
> So hadde I spoken with hem everichon,
> That I was of hir felawshipe anon . . .

It would of course be foolish to suppose that everything in
the Prologue is 'from the life'. Chaucer was too good an artist
and had too lively an imagination to be a mere copyist, even
of life itself. Life was only his raw material, to which he could
on occasion give a more convincing and satisfying shape than
Nature's own. So we can only guess at how far Chaucer drew
upon imparted information and how far upon his own sense
of probability. Did the Knight (or his Squire for him) chatter
at length of the countries he had served in and the battles he
had fought, or did Chaucer himself provide such details as
'At mortal batailles hadde he been fiftene'? and write of
Algezir and Belmarye, Tramissene and Palatye because, like
so many other poets, he could make enchanting music from
place-names? Though quotability is not necessarily a guide to
poetic worth, the creation of memorable phrases is an art in
which great poets excel. Chaucer has a distinguished place
among the makers of immortal lines, and none has been more
often repeated (nor, probably, more often misapplied) than the
conclusion of this passage on the Knight:

> And though that he were worthy, he was wys,
> And of his port as meke as is a mayde.
> He never yet no vileinye ne sayde
> In al his lyf, un-to no maner wight.
> He was a verray parfit gentil knight.

The Knight, we feel, was an impressive person; possibly a little too good to be true, even in the flesh; at any rate Chaucer finds nothing in him to provoke a saving smile. The Doctor of Physic, dealt with rather later, is 'a verrey parfit practisour' portrayed ironically as a know-all, and just as the Knight has his chorus of place-names so the Doctor has his of medical worthies:

> Wel knew he th'olde Esculapius,
> And Deiscorides, and eek Rufus,
> Old Ypocras, Haly, and Galien;
> Serapion, Razis, and Avicen;
> Averrois, Damascien, and Constantyn;
> Bernard, and Gatesden, and Gilbertyn.

The Wife of Bath has no equal of her own sex in English literature, and the only male character on her level is Falstaff. If there is one reason above all others for sometimes wishing that Chaucer and Shakespeare could have been contemporaries, it is that Queen Elizabeth might have commissioned them to collaborate in writing a play showing the Wife and Falstaff in love. The result should have been better than *The Merry Wives of Windsor*. Not until the prelude to her own tale do we get the best of the Wife. In the general Prologue Chaucer goes little further than giving us an inventory—vivid and entertaining— of what she wore: red stockings, new shoes, wimple, spurs,

> . . . and on hir heed an hat
> As brood as is a bokeler or a targe;

she had travelled much, had had five husbands, and knew a great deal about 'remedyes of love'. What is less often re- membered, to her credit, is that at cloth-making she was more skilled than the cloth-workers 'of Ypres and of Gaunt'.

Chaucer's freedom from malice towards his fellows even when his integrity compelled him to strip them naked to the soul is nowhere more plainly shown than in his physical description and characterization of the Summoner. This pimpled, scurfy, scraggy-bearded, lecherous, drunken wretch, this foul-breathed ignorant swindler, whose hideous aspect terrified children but who yet had jurisdiction over all young people in the diocese, still does not tempt the poet to moralize. In fewer than fifty lines he exposes him body and soul as mercilessly as Swift or

Aldous Huxley might have done in a far larger space of prose. Unlike these later satirists, however, Chaucer does not consume himself in a frenzy of hatred and disgust. Nevertheless his satire bites home at least as powerfully as theirs.

As a storyteller and characterizer of men and women Chaucer displayed special abilities and interests that would almost certainly have made him, in a later age, a distinguished novelist. As a poet, however, his eminence depends as much upon his technical command of verse-forms previously unfamiliar in—or even foreign to—English poetry as upon the content of his writings. For these verse forms, as for so much else, he drew largely upon French sources (upon Guillaume de Machault in particular); yet though the skeleton might come from abroad the completed structure was always Chaucer's own. He was not only, as Skeat called him, 'our first great metrist', he was also our first absolute master of rhyme, that essentially artificial device to which only the greatest poets succeed in giving a semblance of inevitability.

Chaucer began, in his translation of *Le Roman de la Rose*, with octosyllabic rhyming couplets and proceeded to heroic (i.e. decasyllabic) couplets in his latest works—e.g. The Prologue to *The Canterbury Tales*. Among his metrical innovations in English were 7-, 8-, 9-, and 10-line stanzas, but it was the first of these, the decasyllabic 7-line stanza rhyming *ababbcc*, that he used most frequently in major works. As will be seen from the extract above (*see* p. 23) it is the metre of *Troilus and Criseyde*. It became a favourite metre with later poets, and after its appearance in *The Kingis Quair* by James the First of Scotland (*see below*, p. 40) became known as rhyme-royal. Chaucer was also the first to experiment in English with the complex measure used by Dante for *The Divine Comedy*, terza rima; but he did not persevere with it after imperfect efforts in *A Compleint to His Lady*.

Being above everything a poet, Chaucer has received less praise than he merits as a prose writer. That he could command beauty in prose can be shown by a brief quotation from his rendering of Boethius's *Consolation of Philosophy*: '. . . the floury yeer yildeth swote smelles in the firste somer-sesoun warminge; and the hote somer dryeth the cornes; and the autumpne comth ayein, hevy of apples; and the fletinge reyn bideweth the

winter'; while the opening sentences of *A Treatise on the Astrolabe*
show a degree of clarity beyond the scope of much of the prose
written more than a century later by the Elizabethans:

> Litel Lowis my sone, I have perceived wel by certeyne evidences
> thyn abilite to lerne sciencez touchinge noumbres and propor-
> ciouns; and as wel considere I thy bisy preyere in special to lerne
> the Tretis of the Astrolabie. Than, for as mechel as a philosofre
> seith, 'he wrappeth him in his frend, that condescendeth to the
> rightful preyers of his frend,' ther-for have I geven thee a
> suffisaunt Astrolabie as for oure orizonte, compowned after the
> latitude of Oxenford; up-on which, by mediacion of this litel
> tretis, I purpose to teche thee a certein nombre of conclusiouns
> apertening to the same instrument. . . . And Lowis, yif so be
> that I shewe thee in my lighte English as trewe conclusiouns
> touching this matere, and naught only as trewe but as many
> and as subtil conclusiouns as ben shewed in Latin in any commune
> tretis of the Astrolabie, con me the more thank; and preye god
> save the king, that is lord of this langage . . .

mechel] much orizonte] horizon con] grant

John Gower

While the works of a writer of outstanding genius are in themselves a priceless asset, as a legacy they may become, in their
luring effect on imitators, a formidable liability. As will appear
later, the greatest individual contribution to English literature,
Shakespeare's plays, laid a stranglehold on English drama for
three hundred years.

Chaucer was the first English writer to be followed by a
group—or, rather, by two groups—of disciples, named by literary historians *the English Chaucerians* and *the Scottish Chaucerians*.
The most prominent of the English group are Thomas Hoccleve
(Occleve), John Lydgate, and Stephen Hawes; of the Scottish,
King James I, Robert Henryson, Henry the Minstrel (Blind
Harry), Gavin Douglas, and William Dunbar. But for each
country a transition poet or two of some importance has first
to be considered.

'O moral Gower', wrote his friend Chaucer towards the end
of *Troilus and Criseyde*, 'this book I directe to thee.' This was
no doubt an instance of Chaucer's naughty irony, for in the
following lines he invites correction from both Gower and

'thee, philosophical Strode', though the poem is not at all likely to have been to the taste of either, nor any 'correction' proposed by them to have been to Chaucer's liking.

John Gower (c. 1330–1408) came of a Kentish family of some wealth, with property also in the eastern counties. He spent most of his time in London, however, had some dealings at Court during Richard II's reign, and died in Southwark. He was buried in the priory church of St. Mary Overy, now Southwark Cathedral, where his effigy on an exceptionally fine contemporary tomb shows him with his three principal literary works beneath his head.

Whereas Chaucer's eager enthusiasm for the English tongue brought it to a fine perfection as an instrument for poetry, and naturalized in his own language all that he borrowed from France and Italy, Gower seems to have laboured for many years under a pedant's mistrust of the vernacular. Of the three long poems by which he is best known, the first, *Speculum Meditantis* (or *Mirour de l'Omme*), relates in French and in highly moral and religious terms, some 30,000 lines long, the struggle between the vices and the virtues for the soul of man; the second, *Vox Clamantis*, was probably written soon after the Peasants' Revolt of 1381, with which it deals in about 10,000 lines of Latin elegiac verse animadverting upon the evil state of the realm; the third, *Confessio Amantis*, in 34,000 lines of English verse, is a compendium of stories from many sources— classical, biblical, medieval—and concerned with the infatuations of passionate love. In this English work Gower caught, as far as he was capable of catching, something of Chaucer's manner; and in it he became, perhaps willy nilly, the first of the Chaucerians. There has been a general inclination to under-rate Gower's achievement as an English poet, mainly because his didacticism and his long-windedness are discouraging to modern readers; but partly also because his was an essentially medieval mind, while Chaucer's was essentially modern. The special interest of Gower lies in the fact that, starting with both feet firmly in the old camp, he was induced—however reluct-antly and whether by Chaucer's example or by the tendency of the age—to move one foot over into the new camp when he had reached the age of about sixty. In spirit he was akin to Langland; as a poetic artist he ultimately became, with

Chaucer, one of the fourteenth-century poets who made it 'impossible in England to use any language for poetry except their own'.[1] The first version (1390) of *Confessio Amantis* included a passage on Chaucer in the form of a message from Venus, beginning

> . . . gret wel Chaucer whan ye mete,
> As mi disciple and my poete:
> For in the floures of his youthe
> In sondri wise, as he wel couthe,
> Of ditees and of songes glade,
> The whiche he for mi sake made

and going on to urge him to crown his work in his 'latere age' with a testament of love to be recorded at the goddess's Court.

The English Chaucerians

Thomas Hoccleve (*c.* 1370–1450) is one of England's earliest autobiographers. The versified *La Male Règle* throws light on his curious personality and also on his money troubles, which are brought into this and other poems for the purpose of begging the authorities to pay what was owing to him as a clerk in the Privy Seal office, where he seems to have worked for about fifty years. Hoccleve's account of his rampagings around the town give a vigorous picture of contemporary London life, but so far as English poetry is concerned his main interest lies in his devotion to Chaucer, whom he praised eloquently and tried with only small success to imitate, principally in an English translation in rhyme-royal of Ægidius's *De Regimine Principum* (Regiment of Princes) intended by Hoccleve as a guide for Prince Henry (afterwards Henry V). A decoration on one of the Hoccleve manuscripts has given us the traditional portrait of Chaucer.

More voluminous than Hoccleve as a poet and much duller both as a man and as a writer, John Lydgate (*c.* 1370–1449) was born in the Suffolk village of Lydgate and became a

---

[1] W. P. Ker: *Medieval English Literature* (Home University Library, 1912). Ker was a generous but judicious appraiser of Gower's work and there is good sense in his hint that a liking for *Confessio Amantis* may be acquired by reading it 'in bits'.

Benedictine in the abbey at Bury St. Edmunds. He had some knowledge of London, and is thought to have visited Paris about 1421, the year in which he became Prior of Hatfield Broadoak in Essex until 1432, when he returned to Bury St. Edmunds. Lydgate's output was enormous, and in a later age he would no doubt have been a Grub Street hack writing on any subject proposed to him. The most—if not the only—amusing thing about him is the distaste, amounting almost to fascination, which the nearly 150,000 lines of his surviving works have aroused in modern literary historians. Lydgate might have agreed with them, for he did not shrink from bewailing his own inadequacy as a poet. Then, it may reasonably be asked, why bother with him? The answer must be that he was extremely popular with readers, and with other poets, for a long time after his death; and his attempts to use Chaucer's verse-forms may, in spite of his own feeble incompetence, have served as a channel of conduction from the Chaucerian age to the Elizabethan. There is ground for regarding with scepticism the common belief that nothing but greatness, alone and unaided, irrigates greatness. Unfortunately the one poem credited to Lydgate which was acceptable to modern readers, *London Lickpenny*, is no longer considered to be by him; but in their heyday *The Troy Book*, *The Story of Thebes*, *The Falls of Princes*, and *The Pilgrimage of the Life of Man* (a kind of Pilgrim's Progress in verse) pleased many; while *The Complaint of the Black Knight* was for some time oddly supposed to be by Chaucer.

Although he belongs to a later generation it is convenient to bring in here Stephen Hawes (c. 1475–1525), the latest of the so-called English Chaucerians before Chaucer's influence became so pervasive that its separate identity was lost and it became merged in the great stream of English poetry from Edmund Spenser onward. Little is known of Hawes's life, beyond that he was a Groom of the Chamber to Henry VII; but he may have been born in Suffolk and educated at Oxford and have travelled abroad. He looked upon himself as a follower of Chaucer, though he was in fact a belated medievalist using verse as a medium for sermonical allegories uneasily wedded to chivalric romance. He was reputed to have so phenomenal a memory that he could recite the works of many

English poets, including Lydgate, of whom he wrote as 'my master', praising his 'perfectness'. Hawes's most notable work was *The Passtyme of Pleasure, or the Historie of Graunde Amoure and La Belle Pucel* (c. 1506), which described the ideal training of a perfect knight and lover, recounting his (allegorical) struggles with giants, and proceeding to his marriage and in due time to his death. It owes little more to Chaucer than the use of rhyme-royal and decasyllabic couplets; but of Hawes, as of Lydgate, we must think not as a poet capable of entertaining or instructing us moderns, but as a duct of poetry. That Spenser owed some debt to Hawes is not seriously questioned, for it is evident that *The Faerie Queene* does perfectly what Hawes had tried but ponderously failed to do; on the other hand it is no longer seriously held that Hawes's *Passtyme of Pleasure* was vitally influential in the making of Spenser's masterpiece.

Besides the bulky works of the Chaucerians already noticed, there were in the fifteenth century a number of outstanding single poems by writers whose names mean little except to scholars. It became habitual after Chaucer's death to father upon him poems of uncertain origin which resembled his in style, and thus were attributed to him *The Flower and the Leaf* (writer unidentified), *The Cuckoo and the Nightingale* (1403: by Sir Thomas Clanvowe), *La Belle Dame Sans Merci* (c. 1450; translated by Sir Richard Ros from the French) until later research established a Chaucer canon. *The Flower and the Leaf* runs to 600 lines in rhyme-royal and employs allegorically the familiar stock-in-trade of Courtly verse—a poet in a garden, knights and ladies, pageantry and games. In *La Belle Dame Sans Merci* (a title which set Keats to writing his shorter and far greater poem) a complaining lover is matched against a lady who adopts a refreshingly common-sense attitude towards his deathly longings by answering that love's sickness causes few deaths—an anticipation of Rosalind's 'The poor world is almost six thousand years old, and in all this time there was not any man died in his own person, videlicet, in a love-cause . . . men have died from time to time and worms have eaten them, but not for love' (*As You Like It*, IV, i). *La Belle Dame* enables us to see how, almost before the Renaissance had dawned, a rationalizing temper was beginning to undermine

the older willingly accepted (however conventional) ritual
make-believe in the relationships of men and women.

Lyric Verse

Outside or alongside the Chaucerian mode, there was in the
fifteenth century a great outpouring of lyric verse, both religious
(including the carols) and secular (including the ballads). The
origin and development of English lyrics, their association with
music from early times, their distribution among the peasantry
on the one hand and the nobility on the other, are matters of
considerable complexity. What is by custom regarded as the
first English lyrical poem, beginning

> Sumer is icumen in,
> Lhude sing cuccu,
> Groweth sed, and bloweth med,
> And springth the wude nu—
> Sing cuccu!

is assigned to the middle of the thirteenth century; while from
the innumerable lyrics that must have been composed after
that date almost nothing (apart from carols and ballads: *see
below*, pp. 43 ff.) has become fixed in popular memory until
the fifteenth-century *Nut Brown Maid*, a lyrical dialogue between the maid and an earl's son in disguise, emphasizing (in
contrast with the tone of so many of the Courtly poems) the
girl's compassion, devotion, fidelity, and resolve to serve her
lover. It is written in 12-line stanzas, each containing three
quatrains, with internal as well as end rhymes, and with
alternating refrains:

> *He* . . . For I muste too the grene-wode goo
> Alone, a banysshed man.

> *She* . . . For in my mynde, of all mankynde,
> I love but you alone.

Among the religious lyrics, none is lovelier or of wider
appeal than

> I sing of a mayden
> that is makeles,
> King of alle kynges
> to here sone che ches.

He cam also stylle
ther his moder was
As dew in Aprylle
that fallyt on the gras

.   .   .   .   .

Moder & maydyn
was neuer non but che.
Well may swych a lady
Gode's moder be.

The grave and haunting music of *Quia Amore Langueo* is on a higher poetic level. This poem exists in several fifteenth-century manuscripts, though the poem itself may be considerably earlier. It is in two parts: in the first the Virgin Mary addresses Man; in the second Christ is the speaker. The following stanza comes from Part I:

O wretch, in the world, I look on thee;
I see thee trespass day by day,
with lechery against my chastity,
with pride against my poor array;
my love abides, thine is away;
my love thee calls, though steal me fro;
turn to me, sinner, I thee pray,
Quia amore langueo.[1]

John Barbour and Henry the Minstrel

Attention has now to be given to the group of Northern writers already mentioned as the Scottish Chaucerians. They and some others between the early fifteenth and the mid-sixteenth century gave the literature of Scotland such prominence as was not to be outdone until the days of Burns and Scott.

Long before any influence from Chaucer's work touched writers beyond the Border, John Barbour (*c.* 1320–95), an archdeacon of Aberdeen and sometime Oxford scholar, had written a 'national epic', *The Bruce* (*c.* 1375), treating of Scotland's war of independence against England, with Bruce and Douglas as its heroes and 'fredome is a noble thing' as

---

[1] The spelling is here modernized. H. S. Bennett's edition of the difficult original includes comparative texts from the several manuscripts (*Quia Amore Langueo*. Faber, London, 1937).

its theme. Except that he exercises poetic licence in the handling of historical material, and that *The Bruce* is properly claimed for the literature of the imagination rather than for the literature of fact, Barbour's work is closer to the interests of students of Scottish history than to those of readers of poetry: yet it has many stirring passages filled with the clangour of battle and the fervour of national aspiration. Notwithstanding that a century separates them, it is logical to mention alongside *The Bruce* Henry the Minstrel's *Wallace* (*c.* 1482), which exalts the later Scottish hero as Barbour's poem does the earlier. But though a greater technical accomplishment is displayed in the verse structure of *Wallace*, less honesty of purpose went to its making. Henry the Minstrel (often called Blind Harry) is himself an ambiguous figure—possibly neither a minstrel nor blind—who put up a possibly fictional front for himself personally, even as he invented wildly fictional episodes in his account of Wallace's exploits in the campaign against the English king. Hatred of the English led Henry into violence against the laws of probability in his poem, but this only served to give it a general and lasting popularity among the uncritical, however much it may have induced educated people to view it with scepticism and distaste. It is a crude blood-and-thunder affair nicely calculated to arouse patriotic passion and anglophobia, yet it has unpolished vigour and occasional rough humour which go some way towards counteracting the fantastic absurdity of its wholesale malversations; moreover, the poet was an accomplished narrator. If only because he used the decasyllabic couplet for *Wallace*, Henry the Minstrel might be put among the followers of Chaucer; but there are in fact other marks of Chaucerian influence.

The Scottish Chaucerians

Of the group to which the term *Scottish Chaucerians* is attached, the first in time was James I of Scotland (1394–1437). While on his way to France (*c.* 1406) as a boy he was captured by an English ship and held in England as a prisoner until 1424, when he returned to Scotland and reigned there for thirteen years. In the last weeks of his imprisonment he married Joan Beaufort, and was both a good husband and an enlightened king. Notwithstanding his virtues he was assassinated, in Perth, at the age of forty-three. While in England he composed a poem of slightly under 1,400 lines in rhyme-royal (*see above*, p. 31), *The Kingis Quair* (The King's Book), the authorship of which has often been in dispute, though scholarly opinion has veered to acceptance of it as James's work. While *The Kingis Quair* imitates Chaucer and other fifteenth-century poets and uses a good deal of the old modish paraphernalia, it does break new ground by substituting genuine emotion for the conventional erotic attitudinizing of the Courtly school. If it has been rightly interpreted, the poem is the testament of James's love and courtship of his future wife, and it presents the love story in a work distinguished by technical skill and poetic art.

Robert Henryson (*c.* 1430–1508) may have been master of the Benedictine Grammar School at Dunfermline, but nothing definite is known of his life. He adopted Chaucerian verse-forms and, with more good sense than other imitators showed, he also followed Chaucer's practice of looking at the world about him with his own eyes, setting down his imaginative interpretation of what he saw. Consequently, although Henryson composed poems with such reminiscent titles as *Orpheus and Eurydice* and *The Testament of Crisseid*, there is in them often a distinct freshness of treatment, genuine human feeling, and more than a little originality of approach, even if it is surprisingly sombre, as in the fate allotted to Crisseid in the *Testament*, where Henryson commits her to the lazar house to end her life as a leper. The fifteenth-century Scots dialect is in general extremely difficult for modern readers, but the following stanza from Crisseid's complaint is clear:

> O Ladyis fair of Troy and Grece, attend
> My miserie, quhilk nane may comprehend;
> My frivoll Fortoun, my Infelicitie:
> My greit mischeif quhilk na man can amend.
> Be war in tyme, approchis neir the end,
> And in your mynd ane mirrour mak of me:
> As I am now, peradventure that ye
> For all your micht may cum to that same end,
> Or ellis war, gif ony war may be

quhilk] which   Be war] be warned   Or ellis war] or else worse

The work of Gavin Douglas (*c.* 1475–1522), Bishop of Dunkeld, is mainly of interest through its threefold character, for the poet was by turns, if not simultaneously, a medievalist, a Chaucerian, and a classicist—producing in the last of these roles a translation of Virgil's *Æneid* (with notable Prologues), thus becoming the first translator of a classical poem into English or Scots. His other principal writings are *The Palice of Honour* (printed *c.* 1553), an allegorical dream poem of the familiar kind, and *King Hart* (not printed until 1786), of a similar pattern though with more evident stirrings of the newer spirit in poetry.

To modern readers William Dunbar (*c.* 1465–*before* 1530) is the best known among this group of Scottish poets, and chiefly for two of his poems: first, *The Lament for the Makaris* (Makers, i.e. poets), an elegy—which he tells us was written when he was sick—on contemporary writers, starting with Chaucer; second, the piece which begins:

> London, thou art of townes A per se.
>   Soveraign of cities, seemliest in sight,
> Of high renoun, riches and royaltie;
>   Of lordis, barons, and many a goodly knyght;
>   Of most delectable lusty ladies bright;
> Of famous prelatis, in habitis clericall;
>   Of merchauntis full of substance and of myght:
> London, thou art the flour of Cities all.

Dunbar's poem, now more than four centuries old, stands in its own right as one of the very few first-rate poems on London. Its refrain, 'London, thou art the flower of cities all', has impressed itself upon the memory of Londoners as deeply as Spenser's refrain to his *Epithalamium*, 'Sweet Thames run softly till I end my song'.

The medieval Scots poets of the post-Chaucer period drew upon three sources of culture: the old Celtic heritage gave them a robust—almost rowdy and sometimes coarse—earthiness of humour; from England and predominantly from Chaucer they derived verse-forms and much of their poetic art; in France they touched one of the fountain-heads of the stream which had so richly fertilized the imagination and fostered the craftsmanship of Chaucer himself, while they also experimented with themes handled by Villon and other contemporary French poets. Dunbar, it is supposed, came of a good family, was educated at St. Andrews, associated for some time with the Franciscan order, wandered in France, then returned to Scotland in Court service, and visited London on a diplomatic mission concerned with the projected match between James IV and Margaret Tudor. This union occasioned Dunbar's *The Thrissil and the Rose*, in which he combines the dream-allegory motive with the mood of a marriage song. *The Goldin Terge* is almost wholly an old-style Courtly poem, but in *To the Merchantis of Edinburgh*, *The Dance of the Sevin Deidly Synnis*, and *The Twa Maryit Women and the Wedo* (The Two Married Women and the Widow), Dunbar is a most vigorous and earthy satirist. His rough humour is displayed in many pieces and his fertile mastery of invective in *The Flyting of Dunbar and Kennedie*, a friendly prearranged bout of verbal all-in wrestling with no holds barred, in which Dunbar himself and a rival poet, Kennedy, are presented as contestants. Whatever their merits and their interest in relation to their age, however, these have all become museum exhibits. *The Lament for the Makaris*, on the other hand, remains a living poem, and even though Dunbar was not alone among the poets in using the phrase which provides its solemn refrain, he uses it with a difference that gives it the tone and reverberating depth of a great tolling bell: *Timor mortis conturbat me.*

> The stait of man dois chainge and vary,
> Now sound, now seik, now blyth, now sary,
> Now dansand mirry, now like to die;
> *Timor Mortis conturbat me.*
>
> . . . .
>
> Vnto the deth gois all estaitis,
> Princis, prelattis, and Potestaitis,
> Bayth riche and pure of all degre;
> *Timor Mortis conturbat me.*
>
> . . . .
>
> He hes done petuouslie devour,
> The noble Chaucer, of makaris flour,
> The Munk of Berry, and Gower, all thre;
> *Timor Mortis conturbat me.*

Potestaitis] powers   He hes done petuouslie devour] [Death] has
piteously devoured   The Munk of Berry (Bury)] John Lydgate

CHAPTER III

POPULAR LITERATURE

Carols and Ballads

ALL poetry began as chanted words, and was at some stage taken up by professional minstrels who became the elaborators and disseminators of poetic material which—starting probably as lays, i.e. short tales in verse—developed by combination and accretion into the full-scale heroic narrative poem, the epic, such as is found in imperfect form in *Beowulf* and at an incomparably higher pitch of accomplishment in Homer. A distinction can be made between *natural* poetry and *cultured* poetry: natural poetry being born of the primitive instinct to create, whereas cultured poetry arises from the desire to give form to inchoate substance. These, the masculine impulse and the feminine impulse, co-exist in the greatest poetry, but comprehension of the early development of literature depends upon an understanding of what is known or can be deduced of the initial and intermediate stages of poetry before it became the highest achievement in verbal expression and perfected art.

Gleemen, bards, minstrels were at one and the same time the ancient forerunners of modern journalists, historians, novelists, and entertainers. Their sung material—more in the nature of a sustained recitative than of a sequence of arias—must have included from time to time news of recent events, dovetailing with older factual stuff passed down orally and intermingled with legends in which fiction embroidered, more or less elaborately, remnants of still older fact. All this, chanted rhythmically to a simple lyre or harp accompaniment, made palatable entertainment during the centuries before a sophisticated culture felt the need for a more complex organization of leisure. No exacting effort of the imagination is needed to conceive of the successive stages through which poetry (always fluid in content and expression so long as it continued to circulate by word of mouth and memory) would pass from minstrels to scribes, in versions differing from each other. The concentration of learning within the ranks of the religious orders in the early medieval period meant that most of the transcribers, if not always the first scribes, were monks who, sometimes skilfully but more often clumsily, endeavoured to Christianize pagan material. From copying other men's verses to the composition of independent works was no great step, hence the proliferation of religious poetry in the Middle Ages; and once a written tradition had been established in this way in religious circles, the production of a secular written poetry was certain to follow as education and general culture advanced.

By Chaucer's time written poetry had for the most part displaced oral poetry among the educated, though for a long time the older mode was still to prevail in popular poetry, mainly in the form of carols and ballads.

Both these types of poetry have a community origin; they arise more from a group impulse than from an individual desire for expression.

The derivation of the word *carol* is uncertain, but that the kind of poem for which it became the generic term was in some way associated with a dance is commonly accepted; and that the dance was originally part of a pagan ritual celebration is most likely. There is evidence to support the opinion that the carol as a dance-song was seasonal in character and probably part of a fertility rite. That such rites must have continued in popular usage long after Christianity came to Britain is unquestionable; and if, as is thought, Christian churches were sometimes built where they would obliterate heathen altars, it would be in keeping to attempt to obliterate also the old ceremonies conducted at those altars and to introduce Christian observances of a countervailing kind.

It is not surprising, therefore, to find that early carols have a wide range of topics and are not confined to any one season. Nor is it surprising, if the pagan equivalents of carols had frequently a fertility reference, that in their Christian reincarnation they became linked particularly with Christmas, the Birth season; or that lullabies, from being a pre-Christian vocal device for soothing a human child, became elevated into songs memorializing the infant Jesus.

But for our present purpose the interest of carols lies in their character as a type of popular poetry; poetry, that is to say, with a folk origin, not a literary one. The recognition mark of such poetry is the repetitive refrain, which tends to become more elaborate and to recur at more distant intervals when the poems are of later dates and more professionally accomplished in technique. The earlier and the nearer to genuine community origin the simpler and more frequent the refrain.

While nothing is known of the actual making of English popular poetry, there is no reason to doubt that the process resembled that still operating among African and other primitive peoples. The essentials are a group of people in movement, either working or dancing, a solo voice (sometimes two, speaking antiphonally), a chorus (usually the whole group), and a theme either set or improvised. The 'soloist' or recitativist chants or intones a brief statement of the theme; if there is a second solo voice the original statement is either repeated or furthered with a second statement; the group then follows with the refrain. The soloist delivers another statement and the procedure is repeated; and so on *ad libitum*. Both 'solo' and refrain are accompanied by (or, rather, they accompany) rhythmical foot and/or body movements of a dance character. If the group is working, the implements (e.g. picks or shovels, adzes, bush knives, flails, paddles) are moved in unison with the refrain, while the brief recitative passages usually fall within the natural intervals—or negative phases—of movement: i.e. the implements will be raised as the recitative is uttered and will be brought down into contact with the earth, tree, undergrowth, corn, or water during the chorus. There is thus a negative phase and a positive phase in the action, an unaccented and an accented. If it is a leisure or a ritual occasion, the recitative and refrain are similarly accompanied by dance-movements (trunk and/or arm and hand movements if the group is seated), but of a more complex kind. The theme, if improvised, usually relates to some occurrence or person of current interest to the group; it may comment on the task in hand, or in general terms upon the condition (weariness, hunger, poverty, etc.) of the participating group; or it may characterize—often unflatteringly—the overseer or a local celebrity.

In some such fashion the folk poetry in which the carols and ballads had their roots must have come into existence—the carols developing into pure lyrical verse, the ballads into narrative lyric. Though the story element in the ballads as we now have them has evidently been through a process, or successive processes, of elaboration and fictionalization, where the refrain is still in simple form the particular ballad has probably undergone little change. Anyone who has in his mind's ear a modern African group-song of the kind sketched above, finds no difficulty in fitting to African rhythm the recitative lines and refrains of *Binnorie*:

> There were two sisters sat in a bour;
> *Binnorie, O Binnorie!*
> There cam a knight to be their wooer,
> *By the bonnie milldams o' Binnorie.*

and so through more than a score of repetitions of each refrain until the whole story has been told of the younger sister drowned by the jealous elder, of the wandering harper who, finding her body by the milldam, made from the dead girl's breast-bone a harp which he carried into her father's hall, where it played of its own accord and sang:

> O yonder sits my father, the King,
> *Binnorie, O Binnorie!*
> And yonder sits my mother, the Queen;
> *By the bonnie milldams o' Binnorie.*
> But the last tune that the harp play'd then—
> *Binnorie, O Binnorie!*
> Was, 'Woe to my sister, false Helèn!'
> *By the bonnie milldams o' Binnorie.*

The popular or folk origin of the ballads could be deduced from the nature and narrow range of subjects treated in them, from the naivety, rapidity, and simple directness of treatment, and from the unquestioning acceptance of marvel and miracle. Seduction, incest, murder within the family and without, the sorrow and tragedy inseparable from these calamities, portents and horrors of supernatural origin, revenges by human hands or by more-than-human agency—these are the materials of the ballads. These are also, of course, the ingredients of crude and ludicrous melodrama on the stage. Yet though they often show, technically as well as in content, plain signs of their hut or cottage origin, the ballads are neither crude nor ludicrous even at their most naive and violent. What saves them, and indeed lifts them to the plane of tragedy, is their utter conviction and sincerity of outlook and their utter simplicity of statement. The narrative lines present the fundamentals of life and death, while the choruses provide a solemn attendant music.

Much of the popular poetry of England and of the northern border country can be assigned to the fifteenth century, though there is no substantial manuscript collection earlier than the middle of the seventeenth century. This, found at Shifnal in Shropshire in 1729 by Thomas Percy (later Bishop of Dromore), is known as the Percy MS., and it was with the publication of Percy's *Reliques of Ancient English Poetry* in 1765 that widespread knowledge of the ballads began. A good many leaves of the original had been destroyed before it came into Percy's hands, but there are nearly 200 poems in the portion he rescued. The other great collection was Sir Walter Scott's *Minstrelsy of the Scottish Border*, published 1802-1803. Many of the ballads are of Scots origin, but the English Robin Hood ballads form the largest group concerned with a single character, the only English ballad hero whose popularity has been maintained down to the present day. The first mention (*c.* 1377) of Robin Hood is in *Piers Plowman* and he became the central figure in many fifteenth-century pieces. About 1500 Wynkyn de Worde printed *A Lytell Geste of Robin Hood*, a long poem which may represent a coalescence of several of the already familiar ballad stories, and illustrate by analogy something of the manner in which the lays of earlier centuries grew into epics.

No hard and fast line can be drawn through the territory of popular poetry to mark the boundary between carols and ballads. The division into sacred and secular gives as convenient a distinction as any, but it must be emphasized that a carol is not exclusively a sacred song for choral or congregational singing at Christmas. Though a refrain is common to both carols and ballads, the tendency was for the refrain to become less marked or to disappear altogether as the two kinds grew increasingly literary and the tradition of oral poetry of popular and communal origin weakened. The 'carol' of *The*

Seven Virgins may be taken as an example of the transitional type:

> All under the leaves and the leaves of life
> I met with virgins seven,
> And one of them was Mary mild,
> Our Lord's mother of Heaven.
>
> 'O what are you seeking, you seven fair maids,
> All under the leaves of life?
> Come tell, come tell, what seek you
> All under the leaves of life?'

After stanzas relating to the Crucifixion the poem ends thus:

> O the rose, the gentle rose,
> And the fennel that grows so green!
> God give us grace in every place
> To pray for our king and queen.
>
> Furthermore for our enemies all
> Our prayers they should be strong:
> Amen, good Lord; your charity
> Is the ending of my song.

Here the mixture of sacred and secular, of finished poetic culture and popular improvisation, of old and less old, brings incongruous elements into a beautiful and devout poem.

Early Plays

In the Prologue to her own story in Chaucer's *Canterbury Tales* the Wife of Bath includes among the many pastimes she had enjoyed 'visitaciouns . . . to playes of miracles'. At the time that was written (c. 1390) miracle plays had been for a century or more a familiar part of the year's round in many parts of England, while as long before as the third quarter of the tenth century the germ, at least, of religious drama was in existence as dialogue spoken by the clergy in church services.

Attempts have been made from time to time to establish an unbroken line of descent from classical Greek tragedy to the early English drama. If a continuous record were extant it might conceivably be possible to draw up a persuasive genealogical table suggesting the family history of various types of

5. The Lover's Confession from Gower's *Confessio Amantis*

16. 'I shoot my arrow at the World,' from Gower's *Vox Clamantis*

17 Detail of John Gower's Monument in Southwark Cathedral

18. Agamemnon in his tent, from Lydgate's *Troy Book*

19. John Lydgate offering *The Pilgrimage of the Life of Man*
to the Earl of Salisbury

Pastores erant i[n] regioue eade[m] uigila[n]-
tes + custodie[n]tes grege[m] suu[m]· et ecce
angelus d[omi]ni astitit iux[ta] illos + timueru[n]t
timore magno ·   iij[us] pastor   / We tib.
telle on · ·   þe myght
Brether What may þis be
þus bright to wan & best   at hand
Whi say ȝe so   obstand
Suche siȝt was neu[er] sene
Before in our[?] ȝolȝoy
Sin me iuelles Wil hit mene
þat wil be hes[?] þo by   a sang
ȝe be Couke by þis siȝt
And iwnes als i orhellez opes
But Was an angel briȝt
þt made þis nobull noyes.   of prophecy
he said a bayn shuld be
in þe bright of bedlem bred
And of þis myues me
our[?] fadros fond be fore   iold kyng
Bot may also þe þo fame
cue in our[?] paso pry mayes
þe angel nemes his name   not i ane
Crist saues þo saued
ȝone briȝhtnes Wil be bryng
unto þt bliffiul bour[?]
ffor soitez shal be bryng / So þo our saues

20. Two pages from the 'Shrewsbury' Mystery manuscript

Surrexit xpc nra ꝓa · paret vos i galilea ·

Crist is rysen witnes tho
by tokones p we haue sen ꝓ mort
Ours hope ours help ours hele is ho
and has bene best sithe we were born
if we wil seke hit for to so
lettes noght ꝓ lessun be forlorn
But gose eue bit to galilee
yer shal zo find hit zow beforn ·

Feria ij in ebdo pasche discipli i cunul cantet

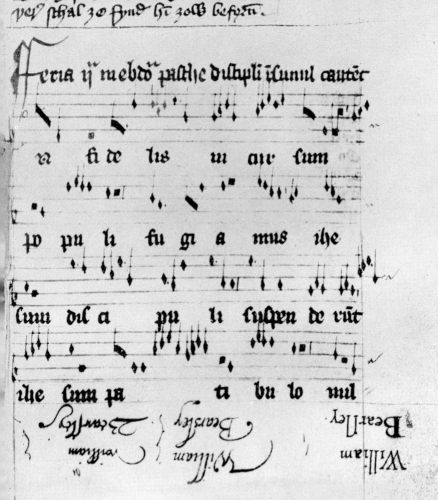

ra   ti de   lis   in   air   cum

po   pu   li   fu   gi   a   mus   ihe

cunu dil a   pu   li   cuspen de rut

ihe cunu et   ti   bu to   mil

William Bearley
William Bearley
Benffay
morgan

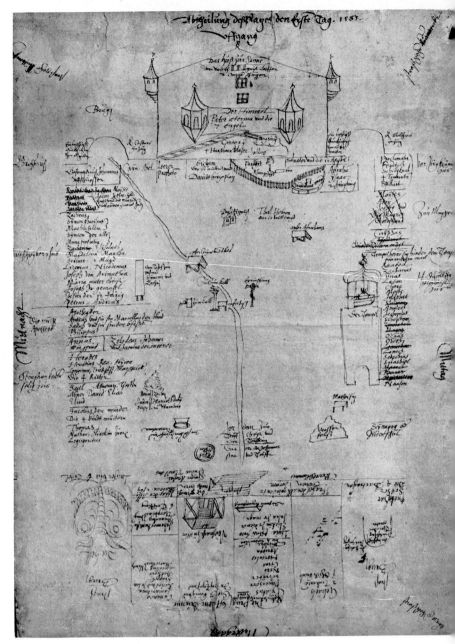

21. Plan of the first day of the Passion Play in the
market place at Lucerne, 1583

22. The stage for the Passion Play of Valenciennes

23. The first page of Wiclif's translation of *The Acts of the Apostles*

drama; but in fact the only link that can be surmised between the classical and the medieval drama is a basic histrionic impulse in the human race.

The great legacy left by the classical Greek dramatists was progressively debased in the Roman theatres, which offered at best, in Seneca and Plautus and Terence, Latin plays presenting formal lifeless situations, often in formal lifeless language; and at worst the Roman theatres and arenas offered debased spectacles in which 'realism' was carried to the ultimate point of actual sexual debauchery and actual murder in the sight of the audience.

It is no wonder, therefore, that with the establishment of Christianity as the state religion, plays and dramatic representations ceased to be a permitted form of entertainment. That the Romans brought stage shows of some kind to England is evident from the preserved remains of the theatre they built at St. Albans (Verulamium), which give an instructive view of the general layout and architectural features of a small classical theatre. But not until the sixteenth century were classical tragedy and comedy, through Roman (i.e. Latin) drama, to have any discernible effect on English literature.

Religionists and moralists who frown upon the theatre and aim to suppress it either by law or by preaching are greatly handicapped by the universal human characteristic that man is an incorrigible actor. From the cot to the coffin we make-believe, and even the most sophisticated cinema-bred modern child is as prone as its most primitive ancestor to live in an imaginative drama—often of surprising fullness and complexity —which runs alongside but rarely invades everyday existence. As the child so the adult. It is common knowledge that for thousands civilized marriage runs on two planes simultaneously —the actual plane and the play-acting imaginative plane in which the parties see each other idealized. Often the gulf between the two causes the ideal to destroy the actual; the play supplants the fact. In statecraft too, though it has been laid down that politics is the art of the possible, the play—the dream of power, or else the dream of human perfectibility—overwhelms the fact. Everywhere and at all times men and women are play-acting, make-believing. The wisdom of the Greeks is seen in relation to this as to so much else: they compensated this human characteristic by making acted drama a significant part of public life, and through dramatic representations in the theatre drained from the citizens' system any souring and disabling tendency to sacrifice the actual to the illusory. Greek tragedy objectified, worked out, and resolved by proxy, orally and visually, the problems and calamities which would otherwise fester in the life of the community. So might a modern playwright of the stature of Æschylus or Sophocles purge twentieth-century man of the nightmare fears with which, by subjective means, he poisons his mind and spirit.

Acted drama is a potent educator, particularly through its visual appeal, for things seen in action come home immediately to many whose ears are insensitive to things heard. It was consequently inevitable that the Church, though it had banished pagan drama, would be compelled at length to open its doors to visual representations of its own Christian drama. Drama was, indeed, implicit in the rite of the Mass.

The earliest impress of what may be called theatrical effects in medieval churches no doubt came from ritual practices at Eastertide, beginning with the covering of the altar crucifix on Good Friday and its unveiling on Easter Day. This simple procedure was later elaborated into the ceremony of carrying the crucifix from the altar on Good Friday and laying it in a nearby structure erected to represent the Sepulchre. On the Sunday it was removed from the sepulchre and restored to the altar. Step by step other episodes from the Gospel story received visual representation during the conduct of the liturgical offices, and when the point was reached at which one of the clergy first impersonated a biblical character Christian religious drama was born. In England this point seems to have been reached by the late tenth century, and to that period the beginnings of English liturgical drama can be dated. Liturgical drama may conveniently be thought of as being in the first phase a kind of sparsely illustrated sacred book; then as becoming gradually more liberally illustrated; and as developing eventually into a volume in which the pictures were so numerous and elaborate that the primacy of the sacred text was challenged. Dramatic representation as a visual aid to unlettered congregations developed into dramatic representation for its own sake and requiring its own dialogue: the liturgical factor dwindled and the increasing emphasis on the alien dramatic element met increasing popularity and enlarging audiences. These tendencies disturbed ecclesiastical authorities and led to the transference of the plays from within the churches to the graveyards outside. This proved unsatisfactory, for spectators crowding into church-yards trampled and desecrated the graves and it again became necessary to change the location to some place beyond the church precincts. However inconsiderable the geographical distance might be, this removal of the plays from sacred ground to village or town was vitally important in the progress, or regress, of English drama from religious to secular.

Once outside the churchyards, responsibility for the organiza-tion and expense of performance fell upon laymen—a responsi-bility which could be met only in places where population and monetary resources were adequate to perform and finance the plays. Since this could be nothing less than a collective enter-prise, control passed to the only secular or semi-secular bodies with authority and standing—the craft guilds. A great deal of scattered evidence of performances in numerous centres has come down to us; but, of the plays that have survived textually, those acted at Chester, York, Coventry, and Wakefield (or in its neighbourhood) are most important. The Chester group contains twenty-five plays; York, forty-eight; Coventry, forty-two; Wakefield (sometimes called the Towneley plays from the fact that the unique manuscript was long in the possession of the family of that name), thirty-two.

A document dated 1415 [1] specifies not only the order of performance of the York cycle but also the particular craft guild by which each play of the forty-eight was performed. This York programme can be regarded as an approximate pattern of the general procedure in other centres. The first three of the York plays deal with phases of the Creation; the next three with God's injunction to Adam and Eve, their dis-obedience, and the expulsion from Eden; the seventh with Cain and Abel; the eighth and ninth with Noah's ark and the Flood; the tenth with Abraham and Isaac; the eleventh with

---

[1] Set out in detail in *York Plays* (the standard text) edited by Lucy Toulmin Smith (Clarendon Press, 1885) and in *English Miracle Plays, Moralities, and Interludes* (with representative specimens and an excellent introduction), edited by A. W. Pollard (8th edn. Clarendon Press, 1927).

Moses and the serpent, Pharaoh, and 'eight Jews wondering and expecting'. With the twelfth the cycle turns to the prophecies of the coming of Christ, and thereafter dramatizes the principal episodes of the Gospel story up to the forty-third play, which takes the Ascension as its subject. The remaining five deal with such topics as the death, ascension, and coronation of Mary and with angels and devils. In other cycles the progression was from the Creation to the Day of Judgment.

The term 'cycle' is apt, for in performance the plays went round in turn from place to place in the particular town on the day of annual performance, which was customarily Corpus Christi day, though there were also plays associated with other occasions in the summer season of the Christian year. Most fortunately, Archdeacon Rogers of Chester set down in the late sixteenth century an account of the manner of presentation. From this document we know that each of the guild companies played on its own four-wheeled travelling stage called a pageant.[1] (In recent times that word has been taken over to designate exclusively a play dealing with local history and usually celebrating a centenary or other anniversary occasion.) The first play was performed soon after daybreak (about 4 or 5 o'clock) at the abbey gates; the second play would follow in the same place, and the rest in succession until the whole cycle had been acted. Meanwhile, the performers of the first play were wheeled on their pageant to the town centre (the 'high cross'), where they played before the mayor, and thence in turn to every street: 'and so every street had a pageant playing before them at one time, till all the pageants for the day appointed were played'. When the action of any episode called for a more elaborate setting, there might be a supplementation of the stage area, either by combining two pageants, or by some scene-changing device, or by using the street as well as the stage. It makes an impressive mental picture to imagine some forty or fifty plays in progress simultaneously out of doors in a small town, with scores of members of the guilds participating, and the rest of the populace in the audiences.

---

[1] The word was no doubt first used for the play and then without differentiation for the wheeled stage. There is no contemporary picture of such a stage.

Although theoretically the aim appears to have been to allot to each guild the play most appropriate to its craft or trade, in practice only a minority could be so fitted. While at York the shipwrights, mariners, and fishmongers found themselves well served with the making and manning of the Ark, the Shepherds' play was done by the chandlers, and the Ascension by the tailors.

An expenses account from Coventry shows that the costs of rehearsals and performances were considerable. These were met by an annual levy on each guild member. Food and drink for the players was paid for out of the funds, and for rehearsals at Coventry it is recorded that, besides much ale and wine, ribs of beef and a goose were bought. The actors received fees on the day of performance, but the system governing the scale of payments is not evident, for whereas God was paid only 2s. (the same as Pilate's Wife and two Knights received each), Herod's fee was 3s. 4d., Pilate's 4s. with 4d. for his son, and Anna's 2s. 2d. Judas and the Devil had 1s. 6d. each, but Peter and Malchus 2d. less. The Minstrel was paid 1s. 1d. It does not appear that either the relative importance or the relative popularity of the characters determined the fee, though it may be that each payment was proportionate to the actor's daily wage at his trade. If popularity had been the criterion, the Devil and Herod would have been as well paid as any, for Herod's bellowing and ranting made him a favourite. He is celebrated in Hamlet's phrase referring to the Player King's speech: 'he out-Herods Herod'; while the Devil must have provided much rough fun, particularly in the later morality plays when he was often accompanied by an attendant who belaboured him with 'a dagger of lath'. This attendant—known as The Vice—became a traditional comic type and settled at length into the stock character whose apotheosis was reached in the Shakespearian Clown.

Nineteenth-century scholars adopted a threefold classification for the medieval plays: *mysteries* (from the French *mystères*), dealing with biblical themes; *miracles*, dealing with incidents in the lives of the saints; *moralities*, dealing with personified abstract virtues and vices. More recently the label *mysteries* has been challenged and mostly abandoned, on the ground that it had not been applied to medieval plays in England until its employment by a collector in the late eighteenth century.[1] Moreover, it is pointed out that there is not in England any separate group of saints plays for which the term *miracles* needs to be reserved. It is now customary, therefore, to follow the medieval English practice of calling all the religious plays *Miracles* whether they are concerned with biblical or with other sacred persons. The term *Moralities* is retained for the plays which deal mainly with personified abstractions, such as Truth, Chastity, Sloth, Lechery, Patience, and many more. A further category, *Interludes*, takes in a type of play which perhaps began as a rough humorous episode interpolated in the Miracles and became through gradual enlargement fostered by its popularity a separate kind, sometimes farcical, sometimes didactic, digressing more and more from strictly religious themes, and coming to be played as a private entertainment within (or in the grounds of) wealthy houses.

With the developed Interludes written by John Heywood (*c.* 1497–1580) we reach works by the first named English playwright, although there have been guesses at the authorship of a few of the early liturgical pieces. Like almost the whole of medieval art the drama was anonymous. It is supposed that the plays in the guild cycles were commissioned from monkish and other clerical authors, since these alone were likely to have the necessary background knowledge and literary skill. But whatever original scripts may have been thus supplied, they could hardly have failed to undergo substantial change in the course of rehearsals and performances from year to year. With so large a body of non-professional actors it would be astonishing if there were no amateur playwrights or improvers or botchers of plays among them; while it is still more likely that there were local wits and clownish fellows who gagged and spoke more than was set down for them. Probably it would not be wide of the mark to suppose that boisterous passages of humour are secular accretions, perhaps improvisations which became incorporated with the authentic text, referring to local and topical affairs. What more likely than that the nagging of

---

[1] L. Toulmin Smith's edition of the *York Plays* carries the sub-title ' The Plays performed by the Crafts or Mysteries of York'. It is possible that in popular speech the word *mysteries* would have been used both for the guilds and for the plays performed by them.

Noah by his Wife in the Chester play of the Deluge was suggested by the plight of some henpecked husband notorious in the town? Or that Mak the sheepstealer in the Wakefield second Shepherds' Play was a thievish character all too well known to those who performed and watched the play? In such passages as these comedy begins to show itself in the distinctively English manner, which changes little in essence though it grows in volume in English writings down to the time of Dickens.

The verse used in the medieval plays has many signs of unskilful cutting, patching, and other maltreatment of the textual material. There were undoubtedly borrowings and adaptations by the players of one locality from those of another: inferior versions of York plays, for example, were performed elsewhere. These and similar corrupt texts may have been disseminated by wandering scribes setting down plays from memory, or they may be due to the normal process of defective oral transmission long before any attempt was made to establish a written text other than the 'parts' used by the individual actors.

The pre-Chaucerian alliterative verse is used extensively in the medieval drama, often with a lingering regard for the old line-structure, as in the York play of the Creation:

> A! mercyfull maker, full mekill as thi mighte,
>   That all this warke at a worde worthely has wroghte
> Ay loved be that lufly lorde of his lighte,
>   That us thus mighty has made, that nowe was righte
>   noghte . . .

> (O merciful maker, how high is thy might / Who all this work at a word worthily hast wrought / Ever loved be that lord beloved for his light / Who us so mighty has made who but now were nought.)[1]

Here and throughout the play affection for head-rhyme is a marked characteristic, four alliterative words being used in many of the lines, rather than the three common to Anglo-Saxon verse. Rhyme is usual in these plays, and considerable use is made of the homely doggerel verse parodied in Chaucer's

[1] From the modernized version by J. S. Purvis in *The York Cycle of Mystery Plays* (S.P.C.K., London, 1951).

Tale of Sir Thopas: e.g. in the Chester play of the Deluge (Noah is speaking after the dove returns):

> Ah lord, blessed be thou aye,
> That me hast confort thus to day;
> By this sight, I may well saye,
> This flood begins to cease.
> My sweete dove to me brought hase
> A branch of olyve from some place,
> This betokenyth God has done us some grace
> And is a signe of peace.

But while the taproots of the plays reach down into the older literature, the medieval drama as a whole introduces a considerable variety of verse forms, tending in the later plays to concentrate on the rhyming couplet, often used with great skill and effect. In addition to the songs clearly indicated as such, there are not a few passages which seem to fit the singing voice most readily—as this in *Mary Magdalen* when the innkeeper greets Mary and Luxuria[1] on their arrival in Jerusalem:

> I am a taverner wytty and wyse,
> That wynys have to sell gret plente.
> Of all the taverners I bere the pryse
> That be dwellyng withinne the cete. . . .

What must be one of the earliest of English drinking songs is given to that amusingly tiresome woman Noah's Wife in the play cited above. She defies Noah when he tells her to come into the ark, and says she will not budge from the land unless she can bring her gossips (women friends) aboard. As Noah grows angrier she becomes more annoying and then breaks into song:

> The flude comes fleetinge in full faste,
>   One every syde that spreads full ferre;
> For feare of drowning I am agaste;
>   Good gossippes, lett us drawe nere
> And let us drinke or we departe,
>   For ofte tymes we have done soe;
> For att a draughte thou drinkes a quarte,
>   And soe will I do or I goe. . . .

[1] An instance of a Morality character encroaching upon a Miracle play.

This English rural alehouse humour is one of the numerous
excrescences imposed upon the biblical stories by the native
authors, who were also skilled in using the plays for more
serious contemporary purposes. The second Shepherds' Play

Everyman and Death

opens with a speech by one of the shepherds which is a complaint
about the condition of his kind—their poverty and other hard-
ships and the ills they are made to suffer by the 'gentlery men'.
There is also acute pathos in keeping with the theme in the
Abraham and Isaac plays, and tragic force in the Crucifixion
episodes. The moods are as various as the many phases of the
sacred record.

The Moralities, unlike the Miracles, rarely gain the willing attention of a modern audience, since abstractions and personifications can have only a loose and precarious hold upon minds accustomed to regard individual men and women and matters of human personality as the vital stuff of drama. *Everyman* (translated in the fifteenth century from a Dutch original) alone among the Moralities transcends the limitations of the medium. It succeeds through a simple clarity which becomes luminously beautiful when Everyman, summoned by Death, finds Fellowship, Beauty, Strength, Discretion, Five Wits, all his trusted companions deserting him; Good Deeds, though weak from neglect by Everyman, remains with him, and Knowledge also, saying:

> Everyman, I wyll go with the and be thy gyde,
> In thy moost nede to go by thy syde.

The Interludes, also, have now a mainly antiquarian interest, and the only examples that need to be mentioned here are *Fulgens and Lucrece* (*c.* 1495) by Henry Medwall, which scholars commend as the first true precursor of English secular drama, inasmuch as the characters (and the comedy characters in particular) exist in their own right and not solely as means to further a moral purpose (*see also below*, p. 175); John Rastell's *The Four Elements* and his other Interludes, which have the interest of being by the brother-in-law of Sir Thomas More, who may have acted in private performances of one or more of them; and *King John* by John Bale, Bishop of Ossory (1495–1563), a curiously interesting piece which injects the beginnings of historical drama into the declining Morality. King John plays his part in the company of such personifications as Nobility, Clergy, Private Wealth (dressed as a cardinal), Verity, Imperial Majesty, Sedition, Dissimulation, England, and so on. Dissimulation, appearing as a fanatical monk, sets out to poison the king, but is himself compelled to drink from the fatal draught, dying before his victim. In spite of its stiff and stilted unnaturalistic manner, Bale's play has some power of compulsion which saves the character of King John from being an altogether lifeless figure.

CHAPTER IV

PROSE IN THE MIDDLE AGES

The Survival of Prose

SUCCESSIVE generations of literary historians and scholars held, somewhat as an article of faith requiring no proof, that English (i.e. Anglo-Saxon) prose was brought to a dead stop when the country was overrun by the Danes in the tenth-eleventh centuries, and that, as a written language, Norman-French poured into a vacuum (except among the learned who used Latin) when William the Conqueror came. This view had hardly been challenged and no evidence brought against it until Professor R. W. Chambers, having written a lengthy introduction to the mid-sixteenth-century *Life of Sir Thomas More* by Nicholas Harpsfield, issued that introduction separately in 1932 as *On the Continuity of English Prose from Alfred to More and His School*.[1]

There could be no questioning that poetry had survived the impact of invasion after invasion, but this could be explained by the fact that, being an oral form, it lodged and persisted in popular memory independently of manuscripts. Moreover, poetry was designed to entertain as well as to inform and instruct, and would therefore be fostered by unlearned and learned alike for the pleasure it gave in times when amusement was hard to come by and long-drawn-out poems tiresome to present-day taste were heard with delight. Whereas the over-stimulated and therefore dulled modern imagination calls for more and more highly condimented entertainment, the medieval public, largely illiterate (or, where literate, ill-supplied with books) and knowing nothing of organized pleasure until playgoing became a national recreation, could find magic in poems which may to our generation represent the acme of tedium. Poetry was then for leisure; and, stored in memory, it could be a private possession of little concern to invaders, who were not to discover until centuries later the technique

---

[1] Published by the Early English Text Society. Reprinted 1951.

of mental conquest through propaganda and the enslavement of language and the arts.

But if poetry, though beginning in public, could be cherished in private, prose was entirely public and essential to the transaction of practical affairs and for all direct intercourse between the victors and the defeated. Thus, after the Norman Conquest French was installed as the official language of the law courts and schools, as well as of the royal Court. Though edicts affecting the populace were for some time necessarily issued in English, Norman-French was adopted more and more for such documents, while Latin held its place as the standard language of religion and higher learning so long as the Church remained unchallenged.

The vernacular, consequently, dwindled except as the medium of everyday communication among the vulgar, and from that source no benefit to literature could be expected. Chambers acknowledges that English ceased to be current for official purposes and also for the writing of history; but it was essential to his thesis in *The Continuity of English Prose* that he should be able to establish an unbroken line for written English literary prose, as distinct from the common spoken tongue. He therefore needed to uncover in some quarter a body of people sufficiently educated to read easily, yet not learned enough to be conversant with Latin, and so far removed from the main current of contemporary life as to remain un-Normanized. Such a body, he suggested, could be found in the nunneries; and he claimed that the English translation from the Latin of the Rule of St. Benedict, which Æthelwold was set to make in the second half of the tenth century, was expressly for nuns, not for monks, since feminine pronouns appear casually in each surviving copy of the translation.

> It would have been a confession of weakness that monks should be supposed unable to study their founder's rules in the original. At any rate, the archetype of our extant copies certainly was for nuns. . . . And here, for the first time, we come across a fact which is the cause of the composition of so much English prose; the fact that women recluses would not be expected to be as familiar as men would be with Latin.

If Chambers's hypothesis is sound—and the case against it (that English prose perished with the coming of the Danes in the late tenth century and was not reborn until the mid-fourteenth century) is harder to sustain—it was in devotional literature that native prose was kept alive during the lean post-Conquest years when Norman-French appeared to be strangling English. And from among the devotional writings the *Ancren Riwle* (*see above*, p. 8) is singled out as having been —through its immense popularity and widespread circulation in several versions and numerous manuscripts—especially serviceable in upholding the English prose tradition until the fourteenth-century revival gave it a vigorous renewal of life. Unless continuity was secured by some such means, it is necessary to believe in a miraculous resurrection of English prose by some near contemporary of Wiclif, and necessary also to account for the impressive fact that Norman-French was at length driven out of its royal, legal, and scholastic strongholds by the supposedly dead English.

Devotional Writings

Historical literature, which in this country began with *The English Chronicle* (started in Alfred's reign, 871–901, and ended in 1154), was carried on by various local chroniclers—at Worcester, Durham, Hexham, Newborough, Devizes, etc.— with *The Peterborough Chronicle* giving a particularly vivid account of troubled times under Norman rule. But poetry and the miracle plays virtually monopolize attention, except for the *Ancren Riwle*, until we come to the succession of writers and translators of prose books beginning with Dan Michel of Northgate, a Canterbury monk, who completed his *Ayenbyte of Inwyt* (The Prick, or Remorse, of Conscience) late in 1340. This translation—or, rather, clumsy rendering—of a late thirteenth-century French work is remarkable as a specimen of the Kentish dialect. 'It treats of the Commandments, the Creed, the Seven Deadly Sins, the Seven Petitions of the Paternoster, and the Seven Gifts of the Holy Spirit.' Chaucer probably based *The Parson's Tale* on the French original (*Somme des Vices et des Virtues* by Friar Lorens, 1279), but *The Ayenbyte of Inwyt* is little more than a disjointed word-book which gropes, term by term, after the English equivalent for the French, with no sense of style or structure. The most memorable thing about it is its title, for 'ayenbyte of inwyt' is in sound more expressive of remorseful inward gnawings than the modern English phrase, *'Prick of Conscience'*, which is also the title of a poem formerly attributed to Richard Rolle of Hampole, a Yorkshire contemporary of the Canterbury Michel and a far more skilful writer of English prose.

Rolle is an engaging character whose personality leaps across the six centuries separating us from him. He was a holy man and a hermit; nevertheless he contrived to attract in the fourteenth century, by 'quasi-amorous ecstasy', the kind of adoring feminine discipleship that fashionable ascetics still enjoy in the twentieth century, though in west London churches and literary coteries rather than in north-country cells. Richard Rolle was born about 1300 at Thornton-le-Dale in Yorkshire and became a scholar at Oxford, leaving the university when he was nineteen and before his studies were completed. Though his writings show that he was not deficient in formal academic learning, he evidently experienced at Oxford a spiritual crisis, for on his return to Yorkshire he arranged that his sister should meet him a short way from their home with garments from which he cobbled a hermit's robe. In a neighbouring church attended by the family of two of his university friends (sons of Sir John and Lady Dalton) he preached a sermon so impressive that they settled him as a resident hermit in a cell on their property. A few years later he moved to another cell near Anderby, where he became the friend and spiritual consultant of Margaret Kirby, a female recluse, for whom he wrote *The Form of Perfect Living*. Finally Rolle settled close by the Cistercian convent at Hampole, near Doncaster. There the nuns made much of him and revered him for his saintliness, and after his death in 1349 tried without success for his canonization.

A peculiar sweetness, though never sickliness, emanates from Richard Rolle's personality and writings. He was a mystic who through solitary contemplation but also through communion with others like-minded achieved union with the Unseen. He drew from solitude the spiritual sustenance that moved him to quiet missionary service among people of all classes. Though he chose poverty for himself, he was at ease with the wealthy and incurred some odium among the narrowly religious on that account. His writings were extremely popular and of wide currency, as the large number of surviving manuscripts shows. With his Commentary on the Psalms (though it is much indebted to the Latin of Peter Lombard) and other writings on the Scriptures he takes a notable place among those who helped to root the Bible in English life and literature. R. W. Chambers claims for Rolle 'a supreme place in the history of English prose', saying that in his writings, notwithstanding their fourteenth-century Yorkshire dialect, we have 'modern English prose. The spelling and form of the words, sometimes the actual vocabulary, may be strange; but the arrangement of the words is modern.' In the passage below (comparing the bee and the righteous man) from a short treatise by Rolle there are few words which cannot be interpreted by a reader of modern English.

The bee has thre kyndis. Ane es þat scho es neuer ydill, and scho es noghte with thaym þat will noghte wyrke, bot castys thaym owte, and puttes thaym away. Anothire es þat when scho flyes scho takes erthe in hyr fette, þat scho be noghte lyghtly ouerheghede in the ayere of wynde. The thyrde es þat scho kepes clene and bryghte hire wyngeȝ.

Thus ryghtwyse men þat lufes God are neuer in ydyllnes. For owthyre þay ere in trauayle, prayand, or thynkande, or redande, or othere gude doande; or withtakand ydill mene, and schewand thaym worthy to be put fra þe ryste of heuene, for þay will noghte trauayle here.

Þay take erthe, þat es, þay halde þamselfe vile and erthely, that thay be noghte blawene with þe wynde of vanyté and of pryde. Thay kepe thaire wyngeȝ clene, that es, þe twa commandementes of charyté þay fulfill in gud concyens, and thay hafe othyre vertus, vnblendyde with þe fylthe of syne and vnclene luste.

scho] she   ouerheghede] raised too high   redande] reading   doande] doing   withtakand] reprehending

John Wiclif
It has been seen that the earliest poetry composed in England was largely concerned with paraphrases of biblical material

and that Ælfric made a prose translation of parts of the Bible in the tenth-eleventh century. Translations of the New Testament and of some books from the Old Testament were also made at various times and approved for use in religious houses, especially in the nunneries. But not until the last quarter of the fourteenth century was a complete translation (and one designed for general lay use) undertaken, by Wiclif and the Wicliffites.

The old picturesque labelling of Wiclif as 'the morning star of the Reformation' does in fact describe him as closely as any phrase can describe so complex a personality living in disturbed times and increasing the disturbances by his own convictions and activities. John Wiclif, like Richard Rolle, was a Yorkshireman, born about 1320 near Richmond in the North Riding, of a family which took its name from Wycliffe-on-Tees. Nothing is known with certainty about his life until he appears in the records as 'master of Balliol' at Oxford in 1360. He was at that time and for years after in good standing with the university and with the papal authorities, for he received ecclesiastical preferment, including a canonry in the Lincoln diocese, where in 1374 he also became rector of Lutterworth, holding the benefice until his death in 1384.

Wiclif lived in the age when the hold of Latin was being challenged by the encroaching vernacular, and it was he more than any other that helped the vulgar tongue to triumph at length over the learned. Yet Wiclif himself for the main part of his life wrote in Latin, and he was much involved in the philosophical controversy between the Nominalists, led by William of Ockham, who held that 'universals or abstract concepts are mere names', and the Realists, supported by Wiclif, who maintained that such concepts have an actual objective existence. Philosophy and theology had not yet, as in modern times, come to represent, respectively, secular and sacred systems of thought, and Wiclif was drawn into a complex of argument which, being concerned with man's relationship with God, led him to conclusions inimical to the prevailing system of Church government from Rome, which imposed monetary levies on the English people hard beset already by tax burdens of their own. Thus Wiclif was by progressive stages implicated in political issues which aligned him with the struggles of the poor against oppression from above. At length he openly challenged the authority of Rome, dissented from most of her doctrines— including, on rational-philosophic grounds, that of transubstantiation—and took the position that the Bible was man's true source of knowledge of God's will. Though the University of Oxford at first acquitted Wiclif of charges made against him at the instigation of the hierarchy, his public denial in 1380 of the doctrine of transubstantiation was open heresy and two years later the university could no longer withstand the demand for his expulsion. By that time, however, Wiclif's prestige was high in the wider sphere beyond academic and ecclesiastical circles, for about 1377 his increasing opposition to the Church had caused him to start his band of Poor Preachers, priests (and, later, laymen also) who lived under a rule of poverty and went about the land preaching and teaching Bible Christianity. By the year of the Peasants' Revolt, 1381, the Poor Preachers had become largely identified with the movements of popular discontent which culminated in that uprising, and, consequently, Wiclif was regarded as politically suspect as well as heretical. Though the Lollards (the name given to the partisans of discontent—from the Dutch *lollærd*, a mumbler or mutterer) were neither founded nor led by Wiclif, and developed an extreme socialistic and anti-religious policy at variance with his beliefs, they were popularly considered to be identical with his followers, no doubt because some at least of the Poor Preachers were inspirers of the Lollard movement.

The last two years of Wiclif's life were passed in his parish at Lutterworth, where, besides preaching, he wrote controversial pieces and worked on his translation of the Scriptures. He died in 1384 after an attack of paralysis. Nearly fifty years later (1428) the Bishop of Lincoln (Richard Fleming, founder of Lincoln College, Oxford) who had himself been condemned as a Wicliffite in 1409, crassly demonstrated (under orders) his recovered orthodoxy by having Wiclif's remains disinterred and thrown into a tributary of the Avon. This resulted only in a popular rhyme of remarkable foresight:

> The Avon to the Severn runs,
>   The Severn to the sea,
> And Wiclif's dust shall spread abroad
>   Wide as the waters be.

F

Credit belongs to Wiclif for organizing the first English translation of the whole Bible, though he himself did but part of the
work, probably the New Testament and portions of the Old.
His style is more archaic than that of some earlier writers of
English prose, and the following passage from the parable of
the prodigal son (St. Luke, xv) shows how far he was from the
intelligible modern prose of the Authorized Version or even
from the prose of Tindale (*see below*, p. 95).

And he seide, A man hadde twei sones; and the ӡonger of hem
seide to the fadir, Fadir, ӡyue me the porcioun of catel, that
fallith to me. And he departide to hem the catel. And not aftir
many daies, whanne alle thingis weren gederid togider, the
ӡonger sone wente forth in pilgrymage in to a fer cuntre; and
there he wastide hise goodis in lyuynge lecherously. And aftir
that he hadde endid alle thingis, a strong hungre was maad in
that cuntre, and he bigan to haue nede. And he wente, and
drouӡ hym to oon of the citeseyns of that cuntre. And he sente
hym in to his toun, to fede swyn. And he coueitide to fille his
wombe of the coddis that the hoggis eeten, and no man ӡaf hym.
And he turnede aӡen to hym silf, and seide, Hou many hirid
men in my fadir hous han plente of looues; and Y perische here
thorouӡ hungir. Y schal rise vp, and go to my fadir, and Y schal
seie to hym, Fadir, Y haue synned in to heuene, and bifor thee;
and now Y am not worthi to be clepid thi sone, make me as
oon of thin hirid men. . . .

Very little information concerning Wiclif's helpers in the
work of translation has been handed down. Part of the Old
Testament is attributed, however, to Nicholas of Hereford, who
recanted after being for a while the leader of the Lollards;
while John Purvey, who also recanted in 1401 after imprisonment for heresy, had been Wiclif's chief assistant at Lutterworth
and completed a revision of the whole translation about 1388.

Walter Hilton's *Scala Perfectionis* (The Scale, or Ladder, of
Perfection), written in English and embodying translated
passages from the Scriptures, shows a further stage of development in vernacular prose. Hilton, an Augustinian canon at
Thurgarton, Nottinghamshire, had some of the devotional
fervour of Richard Rolle, some of his common sense, and occasionally also a touch of his literary charm.

Mandeville

Much scholarly investigation was directed to the fourteenth-century book called *Mandeville's Travels* before it was determined to be a deception, almost certainly written by a Belgian notary-public, Jean d'Outremeuse, author of a bulky prose chronicle, *Miroir des Histoires*, and other writings in prose and verse.[1] He filched his Mandeville material from various sources—books of travel, descriptions of pilgrimages, and legendary romances, all concerned with Eastern lands—twisted the originals in the

An illustration from *Mandeville's Travels*

attempt to cover his tracks as a shameless plagiarist, invented when invention was easier than stealing, and fathered the compilation upon an English knight and physician buried at Liège in 1372, whose epitaph had been misread by others, thus causing him to become known posthumously as Sir John Mandeville. It is possible that d'Outremeuse was acquainted with 'Mandeville', and to the question 'why a book made by one man should have circulated under the name of another' Hamelius replies that the real author had reason to fear the ecclesiastical authorities, since the *Travels* contains controversial matter obnoxious to the Church; indeed, Hamelius goes further and suggests that the book was put out as an anti-papal pamphlet in disguise. What is beyond doubt is that d'Outremeuse, whatever his motive, succeeded in fabricating

[1] For a discussion of the whole problem of the authorship of the *Travels* see the two-vol. edition by Paul Hamelius (Early English Text Society, 1919, 1923).

a work which has been found highly entertaining by readers during six centuries, however blameworthy he might be as a liar and a heretic.

The original version in French seems to have been completed shortly before 1370. It was rendered into English by an anonymous translator whose knowledge of French was imperfect, if the earliest surviving manuscript (belonging to the first quarter of the fifteenth century) contains his work.

The imaginary traveller is represented as journeying to the Holy Land and other countries of the Middle East and afterwards to the lands beyond. There is a good deal of dubious theological material, but the lasting attraction of the *Travels* comes from its wealth of incredible wonders and fascinating marvels. The translation is of little account as English prose, and the typical passage below is slightly paraphrased, with the exception of the one (here italicized) sentence retained as an illustration of the translator's South-East Midland dialect.

In that island [Ceylon] is a great mountain in the middle of which is a great lake. And the people of the country say that Adam and Eve wept upon that mountain for a hundred years after they were driven out of paradise and that their tears filled the lake, in the bottom of which men find many precious stones and great pearls. In the lake grow many reeds and large canes, within which are numerous crocodiles and serpents and great water-leeches. *And the kyng of þat contree ones euery ʒeer ʒeueth leve to pore men to gon in to the lake to gadre hem precyous stones & perles by way of almess for the loue of god þat made Adam.* And all the year men find enough. For protection against the vermin in the lake they anoint their arms and their thighs and their legges with an ointment made of a kind of fruit, called lemons [limes], like small [peaches],[1] and then they have no dread of the crocodiles or other venomous vermin. . . . And the men of that island say that the serpents and wild beasts of the country will not harm or touch with evil any stranger, but only men born in the country. In that land and other round about there are wild geese with two heads, white lions as big as oxen, and many other beasts and birds not seen among us. The surrounding sea is so high that it seems as though it might hang from the clouds and cover the whole world; and it is a great marvel that it might do so, but that, only through the will of God, the air sustains it.

[1] The translator rendered *pêches* as *pesen* (peas).

Other Translations

The history of English prose in the second half of the fourteenth and throughout the fifteenth century is largely a history of translations. *Mandeville's Travels* had little distinguishable influence upon the course of literature in England, but it appealed to that sense of the marvellous which is inherent, however often latent, in Englishmen and which was to be stimulated by many genuine travellers' tales in the Age of Discovery. The need for translations of soberer and more learned works than the Mandeville book increased when the native language ousted French after the statute of 1362 had re-established English as the language of the law courts. By the end of the century English had superseded French in the schools also, and Latin was slowly but inevitably losing ground.

It fell to John Trevisa (1362–1412), a dissident Oxford scholar who became vicar of Berkeley in Gloucestershire, to translate at the request of Lord Berkeley, to whom Trevisa was chaplain, two encyclopædic works, *De Proprietatibus Rerum* by Bartholomæus Anglicus, settled as a professor of theology in the University of Paris, and the *Polychronicon* by Ranulf Higden, a Chester monk. The first of these is a voluminous thirteenth-century compendium of natural science; the latter an eclectic universal history from the Creation to the fourteenth century, taking in geography as well as much mythical lore. Both were valued as basic works of learning, though they have since fallen to the level of literary curiosities.

Of more enduring interest is that vast storehouse of tales, the *Gesta Romanorum*: 'perhaps there has been no work among those composed before the invention of printing, of which the popularity has been so great and the history so obscure'.[1] As originally put together in Latin it derives from 'oriental apologues, monkish legends, classical stories, tales of chroniclers, popular traditions, and other sources which it would be now difficult and perhaps impossible to discover'. Though it is an omnibus of fiction, its purpose was religious and moral, being intended to provide preachers with palatable illustrations for their discourses. Each anecdote is followed by a 'moralite' or a 'declaracio' which presses what had gone before into a

---

[1] Sidney J. H. Herrtage: *The Early English Versions of the Gesta Romanorum* (Early English Text Society, 1879).

Christian mould. Thus, the story of Lear and his daughters (which in one version of the *Gesta Romanorum* is changed to the Emperor Theodosius and his three daughters) has as its 'moralite' the statement that the king or emperor is 'ech worldly man', the first daughter (Goneril) is 'the worlde', the second (Regan) is 'thi wif, or thi childryn, or thi kyn', and the third (Cordelia) 'is our lord god, whom we lovith to litell; But if we come to him in tyme of oure nede with a clene hert and mynde, withoute doute we shull have help of him against the king of egipt, [i.e.] the devil; and he shal sette us in oure heritage, [i.e.] the kyngdome of heven.'

The Latin *Gesta Romanorum* is ascribed to the earlier part of the fourteenth century and was known to Boccaccio, who drew upon it in the *Decameron* (written 1348–58); the earliest manuscript in English belongs to *c.* 1440. In addition to the Lear story (which had appeared in English earlier: *see above*, p. 8), the *Gesta Romanorum* contains the caskets episode used in *The Merchant of Venice*, the story of Constance used by Chaucer and Gower, and originals for certain lesser works. An even vaster compilation with a similar purpose, though differing in scope and in the nature of its material, is *The Golden Legend* (*Legenda Aurea*), an English version of which existed before Caxton issued his extremely popular enlarged edition (*see below*, p. 83).

Pecock and Fortescue

As examples of argumentative prose, Bishop Reginald Pecock's *The Repressor of overmuch blaming of the clergy* (*c.* 1455) and *The Donet* ('þe "donet" or "key" of goddis lawe, or ellis þe "donet" or "key" of cristen religioun') (*c.* 1443–9), and Sir John Fortescue's *On the Governance of England, otherwise called The Difference between an Absolute and a Limited Monarchy* (*c.* 1475), are outstanding, as much for their style as for their content. Pecock was not a graceful writer and he is much inferior to Fortescue in clarity of statement, but he wrote a full-bodied prose and he was a resourceful if inelegant word-maker who did not permit himself to be confined within the limits of the current English vocabulary. Though he wrote against the Lollards, Pecock was himself branded as a heretic for seeking to confute his opponents by reason, thus conceding (so his ecclesiastical superiors judged) that the Lollards had a case which should be met by argument rather than by outright condemnation. Faced with the choice of the stake or of recantation Pecock chose the latter, and stood at St. Paul's Cross while his writings were burnt beside him and the mob howled at him. The last word was with Pecock's spirit, however, for after his death some time later the Church authorities complained that his works were circulating much more widely than while he was alive.

Fortescue, who began as a Lancastrian and became Chiei Justice, was also compelled to change sides. After the House of York had triumphed he prudently, and perhaps sincerely, claimed that new evidence which had come to his notice enabled him to support the new regime and convinced him that he had previously been mistaken in upholding the cause of the other party. His case is presented with remarkable skill and every appearance of conviction, and *The Governance of England* is notable also as the first English treatise on constitutional rule.

The Paston Letters

In the Paston Letters we have a large body of unprofessional prose concerned with personal and domestic matters, and with current events seen from a family angle, which is valuable as enabling us to see how the English language was written by average men and women in the fifteenth century. The Pastons were a Norfolk family whose preserved correspondence overlaps three generations, *c.* 1440–88. The letters are perhaps more interesting as history than as literature; nevertheless, the varieties of character displayed in them, their exposure of the best and the worst of human behaviour, the loves and hates, the hopes and dreads, the gentlenesses and brutalities, the meannesses and generosities of men and women—all this is, at the least, raw material from which literature is made by writers more imaginative than the Pastons were. From material far less varied and exciting than theirs Dorothy Osborne produced her spontaneous masterpieces of the letter-writing art in the seventeenth century.

Juliana of Norwich and Margery Kempe

Two women writers who come by right into the present chapter—Dame Juliana of Norwich (*c.* 1343–*after* 1413) and

Margery Kempe of Lynn (*c.* 1373–*c.* 1438)—are in the strict sense outside its scope, for neither made a fruitful contribution to English prose in their own time. Juliana's *XVI Revelations of Divine Love*, which belongs to the same category as the writings of Richard Rolle and Walter Hilton and the anonymous *Cloud of Unknowing* (late fourteenth century), has come to be in the present century one of the cherished works in the small body of English mystical literature, but no manuscript of earlier date than the sixteenth century is known. Juliana says: 'These Revelations were shewed to a simple creature unlettered, the year of our Lord 1373, the Eighth day of May. Which creature had afore desired three gifts of God. The First was mind of His Passion; the Second was bodily sickness in youth, at thirty years of age; the Third was to have of God's Gift three wounds . . . that is to say, the wound of very contrition, the wound of kind compassion, and the wound of steadfast longing toward God.'[1] When she was 'thirty years old and a half' she had a serious illness and was thought to be dying. She tells of how her sight began to fail and of how she lost all feeling in her body: 'And then I weened in sooth to have passed'. But suddenly she was conscious of being made whole again and she experienced the first of her Revelations or, as she usually calls them, 'Shewings'. There followed fourteen more, between 4 and 9 o'clock of the same morning, and the last on the following night. In this series of shewings the Lord revealed Himself to her spiritual vision, and at the end of the book she sums up the 'meaning' of the experience:

> . . . from that time that it was shewed I desired oftentimes to learn what was our Lord's meaning. And fifteen years after, and more, I was answered in ghostly understanding, saying thus: *Wouldst thou learn thy Lord's meaning in this thing? Learn it well: Love was His meaning. Who shewed it thee? Love. What shewed He thee? Love. Wherefore shewed it He? For Love. Hold thee therein and thou shalt learn and know more in the same. But thou shalt never know nor learn therein other thing without end.* Thus was I learned that Love was our Lord's meaning.

In 1501 Wynkyn de Worde printed a thin pamphlet titled *A shorte treatyse of contemplacyon taughte by our lorde Ihesu cryste, or*

[1] *Revelations of Divine Love*: A version from the MS. in the British Museum edited by Grace Warrack (Methuen, London, 1901).

taken out of the boke of Margerie kempe of Lynn, but the original
from which this excerpt came was unknown until the complete
manuscript (of about the year 1440) in a unique copy was
identified in 1934 and first published in its original Middle
English form in 1940.[1] Unfortunately the book was not written
by Margery Kempe herself, but is a transcript by a copyist
named Salthows from an earlier manuscript made by a priest,
who had in turn rewritten the first version taken down from
Margery's own account by 'a man dwellyng in Dewchlond
[Germany] which was an Englyschman'. The book as we have
it is thus not less than a fourth-hand rendering. Scholars have
concluded from internal evidence, however, that though
Margery Kempe was illiterate and could neither have written
her own story nor read back what was written, the manuscript
does provide a reliable account of her experiences as told orally
by herself.

That Margery was an hysteric is beyond doubt, but since the
spiritual ecstasies of genuine mystics have often appeared in the
guise of hysteria, her visions and transports, her cryings and
roarings, do not invalidate her remarkable story, which also
has some of the attractions of a travel book—and occasional
touches of unconscious humour, as when in the early pages
mention is made of her vanity and family pride. She would
not be content, as her husband was, with the goods that God
had provided, but ever desired more and more. So she took
up brewing for three or four years in Norwich, but the ale
always went wrong. Then she set up as a miller to grind corn
in a horse-mill, but the horses refused to work. Here (modernized) is a glimpse of her hired man's failure with one of
the horses:

> Sometimes he led him by the head, sometimes he beat him, and
> sometimes he cherished him, and all availed not, for he would
> rather go backward than forward. Then the man set a sharp
> pair of spurs on his heels and rode on the horse's back to make
> him draw, but that was no better. Then he put the horse back into
> the stable and gave him food and he ate well and freshly.

Margery Kempe went to consult Dame Juliana of Norwich
about her visions and revelations and was counselled ' to be

---

[1] S. B. Meech and H. E. Allen: *The Book of Margery Kempe* (Early English
Text Society, 1940).

obedient to the will of our Lord God and to fulfil with all her might whatever He put in her soul if it were not against the worship of God and profit of her fellow Christians, for if it were it was not the influence of a good spirit but rather of an evil spirit'. She had her first major ecstasy during a visit to the Holy Land:

> . . . whan þei cam vp on-to þe Mownt of Caluarye, sche fel down þat sche myght not stondyn ne knelyn but walwyd & wrestyd wyth hir body, spredyng hir armys a-brode, & cryed wyth a lowde voys as þow hir hert xulde a brostyn a-sunder, for in þe cite of hir sowle sche saw veryly & freschly how owye Lord was crucifyed. Beforn hir face sche herd and saw in hir gostly syght þe mornyng of owyr Lady, of Sen John & Mary Mawdelyn, and of many oþer þat louyd owyr Lord. & sche had so gret compassyon & so gret peyn to se owyr Lordys peyn þat sche myt not kepe hirself fro krying & rorying þow sche xuld a be ded perfor. And þis was þe fyrst cry þat euyr sche cryed in any contemplacyon. And þis maner of crying enduryd many ȝerys aftyr þis tyme . . .

walwyd] wallowed   xulde] should   brostyn] burst   mornyng]
mourning   louyd] loved   ȝerys] years.

She invariably speaks of herself in the third person, often as 'this creature' or 'the creature', yet in spite of this sustained attempt at depersonalization Margery Kempe breaks through as a real person, though (as secular readers may feel) not always as a pleasant one. For example, the creature's son was a worldly young man whom she prayed God to chastise if he did not live purely. Then the son went abroad on his business as a merchant, fell into lechery, and soon afterwards his face became covered with 'whelys & blobberys' (pimples and pustules) as though he were a leper. She then tells, not without some taint of priggishness and slight geographical irrelevance, of how, when at length he came for her blessing, 'so long she prayed for him that he was clean delivered of his sickness and lived many years after and had a wife and a child, "blessed be God," for he wedded his wife in Prussia'. A few years later he came home a reformed character and then went on pilgrimage to Rome and elsewhere.

Both as a mystic and as a woman Margery Kempe is the

most memorable real-life character that the literature of the
Middle Ages has preserved for us, and her autobiographical
narrative is in its special way as important a twentieth-century
recovery as Boswell's journals.

Malory

Until the 1930s Sir Thomas Malory's writings, the greatest
prose work of the later Middle Ages, were known to modern
readers only in the book edited and printed by Caxton in 1485
as *Morte Darthur*. In 1934, however, a manuscript lacking a
few pages at beginning and end, and therefore without a title
page, was recognized in the Fellows' Library of Winchester
College as a fifteenth-century copy of Malory. Certain textual
peculiarities showed that it could not be the version from which
Caxton worked, but it was evidently from the same ultimate
source as Caxton's and it enabled Professor Eugène Vinaver
of the University of Manchester to establish a text as close as
possible to Malory's own, so far as that can be deduced from
the evidence available. The result is an absorbing book for
general reading as well as a treasure for students. This edition [1]
is the product of a minute comparison of the manuscript with
the only surviving copies of Caxton's printed book, one in the
Rylands Library, Manchester, the other (with some textual
differences due to corrections made in type after the first
printing) in the Pierpont Morgan Library, New York. It has
now been shown that Caxton's purpose was to combine into
a single continuous narrative what Malory had conceived as
eight separate stories, linked only by their common presentation
of phases and aspects of the Arthurian legends drawn from
different sources. After five hundred years, therefore, we are
now given an unhindered view of one of the most valued works
in the English language, written in the mid-fifteenth century
by one of the most enigmatic of English writers.

It remains a paradox, however, that what poets and many
others have for centuries accepted as a mystical and spiritually
enobling body of legends should have been presented at its

---

[1] *The Works of Sir Thomas Malory*, edited by Eugène Vinaver (3 vols.
Clarendon Press, 1947); to appear in one volume, without the critical ap-
paratus, in the Oxford Standard Authors Series, 1954. Caxton's text is
given in the Everyman's Library edition of *Morte Darthur* (2 vols. Dent).

finest by a man with a long and desperate criminal history. Those who hold that only noble persons write noble books have sought to resolve the paradox by postulating two Malorys— Sir Thomas the writer, and Sir Thomas the criminal; but there is no evidence to support that theory, which is also weakened positively by the information given in his book(s) by the author that he was a prisoner: e.g. at the end of the first of the eight tales as printed by Vinaver he describes himself as 'a knyght presoner, sir Thomas Malleorré'. Considering his record, modern readers may find something sanctimonious in the prayerful endings to which he inclined, as in the final address to the reader copied in Caxton's edition:

> I pray you all, gentlemen and gentlewomen that readeth this book of Arthur and his knights from the beginning to the end, pray for me while I am alive, that God send me good deliverance. And when I am dead, I pray you all, pray for my soul. For this book was ended the ninth year of the reign of King Edward the Fourth, by Sir Thomas Malory [Maleoré], knight, and Jesus help him by His great might, as he is the servant of Jesus both day and night.[1]

But repeated sin and repeated contrition would be less noted for shocked comment in Malory's time than now; while, viewed in historical perspective, there is no certain psychological ground for charging Malory with hypocrisy or even insincerity. It is enough to contemplate his life with cool interest and his writings with deserved respect.

The only known Sir Thomas Malory of the period was born between 1400 and 1410 of a family with estates at Newbold Revell in Warwickshire and Winwick in Northamptonshire, to which he succeeded c. 1433–4. He served with the Earl of Warwick's forces in France in 1436 and married soon after. In 1443 his name first appears in court documents on an apparently unproved charge of theft, but seven years later, at the beginning of 1450, there opened eighteen months of serious crime which for variety can rarely have been equalled in so short a period. He took part in an ambush planned (unsuccessfully) to murder Humphrey, Duke of Buckingham; raped, stole, extorted money, cattle, and sheep; was arrested, but escaped by swimming a

---

[1] Modernized.

moat, and almost immediately after (as one of a gang) broke on two successive days into Coombe Abbey, near Coventry, stealing money and church property and insulting the abbot. From about August 1451 to the middle of 1454 he was in prison, except for one short interval of freedom. When in May of the latter year he was released on bail he shared in cattle raids and horse-stealing forays, and in October 1454 was sent to Colchester gaol, whence he broke out in a fortnight, only to be charged again in November. Although twelve months later he received a royal pardon, in February 1456 he was brought before the King's Bench. In the same year, nevertheless, he sat in Parliament for Warwickshire, relapsing shortly afterwards to Ludgate prison. Late in 1457 he was again on bail, and in 1460 was committed to Newgate. Between times there is news of him in Warwickshire (1459); in the train of Edward IV in Northumberland (1462); and with the Duke of Warwick's men at the siege of Alnwick (1463). Twice in 1468 he was specifically excluded from general writs of amnesty. He died in 1471 and was buried in St. Francis's Chapel, Greyfriars, near enough to Newgate to suggest that he may again have been a prisoner there.[1]

Malory completed his Arthurian writings during the year 1469–70, fifteen years before Caxton issued the printed version. The discovery of the Winchester manuscript made it possible to determine that Malory began by adapting in fifteenth-century prose the English fourteenth-century alliterative poem *Morte Arthure*, which recounts the legendary triumphs of King Arthur against the Romans and his crowning as emperor by the Pope. Vinaver suggests that Malory intended the victories of Arthur to be read as an analogy of those of Henry V and that he therefore broke off his prose transcription of the alliterative *Morte Arthure* at the crowning and return of Arthur to England, instead of carrying the story on to the death of Arthur as the old poem does. His first tale having been thus finished, Malory —during a period of unknown length—proceeded to adapt from the French other Arthurian episodes, treating each as a

---

[1] A fuller account of his delinquencies is given by Sir E. K. Chambers in the chapter on Malory in *English Literature at the Close of the Middle Ages* (Oxford History of English Literature, vol. 2, part 2, Clarendon Press, 1945).

self-contained unit, simplifying the narrative method, but not attempting to smooth away overlapping and inconsistencies as between one tale and another. The order in which the eight tales are bound up in the manuscript is not the order of composition.

When Caxton essayed to make a single narrative from

Sir Lancelot in his madness

Malory's series, he was attempting to produce from a group of short stories what would now be described as a novel; but he did not work as a conscientious literary craftsman shaping and dovetailing the material into a unified whole. He 'edited' Malory, rather unskilfully, following the original text closely in most places, though with substantial reductions in length, and adopting a different system of division by splitting the eight tales into twenty-one 'books' or parts. As a consequence of Caxton's slack editorial method many discrepancies and inconsistences remain, while the title attached to the whole is inappropriate since *Morte Darthur* relates only to the final section in Caxton.

It is largely from Caxton's Preface that subsequent generations of readers have obtained the notion that Malory was
animated by a high moral and spiritual purpose in 'his' *Morte
Darthur*. Nothing is known of Malory's purpose, beyond the
obvious service of rendering into contemporary English a body
of popular stories, one at least of which (King Arthur and the
Romans) was capable of being given a topical interest. A
thorough-going appreciation of religious poetry is not confined
to religious people; nor is the fact that Malory's life was incongruous with his tale of the quest of the Holy Grail sufficient
in itself to convict him of hypocrisy. The Arthurian legends, as
Caxton observed, are compacted of 'cowardyse, murdre, . . .
hate, . . . and synne' as well as of 'chyvalrye, curtoyse, hu-
manyte, frendlynesse, hardynesse, love, frendshyp, . . . vertue';
and readers not already habituated to Christian doctrine would
not of a certainty draw from Malory the conclusions that
Christians traditionally draw. So far as literature is concerned
Malory's writings are a magnificent repository of story material,
while his prose has the merit of directness in straightforward
narrative and the virtues of rhythm and cadence and balance
in passages where tragic pathos or other deep emotion demands
a fit medium of expression.

Than sir Bedwere toke the kynge upon hys bak and so wente
with hym to the watirs syde. And whan they were there, evyn
faste by the banke hoved a lytyll barge wyth many fayre ladyes
in hit, and amonge hem all was a quene, and all they had blak
hoodis. And all they wepte and shryked whan they saw kynge
Arthur.

'Now put me into that barge,' seyde the kynge.

And so he ded sofftely, and there resceyved hym three ladyes
with grete mournyng. And so they sette hem downe, and in
one of their lappis kyng Arthure layde hys hede. And then the
quene sayde,

'A, my dere brothir! Why have ye taryed so longe frome me?
Alas, thys wounde on youre hede hath caught over-much coulde!'

And anone they rowed fromward the londe, and sir Bedyvere
behylde all the ladys go frowarde hym. Than sir Bedwere cryed
and seyde,

'A, my lorde Arthur, what shall becom of me, now ye go
frome me and leve me here alone amonge myne enemyes?'

'Comforte thyselff,' seyde the kynge, 'and do as well as thou

mayste, for in me ys no truste for to truste in. For I muste into
the vale of Avylyon to hele me of my grevous wounde. And if
thou here nevermore of me, pray for my soule!'

But ever the quene and ladyes wepte and shryked, that hit
was pité to hyre. And as sone as sir Bedwere had loste the syght
of the barge he wepte and wayled, and so toke the foreste and
wente all that nyght. . . .[1]

No two men could have had lives more unlike than those of
the fifteenth-century Malory and the seventeenth-century
Bunyan, except for their inside knowledge of gaol; yet as
natural prose artists no other two English writers have a
closer affinity.

[1] Vinaver, vol. III, pp.1240–1 ('The Most Piteous Tale of the Morte
Arthur Saunz Gwerdon').

CHAPTER V

RENAISSANCE AND EARLY TUDOR LITERATURE

THE ferment of humanitarian and anti-authoritarian thought and conviction working in England in the fourteenth-century—manifested politically in the Peasants' Revolt and through literature in *Piers Plowman* and the prose writings of Wiclif and others—suggests that the foundations of the Middle Ages were cracking and crumbling several generations before the date, 1453, often set down as the beginning of the Renaissance and therefore of 'Modern Times'. The impulses behind the challenge to Church and State prepared men's minds for the new and new-old ideas which were to flourish in a wild tangle of good and evil in the sixteenth century, consequent upon (*a*) the invention of printing in the mid-fifteenth century, (*b*) the capture of Constantinople by the Turks from the Christians, (*c*) the opening of the Age of Discovery through the voyages of Columbus in the 1490s, and (*d*) the sixteenth-century Protestant Reformation. To the intellectual fruits of this complex of events the term *Renaissance* or, alternatively, *Revival of Learning* is applied; though the Revival of Learning was truly a rebirth of man's mind, and also—and perhaps more potently —of his imagination, not merely a restirring of either.

Extensive new vistas opened up as the physical world and the metaphysical broke through their boundaries as hitherto conceived. Doubts crept in concerning the supposed theocentric universe, while the competing idea of a homocentric universe lured the daringly atheistic. It was then that the first step was made towards Swinburne's defiant 'Glory to Man in the Highest, for Man is the master of things', written more than four centuries later.

Printing and Translating

While books were limited to handwritten copies there could be no more than a narrow dissemination of knowledge through small pockets of learning in the religious houses and the few universities, which were also under ecclesiastical jurisdiction. In the first quarter of the fifteenth century woodcut pictures began to be impressed in spaces left for them in manuscripts, and through a simple and inevitable development words as well as designs soon came to be cut on the wooden blocks. But this laborious process required an entirely fresh set of blocks for each new book, and there could be no really rapid multi-plication until the practice was adopted of cutting moulds of separate letters from which 'type' could be cast on metal 'bodies' of uniform height, every letter and other character on a separate stem of metal, so that they could be arranged in the required order as words, to be separated again when the pages were printed, and reassembled for the next book.

Nothwithstanding other claims, there seems no doubt that Gutenberg was the actual inventor of printing with movable types so exactly proportioned in girth and depth as to enable them, in any combination, to fit exactly and to be impressed evenly, after inking, on paper or parchment or vellum. The solution of this technical problem occupied the best part of two decades.[1] Johann Gensfleisch zum Gutenberg worked first at Strasbourg and then at Mainz and his invention was perfected in the period 1440–50. As he apparently fell out with his financial backer before completing any of the books on which he was working, Gutenberg's name does not appear on any surviving volume, not even on the so-called Gutenberg Bible, which was finished by others after the dissolution of his partnership.

The art and business of printing spread quickly from Germany to Italy, Switzerland, France, the Netherlands, and east European centres. Presses were at work in those parts before printing in English was begun in 1474 at Bruges by Caxton, who returned (1476) to England to establish the first printery there, at Westminster.

William Caxton, born in Kent *c.* 1422 and apprenticed in 1438 to a silk mercer, settled in the Netherlands as a young man and rose to be Governor of the English Company of Commercial Adventurers in the Low Countries and a negotiator

---

[1] For a succinct account of the beginnings and later developments see *The Printed Book* by John Carter and Brooke Crutchley (Cambridge University Press, 1951).

and adviser in the household of the Duchess of Burgundy. It is thought that he began to practise printing in Cologne, where he was living in 1471. By 1474 he was again at Bruges, whence he issued in that year his translations (from the French) of *The Recuyell of the Historyes of Troye* and *The Game and Playe*

The Game and Playe of the Chesse

of *the Chesse*, the first books printed in English. Bringing the necessary equipment to England, he continued his work as printer and translator, producing a succession of small books (including minor works by Chaucer) before publishing the first printed edition of *The Canterbury Tales* in 1478, Gower's *Confessio Amantis* in 1483, and his own versions of *The Golden Legend* (1483) and *Morte Darthur* (1485). He died in 1491.

As a disseminator of literature Caxton was invaluable ;[1] as a

---

[1] With the advent of printing came also the birth of the book trade and of the economic considerations inseparable from it. Caxton safeguarded part of his capital outlay by assurances of support from the Earl of Arundel, thus

writer of prose he showed the characteristic reluctance of other translators in the fourteenth-fifteenth centuries to use simple straightforward English. It was their habit to employ coupled words for the rendering of a single term, possibly because they were often unsure of the precise English equivalent and eluded the problem by offering alternatives. Thus, in Caxton, 'founden and maad', 'to doo well and good', 'ease and ydleness', 'most grettest and hyest', 'slouthe and ydleness', 'occupacion and besynesse', 'grete pleasyr and delyte', 'to accepte and take'. This mannerism extended from Caxton's translations to his own independent writings, and through him and others tended to set a pattern for printed prose which, in a highly self-conscious and elaborated form, terminated in the excessively stylized *Euphues* by the Elizabethan John Lyly (*see below*, p. 154).

Although he belongs to the next generation, it is convenient to bring in here another translator, John Bourchier, Lord Berners (1467–1532), whose rendering from the French of Jean Froissart's *Chronicles* of (as Berners's title-page ran) 'Englande, Fraunce, Spayne, Portyngale, Scotlande, Bretayne, Flaunders, and other places adioynynge' was for long a favourite book in England after its appearance in the 1520s, the translation having been undertaken at Henry VIII's request. Berners wrote an elaborate ornamented English which must be taken into account as a factor that helped to shape the style of Lyly and other Elizabethan prose writers. His material was for the most part serious history, and as such it was serviceable in both content and method to historians in the later part of the century. The account in the *Chronicles* of the march on London by the bands led by Wat Tyler, Jack Straw, and John Ball at the time of the Peasants' Revolt is but one among the many stirring episodes in the book, the narrative interest of which is maintained, however far it may come

introducing the system of patronage—noble, ecclesiastical, or political—which prevailed (though often subject to piratical attack) until, in the eighteenth century and after, the book-buying public was large enough to bring in a democratic, though not invariably more enlightened, form of patronage. The relationship—a vitally important one—between literature and the book trade will be briefly surveyed in Vol. II of the present work. For a comprehensive history of the subject from earliest times see *Publishing and Bookselling* by F. A. Mumby (revised edn.) (Cape, London, 1949).

short of modern standards of historical accuracy. Berners was wordy, but he could sense the value of a vivid phrase, as in the account of the battle of Crécy: 'Then the English archers stept forth one pace and let fly their arrows so wholly and so thick, that it seemed snow.' Of Berners's several translations nothing else has continued to be read, but a point of interest in his rendering of the popular French romance *Huon of Bordeaux* is that it introduced Oberon into English literature.

The Revival of Learning

In the late fourteenth century Italian scholars began to show a reawakened interest in the classical writings of ancient Greece and Rome, and teachers of Greek established themselves in Florence, Venice, and elsewhere in Italy. Hundreds of manuscripts of the works of antiquity were carried from Greece into Italy during the early decades of the fifteenth century, while universities increased and flourished. By the crucial year 1453, when the Turks captured Constantinople, Italy was therefore well prepared to profit by the inrush of learned men and the further inpouring of manuscripts from the fallen metropolis of the East Roman Empire. But the great part played by Italy in spreading Renaissance learning throughout Europe cannot be isolated from the impetus to intellectual awakening provided earlier by Dante (1265-1321), Petrarch (1304-74), and Boccaccio (1313-75). Though Dante's outlook was almost wholly medieval, his exaltation of Virgil and his own greatness as a poet, both spiritually and æsthetically, could not fail to be a stimulus of the highest importance in the early Renaissance period. Petrarch's position is far more difficult to assess, apart from English use of the Petrarchan form in sonnet structure; but Boccaccio, though he died before the first birthpangs of the modern world were even dimly apparent, prefigured in himself the modern man, concerned more with humanity and the temporalities than the true medieval mind could condone.[1] Both by the greatness of its three native poets and by the deep learning of its next generation of scholars, Italy became the intellectual reservoir of sixteenth-century Europe, while through

---

[1] It is necessary, however, to recognize that Boccaccio's *Decameron* was not his only work, and that his *Olympia* may have been a source of inspiration for so unworldly an English poem as *Pearl* (*see above*, p. 10).

its painting and sculpture even more than through its poetry it became the æsthetic reservoir also.

The English Renaissance

In Italy the Church stood firm amid the swirling and conflicting currents of secular enlightenment, mainly by taking into itself through the Renaissance popes and other ecclesiastics much of the spirit of the age, and by becoming itself the chief patron of the arts. However incongruously, Renaissance art in Italy was for the most part religious art, in the sense that the bulk of it was directed to church decoration. Such men as Leonardo da Vinci and Michelangelo were doubtless uneasy sons of the Church, but among the great art-workers only Benvenuto Cellini's conduct was notoriously and incorrigibly scandalous.

In Germany, the Netherlands, and England the Renaissance and the Reformation entwined—though neither intentionally nor appropriately. In England one strand comprised the austere and learned Grocyn, Linacre, Colet, and Thomas More (with Erasmus as a distinguished and influential visitor from the Low Countries); the other and later strand included rascally playwrights and pamphleteers, Marlowe, Greene, Nashe, and others. But while the first group represents the sacred and the other the profane, they are of equal importance in the English Renaissance—the one for its profound Christian scholarship, the other for its fiery pagan imagination.

Though Langland and Wiclif had been outspoken critics of clerical corruption, they were loyal sons of the Church and were as reluctant as John Wesley was to be in the eighteenth century to break away from constituted spiritual authority. If Henry VIII had not been a determined polyamorist to whom divorce or some more drastic means to annulment of marriage was a recurrent necessity, the break with Rome would probably not have come in his reign, More and others would have died naturally, and the whole of subsequent English history might well have been different. The turn of events which broke the hegemony of Rome made Renaissance humanism [1] an inter-

---

[1] The words *humanist* and *humanism*, unavoidable in writing about the Renaissance, are more frequently used than precisely defined. In the narrowest original sense a humanist was a scholar-grammarian, one absorbed in 'the humanities', which the Concise Oxford Dictionary defines as 'polite scholarship, especially of Latin and Greek classics'. In later

national intellectual movement, with Erasmus (1467–1536) at its head. He was introduced to England in 1499 by Lord Mountjoy, one of his young pupils, and during his first six-months' stay he met and greatly admired the learning of Colet and More, and also of William Grocyn (? 1446–1519) and Thomas Linacre (? 1460–1524) both of whom had studied Greek in Florence. Erasmus was again in England in 1506 and it was then that Colet persuaded him to direct his scholarship to the Greek New Testament, of which he issued an annotated text in 1516.

Since little but the names of Grocyn and Linacre now remain in memory it is proper to stress that as teachers of Greek (almost the first in England) at Oxford, and through their direct personal contact with Erasmus and Colet, they were outstanding in the Revival of Learning in England.

John Colet (? 1467–1519), Dean of St. Paul's Cathedral and founder of St. Paul's School, was a staunch advocate of reform within the Church, and his demand that the reform should begin with higher standards among the episcopacy itself caused the Bishop of London to lodge an unsustained charge of heresy against his Dean. As preacher, as theological lecturer at Oxford, and as an educational innovator Colet greatly promoted contemporary enlightenment, and the school he founded still flourishes.

Erasmus's own writings, being by a foreigner and in Latin, are no part of English literature, but they are essential documents of the whole Renaissance movement and even in translation *The Praise of Folly*, the *Colloquies*, and his personal Letters are as attractive as they are important.

Sir Thomas More

It is a literary misfortune that More's most famous work, *Utopia*, perhaps the first book of universal interest by an Englishman, was not written in English by its author but had to wait thirty-five years before it was translated from the Latin by Ralph

usage the words have taken on overtones which give them a much wider application, wider even than the C.O.D. definition of humanism as 'devotion to human interests; system concerned with human (not divine) interests or with the human race (not the individual)'. In modern times a combination of liberal scholarship, tolerance, compassion, humour, and integrity constitutes the ideal of humanism, however seldom realized.

Robynson, sixteen years after More was beheaded. We have therefore to turn to lesser works in order to judge of More's English prose style.

Without underestimating his rank as an author it can be said that his personal character has impressed posterity even more than his literary genius. He was the humanist without equal. Born in 1478, the son of Sir John More, a London lawyer and later a judge, he served as a youth in the household of Cardinal Morton [1] and, having displayed remarkable mental gifts, was sent by him to Oxford, where as a pupil of Linacre and Grocyn he developed a passion for Latin and Greek studies. He followed his father's profession and was called to the Bar, becoming highly reputed also as a lecturer in London on philosophical and historical aspects of St. Augustine's *De Civitate Dei*. After a brief term as member of parliament he retired into private life, but was later sent as an envoy to the Netherlands and thereafter filled a succession of offices before he became Lord Chancellor in 1529, having been knighted by Henry VIII in 1521. In 1534 he declined to take the general oath which purported to uphold the Succession Act of that year (regularizing the position of Anne Boleyn's children in the royal line), but which More believed to be aimed against the authority of the Pope as head of the Church. After imprisonment in the Tower of London he was charged with high treason, condemned to death, and executed on Tower Hill 6 July 1535. John Fisher, Bishop of Rochester and Chancellor of Cambridge University (who had persuaded Erasmus to become lecturer in Greek at Cambridge), was condemned on a similar charge and beheaded a fortnight earlier. Three hundred years afterwards, in 1935, both Fisher and More were canonized by the Church for whose tenets they had accepted martyrdom. The biography of More by his son-in-law, William Roper, and the paintings and drawings of the family by Holbein, have fixed for all time the benign and serene life of the Mores' patriarchal household at Chelsea on the outskirts of London.

More wrote *Utopia* in two parts in 1515–16 when he was about thirty-six, the publication of the original Latin edition at

---

[1] More's unabating admiration for the Cardinal is shown by the tribute he worked into the early pages of *Utopia*.

Louvain in 1516 being supervised by Erasmus. Translated into German in 1524, into French in 1530, and into Italian in 1548, the book was available in their own languages to the peoples of a large part of the European continent before Robynson's English translation was printed, also at Louvain, in 1551. Even then it was proscribed in England, for More was still accounted a traitor and his book a subversive satire.

Utopia was a product both of the Revival of Learning through its debt to Plato and of the contemporary Age of Discovery through its link with Amerigo Vespucci's account of his voyages and Columbus's later 'discovery' of America, for these planted in More's imagination the idea of the island called Utopia (Greek *ou topos*, no place). In modern colloquial usage the word has come to signify a state of final and therefore static perfection, though this interpretation can no more accurately be given to Utopia than to Plato's Republic. Each is a thinking-out by a single mind of a scheme of government and social organization based upon a rational system and a conception of justice which, in the one instance, appeared valid to a Greek in the fifth century B.C. and, in the other, to an Englishman in the sixteenth century A.D. Though each of the two books has been taken as a pattern for much subsequent thinking, and each embodies notions original in its own age but since become practical commonplaces long ago accepted, the truth about every paper Utopia is that it is coloured by prejudices and limitations peculiar to the writer and by some at least of the makeshift customs and convictions peculiar to his time.

While Utopia has certain features of an embryonic novel, its 'story' is slight and somewhat involved and tedious. It introduces actual persons, including More himself and Peter Giles, secretary to the municipality of Antwerp, where they encounter a stranger, 'a man well stricken in age, with a black, sunburnt face, a long beard, and a cloak cast homely about his shoulders, whom . . . forthwith I judged to be a mariner'. This fictional character, Raphael Hythloday, is described as having been on Vespucci's last three voyages. Contriving to be left behind 'in the country of Gulike', he ventured thence into other parts by land and by water and at length reached the Island of Utopia, governed by King Utopus.

The Island of Utopia

The 'description of Utopia, with a large declaration of the
political government, and of all the good laws and orders of the
same island', is given in Part II, the first part being concerned
mainly with preliminary conversation between More, Giles,
and Hythloday, during which a number of animadversions are
made upon the condition of England. Hythloday attacks the

imposition there of capital punishment for thieves, and attributes the prevalence of robbery to the large number of former retainers of the wealthy, cast adrift when their masters die and left to wander at large without employment. He also dwells upon what was at the time both a major economic problem and also an explosive social question: namely the widespread enclosures of arable land to provide additional pasturage for sheep required to expand the wool trade, then a staple asset in the national budget. In the course of an uncompromising denunciation Hythloday says: 'Your shepe that were wont to be so meke and tame, and so smal eaters, now, as I heare saye, be become so great deuowerers and so wylde, that they eate vp and swallow downe the very men themselves.'[1] He goes on to attack the 'noblemen and gentlemen; yea, and certain Abbots' who 'leave no ground for tillage, they enclose all into pastures; they pluck down towns, and leave nothing standing, but only the church to be made a sheep-house'. The great 'wool churches' of East Anglia, Devon, and other parts of the country, now one of the glories of English architecture, were to More, speaking through Hythloday, nothing better than sheep-houses founded upon the impoverishment of the food-growing community.

Against a background of such actual discontents More posed the institutions of his imagined Utopia. There, an annual interchange between town dwellers and countryfolk ensures a general knowledge of both rural and urban needs and occupations. Inasmuch as More was greatly disturbed by the multitude of idlers in his own country, it is in keeping that in Utopia all, women as well as men, are taught a craft and set to work; but the working day is limited to six hours and provision is made for a rational and enlightened use of leisure. Social organization is on a patriarchal basis, and local density of population is controlled by the transfer of any surplus of 14-year-old children in one family group to another having less than its quota: 'the whole island is, as it were, one family or household'. 'War and battle as a thing very beastly' the Utopians abhor, yet they train both men and women in military skill and discipline lest there should be need to defend their own country or to aid their friends against invasion and tyranny. Iron is their most precious

---

[1] Except for this sentence, which reproduces the orthography of Ralph Robynson's translation, the quotations from *Utopia* are modernized.

metal, and to show contempt for gold they use it only for mean utensils and for chains and gyves for their bondsmen—who, by modern humanitarian standards, constitute a very strange order in a utopian society. More discourses at considerable length on religion and philosophy in Utopia, as well as upon the system of government. In matters of belief a large tolerance prevails.

Utopia created in English literature a genre which has since produced such fables, romances, and treatises as Francis Bacon's *The New Atlantis* (1626), Samuel Butler's *Erewhon* (1872), W. H. Mallock's *The New Republic* (1877), Richard Jefferies' *After London* (1885), W. H. Hudson's *The Crystal Age* (1887), William Morris's *News from Nowhere* (1891), and H. G. Wells's *A Modern Utopia* (1905). While none of these could equal their great forerunner in basic originality, they provide evidence enough of More's lasting impression upon social and political thought, and of his unique contribution in establishing a literary form which seems unlikely to lose its attraction for speculative minds.

More's place among writers of English prose has been a matter of fluctuating opinions, ranging between those who hold that he is of little account in this respect and those who share the view taken by R. W. Chambers that 'More was the first Englishman to evolve an effective prose, sufficient for all the purposes of his time: eloquent, dramatic, varied. More can write a prose which is good equally in argument or in narrative, in carefully constructed passages of sustained eloquence, or in rapid dialogue . . .'.[1] There would be less dispute under this head if it were not that More's authorship of *The History of King Richard III* is questioned. This short English work was found among his manuscript remains and accepted as his by early editors. It has since been suggested that it shows 'an asperity of tone, an eager partisanship' uncharacteristic of More, and that it was originally written in Latin by Cardinal Morton and translated into English by More. Even if this could be proved, the English prose would still be More's. Whether the narrative was originally his or Morton's, the existing work is a masterpiece of historical and biographical writing. The characters are drawn brilliantly and with independence of judgment, for if Richard himself is the familiar triple-dyed villain of popular melodrama, his mistress, Jane Shore, appears not as

[1] *Op. cit.* (*see above*, p. 59).

a wanton meeting a deservedly miserable end but as an intensely pathetic if not positively tragic figure. And inasmuch as a great deal of the book's merit is in the force and swiftness of its English style, there would be little real credit to withdraw from More if a Latin original by Morton or another were found. The murder of the two young princes in the Tower of London is among the events described in *The History of King Richard III*, which begins before Richard took the throne. The account of the circumstances leading up to the execution of Lord Hastings on a trumped up charge of treason is an excellent piece of narrative writing, introduced with dramatic skill:

> [The Protector] sayd vnto the Bishop of Elye: My lord you haue very good strawberies at your gardayne in Holberne, I require you let vs haue a messe of them. Gladly my lord, quod he, woulde God I had some better thing as redy to your pleasure as that. And therwith in al the hast he sent hys seruant for a messe of strauberies. The protectour sette the lordes fast in comoning, and therupon prayeng them to spare hym for a little while departed thence. And sone, after one hower, betwene .x. and .xi. he returned into the chamber among them, al changed, with a wonderful soure angrye countenaunce, knitting the browes, frowning and froting and knawing on hys lippes, and so sat him downe in hys place; al the lordes much dismaied and sore merueling of this maner of sodain chaunge, and what this should him aile.

    comoning] communing   froting] chafing   merueling] marvelling

Didactic Prose

Among the most widely read authors in the first half of the sixteenth century was Sir Thomas Elyot (*c.* 1488–1546), a man of extensive interests who drew from classical sources a mass of varied information which he purveyed in a series of books designed as guides to living. So far as any such existed at that time, Elyot was a 'popular educator', and his usefulness lay chiefly in his being the first to bring within the orbit of the Revival of Learning a large body of people whose intellectual needs could not have been served by the more rarefied scholarship of Erasmus, More, and their circle.

Elyot compiled *The Castel of Helth*—'full of prescriptions and remedies largely selected from Galen and other medical authorities of antiquity'—and *The Dictionary of Syr T. Eliot* (Latin-English). His numerous other publications included *The Education or Bringinge up of Children* and *The Rules of a Christian lyfe*, but the most successful with his contemporaries and the only one still read is *The Boke of the Governour*, a complete guide for members of the governing classes. It deals not only with the upbringing, education, and moral training of 'the governor' but also with his amusements and æsthetic development—in short, with the making of a paragon steeped in classical humanism. This is not all that Elyot's book sets out to do, however, for it also compares and arbitrates between the various types of government, and (not surprisingly since Henry VIII was something of a patron to the author) it comes out in support of monarchy as the ideal system. For us, Elyot's prose style is a major point of interest: or, rather, his sharing with many others in that period, and during long after, the inability to write straightforward lucid prose. In *The Governour* Elyot's skill is intermittent, and the following quotation shows him tortuously encoiled in a single sentence:

> . . . If a man, beinge determined to equitie, hauynge the eyen and eares of his mynde set onely on the trouthe and the publike weale of his contray, will haue no regarde to any requeste or desire, but procedeth directely in the adminystration of iustyce, than either he whiche by iustice is offended, or some his fautours, abettours, or adherentes, if he him selfe or any of them be in seruice or familiaritie with hym that is in auctoritie, as soone as by any occasion mention hapneth to be made of hym who hathe executed Justyce exactely, furthe with they imagine some vice or defaute, be it neuer so little, wherby they may minysshe his credence, and craftly omittyng to speke any thyng of his rygour in Justyce, they wyll note and touche some thynge of his maners, wherein shall eyther seme to be lyghtnes or lacke of grauitie, or to moche sowernes, or lacke of ciuilitie, or that he is nat sufficient to receyue any dignitie, or to despeche matters of weyghtye importaunce, or that he is superfluous in wordes or elles to scarse. (*Book* III, *ch.* xxvii. 1531 *edition.*)

fautours] favourers   furthe with] forthwith

If the sermons of Hugh Latimer (*c.* 1484/8–1555) as printed are in their original form as delivered by the preacher, spoken

prose in the first half of the sixteenth century did not suffer from
the halting elaboration which hampered so much of the bookish
prose. Latimer, a Cambridge scholar and later Master in Theology at Oxford, was first caught up in the cross-currents of
dogma in the reign of Henry VIII, but he submitted to the
official articles of faith and was made Bishop of Worcester in
1535. He was in trouble again before the end of that decade,
but it was not until Mary's accession in 1553 that he became
fatally involved. Convicted of heresy, he was burned at Oxford
in 1555. His two most famous sermons, *On the Card* and *Of the
Ploughers*, were preached in 1529 and 1548 respectively, the first
at Cambridge, the other in London at St. Paul's. The latter
included a lengthy rebuke to the wealthy burgesses of the City,
which ran in part:

> . . . But London cannot abide to be rebuked: such is the nature
> of man. If they be pricked, they will kick; if they be rubbed on
> the gall, they will wince; but yet they will not amend their
> faults, they will not be ill spoken of. But how shall I speak well
> of them? If you could be content to receive and follow the word
> of God, and favour good preachers, if you could bear to be told
> of your faults, if you could amend when you hear of them, if
> you would be glad to reform that is amiss; if I might see any such
> inclination in you, that you would leave to be merciless, and
> begin to be charitable, I would then hope well of you, I would
> then speak well of you. But London was never so ill as it is now.
> In times past men were full of pity and compassion, but now
> there is no pity; for in London their brother shall die in the
> streets for cold, he shall lie sick at their door between stock and
> stock, I cannot tell what to call it, and perish there for hunger. . . .

William Tindale (*c.* 1490–1556), a more fiery character than
Latimer, met with a similar fate, being burned at Vilvorde in
1535. He went from London to the Continent in 1524 to complete his translation of the New Testament (1525), the purpose
of which is stated in his Prologue: 'lyght shulde be shewed to
them that walke in dercknes where they cannot but stomble
and where to stomble ys the daunger of eternall dammacioun'.
He also translated portions of the Old Testament (mainly the
Pentateuch, *c.* 1530, and Jonah, 1531) and the makers of the
Authorized Version of 1611 were much indebted to his work,
as can be seen if the following, together with Wyclif's version

of the same passage (*see above*, p. 66), is compared with the A.V.

> . . . I will aryse, and goo to my father and will saye vnto him: father, I have synned agaynst heven and before the, and am no moare worthy to be called thy sonne, make me as one of thy hyred servauntes. And he arose and went to his father. And when he was yet a greate waye of, his father sawe him and had compassion, and ran and fell on his necke, and kyssed him. And the sonne sayd vnto him: father, I have synned agaynst heven, and in thy sight, and am no moare worthy to be called thy sonne.

The English Bible (1537) prepared by Miles Coverdale (1488–1568), sometime Bishop of Exeter and later rector of St. Magnus the Martyr, London Bridge, had an origin and history too complicated to be detailed here. It relied to some extent upon Tindale's translation and served as a further aid to the A.V. A second edition (1537) was the first Bible printed in England: while the 1539 version, also superintended by Coverdale and known as the Great Bible, was the first officially ordered to be read in churches. A further edition of this, in 1540, was called Cranmer's Bible from the Preface written for it by the archbishop.

Thomas Cranmer (1489–1556), after a chequered career which led him to the archiepiscopal throne of Canterbury under Henry VIII and to the stake at Oxford under Mary, achieved literary immortality with the English Prayer Book under Edward VI (1549; revised in 1552). Not even the Authorized Version of the Bible surpasses in beauty and dignity the prose of Cranmer's Prayer Books; and since, like the A.V., it has sounded in the ears of millions weekly if not daily throughout four centuries, its contribution to the writing and speaking of English can no more be doubted or estimated than can the contribution of rain to the English rivers.

The End of the Older Poetry

Before English poets came under the spell of Renaissance tendencies from Italy, which fostered the *art* of poetry, giving a new importance to form and often making the thing said of no greater account than the manner of saying it, two writers —one an Englishman, the other a Scot—ushered out the older poetry with peculiar distinction. Neither received popular at-

placas of bellap many eften

24. Hares with trumpet and
bagpipes

25. A popynjaye

a popyn iaye

6. A girsaunt
   (giraffe)

þon þe day in þe londe a nio
ge wischeo þese cooyeos sleep
nion and etep hem gynntyn
ge and þey haue no tonge

slotteo as siit kéye sonnes
and þer bep þyono al bifine
And þer bep oper beeftes as
sget as steeos þat men calle

Sir saunt

from *Mandeville's Travels*

27. The Barons of Cornwall grieving,

28. The Dead Maid of Astolat, from *Morte Arthur*

29. The Woodcutter

30. The Printer

31. The Papermaker

32. The Bookbinder

from *Panoplia Omnium Artium* by Hartmann Schopper

33. Caxton presenting his *Recuyell of the Historyes of Troye* to Margaret of York

FAMILIA THOMÆ MORI ANGL: CANCELL:

Thomas Morus Æt:50. Alicia Thomæ Mori uxor Æt:57. Iohannes Morus pater Æt:76. Iohannes Morus Thomæ filius Æt:19. Anna Crisacria Iohannis Mori Sponsa Æt:15. Margareta Ropera Thomæ Mori filia Æt:22. Elisabeta Dauncia Thomæ Mori filia Æt:21. Cæcilia Heronia Thomæ Mori filia Æt:20. Margareta Giga Clementis uxor Mori filiabus Condiscipula et cognata Æt:22. Henricus Patensonus Thomæ Mori moric: Æt:40.

34. Sir Thomas More and his Family, by Hans Holbein the Younger

35. More and his Friends listen to Raphael's tale, by Ambrosius
Holbein, from More's *Utopia*

36. John Skelton

37. Title-page of the *Great Bible*, 1539

38. St. Matthew from Tindale's
translation of the *New Testament*

39. William Tindale

tention between the time of his death and the present century, but latterly John Skelton (*c.* 1460–*c.* 1528) has been 'rediscovered' by many readers and by broadcasters, while *The Satire of the Three Estates* by Sir David Lyndsay (1490–1555) came back into favour in Scotland when a modernized and much abbreviated version was staged at the Edinburgh Festival in 1948 and after.

Too little is known about Skelton's early life to allow of more than guesses as to his place of birth, but he probably came of a Cumberland family living in Norfolk. He was almost certainly a graduate of Cambridge, but the first definite knowledge of him is that both Oxford and Cambridge (and also Louvain) accorded him the title of Laureate, which he delighted to use as if it were a master weapon to confound his rivals and unfriendly critics. That he was as well thought of at Court as in the universities is suggested by his appointment as tutor to the young Prince Henry (afterwards Henry VIII). Caxton wrote of him (in the preface to *The Boke of Enydos* [1]) in terms which show that Skelton was acknowledged to be a well-informed classical scholar and skilled translator.

In 1498 he entered the Church and within a few years became Rector of Diss in Norfolk. He married either before deciding to take Orders or secretly afterwards, and, wives being forbidden to clerics, he laid himself open to the accusation of concubinage. He is said to have answered the accusation by bringing his wife and child into the church on the following Sunday, rebuking the scandalmongering congregation a little disingenuously for complaining against him without due cause. Such performances earned him the local reputation of being fitter for the stage than for the pulpit.

Skelton vented the indignations of a born reformer with a lashing tongue and a vitriolic pen, and lines in his poem to 'Mistress Anne, of The Key in Thames Street', can fairly be applied to himself:

> . . . Yet is your tongue an adder's tail,
> Full like a scorpion stinging. . . .

His satirical bolts were aimed at many, but the heaviest and most at Cardinal Wolsey, whom he attacked again and again

[1] Described by an editor of Caxton as 'a translation of a silly French novel based upon the Æneid of Virgil'.

H

vituperatively and sometimes scurrilously. As a consequence of this feud against the most powerful man in England Skelton was at length compelled to protect himself from arrest by taking sanctuary at Westminster, where he died six years later at the age of about seventy and was buried in St. Margaret's beside the Abbey.

Skelton was the most considerable and original poet in the two centuries between Chaucer and Spenser, though he was a wilding in contrast with them: for whereas their poetry is carefully bred and impeccably cultivated his appears often to be improvised and deliberately shagged. But this appearance is delusively far from reality, for any apparent artlessness in Skelton may be nothing less than cunningly premeditated art controlled by a unique sour-sweet humour which was, by turns, obscene and tender. *The Tunning of Elinor Rumming* is a scarifying panorama of the loathly women—landlady and customers —who infest Elinor Rumming's alehouse at Leatherhead in Surrey. Its morality is unexceptionable, for the disgustingness of those scrabbling subhuman creatures should shock the indecent into decency; while as a literary feat the poem is brilliant in its precise adjustment of means to effects. The characteristic 'Skeltonic' metre (short lines often of only four syllables), matched with a resourceful and often rude vocabulary, is used with surprising flexibility and made to serve a wide range of moods, from the satirical repulsion of *Elinor Rumming* to the playful charm and delicate humour (and the mock ferocity against Gyb the cat who kills young Jane's pet bird) in *The Boke of Phyllyp Sparowe*. This, Skelton's masterpiece, handles a tiny theme with unfaltering dexterity. The first half of the poem is put into the girl's mouth and she is presumed to be the speaker in this passage:

What I remember agayn
How mi Philyp was slayn,
Neuer halfe the payne
Was betwene you twayne,
Pyramus and Thesbe,
As than befell to me:
I wept and I wayled,
The tearys downe hayled;
But nothynge it auayled
To call Phylyp agayne,
Whom Gyb our cat hath slayne.

Gib, I saye, our cat
Worrowyd her on that
Which I loued best:
It can not be exprest
My sorrowfull heuynesse,
But all without redresse;
For within that stounde,
Halfe slumbrynge, in a sounde
I fell downe to the grounde

. . . . .

It had a veluet cap,
And wold syt vpon my lap,
And seke after small wormes,
And sometyme white bred
 crommes;
And many tymes and ofte
Betwene my brestes softe
It wolde lye and rest;
It was propre and preste.
Sometyme he wolde gaspe
Whan he sawe a waspe;
A fly or a gnat,
He wolde flye at that;
And prytely he wold pant
Whan he saw an ant;
Lorde, howe he wolde pry
After the butterfly!

 . . . . .

. . . vengeaunce, I aske and crye,
By way of exclamacyon,
On all the hole nacyon

Of cattes wylde and tame;
God send them sorowe and shame!
That cat specyally
That slew so cruelly
My lytell prety sparowe
That I brought vp at Carowe.
 O cat of carlyshe kynde,
The fynde was in thy mynde
Whan thou my byrde vntwynde!
I wold thou haddest ben blynde!
The leopardes sauage,
The lyons in theyr rage,
Myght catch the in theyr pawes,
And gnawe the in their iawes!
The serpentes of Lybany
Myght stynge the venymously!
The dragones with their tonges
Might poyson thy lyver and
 longes!
The mantycors of the montaynes
Myght fede them on thy braynes! [1]

worrowyd] choked stounde] instant sounde] swoon preste] sprightly
Carowe] Carrow (near Norwich) carlyshe] churlish manticor] fabulous creature with a lion's body, a human head, porcupine's quills, and a scorpion's tail.

In other metres Skelton wrote impressive religious poems (e.g. *Woefully Arrayed*) and the beautiful lullaby *Lullay, Lullay, Like a Child*, which appeal more immediately than do such larger pieces as *The Bowge of Court*, showing Skelton as a master of disillusion; and *Speak Parrot, Colin Clout*, and *Why Come Ye Not to Court*, satires more or less violently against Wolsey. He could also turn not only such homely rural ditties as *Jolly Rutterkin* and *Mannerly Margery Milk and Ale*, but also the attractive lyrics addressed to the Countess of Surrey, Lady Elizabeth Howard, Margery Wentworth and others in *The Garland of Laurel*. In these, Skelton, who in many respects belongs to the medieval world, reaches forward to the Elizabethan age. It was his misfortune but is our advantage that he was a transition poet. Caught between two periods he could not belong wholly to either, and therefore exhibits to us something of the emergence of the one from the other.

[1] *The Poetical Works of John Skelton*, edited by Alexander Dyce (2 vols. London, 1843). A modernized text is provided in Philip Henderson's edition, based on Dyce (Dent, London, 1931).

It is as a transitional work that his one surviving play is of particular interest. *Magnificence* (called 'a Goodly Interlude and a Merry', though it is in fact a Morality play and hardly merry) introduces Wealthful, Felicity, Liberty, Measure (i.e. Moderation), Fancy, Counterfeit, Countenance, Crafty Conveyance, Cloaked Collusion, Courtly Abusion, Folly, Adversity, Poverty, Despair, Mischief, Goodhope, Redress, Sad Circumspection, Perseverance, with Magnificence himself as the central figure. The main weakness of this over-long and mostly tedious work, if considered as drama, is that the list of characters by itself reveals the theme and imposes upon the author the necessity of creating dramatic interest through treatment and style alone. Skelton fails in this. It is fair to add, however, that the fault is inherent in the limitations of morality plays as such, since personified abstractions are inevitably static, and a morality playwright can therefore put his trust in little but the dignity of stark simplicity and economy of statement. *Magnificence* was bound to fail by this test, for Skelton was voluminous and diffuse, always readier to amplify than to prune; yet his play, if considered as a literary experiment, represents a genuine attempt to carry English drama a step forward. Morality plays had previously been concerned not merely with personified abstractions but also with very broad, even crude, moral generalizations. The distinction of Skelton's *Magnificence* was that it had for its own time a peculiar immediacy as 'a Wolsey play'. Though it was obviously intended as a warning to the young Henry VIII against ruinous extravagance, the central figure cannot be wholly divorced from Wolsey personally, however much it may embody a prophetic shadow of what might befall the king himself if he did not draw back from the pitfalls of luxury. That *Magnificence* had other current significances is probable: e.g. the discussion in an early scene on liberty free (i.e. licence) or liberty controlled by moderation sounds a note of urgency.

Beyond such contemporary allusions, and the stumbling endeavours to give new life to a moribund literary type, Skelton's play has the interest of making a tentative approach to a theme which was to become obsessive in Elizabethan drama. Poverty says to Magnificence:

> Syr, remembre the tourne of Fortunes whele,
> That wantonly can wynke, and wynche with her hele.
> Nowe she wyll laughe; forthwith she wyll frowne;
> Sodenly set vp and sodenly pluckyd downe;
> She dawnsyth varyaunce with mutabylyte,
> Nowe all in Welth, forthwith in Pouerte;
> In her promyse there is no sykernesse;
> All her Delyte is set in Doublenesse.[1]

wynche] kick   sykernesse] security

But whereas the Elizabethans take the final turn of Fortune's wheel as the mainspring of tragedy, Skelton burkes the very issue from which he could have drawn genuine dramatic power in *Magnificence*. When retribution begins to assail the chief character the play does for the first time (Scene 26) show signs of life, but instead of reaching a tragic climax through calamity it fades out on a dim note of repentance. Morality is served while drama is wrecked.[2]

Among the dramatis personæ in *Magnificence* only Courtly Abusion has glimmerings of individuality, as a popinjay akin to Osric in *Hamlet*. The technical literary interest of the piece consists partly in Skelton's manipulation of the metres, chiefly the Chaucerian seven-line stanza (rhyme-royal), rhyming couplets, and Skeltonics—upon which variations of stress and line-length are ingeniously played, with frequent harking back to the older English alliterative line which obviously fascinated Skelton. The passages of cut-and-thrust dialogue (the sustained rapid exchange of single-line speeches between Fancy and Folly

[1] *Magnyfycence*, edited by Robert Lee Ramsay (Early English Text Society, 1908). Dr. Ramsay's Introduction is an exhaustive study of Skelton's play in every aspect.

[2] The tragic intensity which eluded Skelton (or was not to his purpose) in *Magnificence* abounds in George Cavendish's *Life of Wolsey*, written about 1557. Though this biography was not published until long after Shakespeare's death, one of the manuscript copies that are known to have been in circulation must have impressed him deeply, for he based the Wolsey passages in *Henry VIII* on Cavendish and sometimes adopted the biographer's words with no more change than their translation into blank verse required. Cavendish was a faithful servant of Wolsey, but his personal devotion did not dull his critical perception. English biography had a distinguished beginning with this book and William Roper's and Nicholas Harpsfield's lives of Sir Thomas More. Cavendish's work, alike in its skilful selection and direction of material, in its prose style, and in its presentation of character is a masterpiece of biographical art.

in Scene 17 and between other characters elsewhere) may have been a product of Skelton's classical studies, for this device (*stichomythia*) goes back to Greek tragedy.

Few poets have had a fuller command of rhetoric than Skelton, and the *Poems Against Garnesche* (a prominent member of Henry VIII's Court) abound with picturesque abuse. But 'Gup, gorbellied Godfrey, gup, Garnesche, gawdy fool!' and all the rest was perhaps little more than paper fighting, a literary tournament staged by request to amuse the king.

In Alexander Barclay (*c.* 1475–1552), author of *The Ship of Fools*, Skelton had a genuine enemy who attacked him in print more than once and was particularly scornful of *Philip Sparrow*; yet Skelton was indebted to Barclay's chief poem for certain features in his own writings. Barclay, a Scot, was educated at the English universities and probably travelled on the Continent, for he had a good knowledge of French and some at least of German. After holding various clerical appointments in the provinces he became rector of All Hallows, Lombard Street, London, very shortly before his death. Of his fairly numerous writings none is now of even indirect importance except *The Ship of Fools* (1509), adapted from an extremely popular German work, *Narrenschiff*, written or compiled *c.* 1494 by Sebastian Brandt. Barclay relied more upon the Latin and French translations than upon Brandt's own work, and he also added a good deal of original matter. Indeed, in his hands the book (put into rhyme-royal) became an English compendium of reform, for Barclay exposes a multitude of vices and abuses, and castigates liberally: lawyers, students, clerics, public officials, and others. Medieval in conception and belonging at root to the allegorical tradition, *The Ship of Fools* nevertheless displays more interest in human character than in moral abstractions. After its immediate popularity as a work of social protest had lessened, its literary effect remained—even if it was not always openly evident—as a contribution to the growth of interest throughout the sixteenth century in the nature and actions of men and women.

Sir David Lyndsay (1490–1555) resembled Barclay in being primarily concerned with the sorry state of society and in owing a formal debt to Chaucerian verse. Unlike Barclay his vision was concentrated on Scotland and its affairs, and his writings belong entirely to Scottish literature. He was a close personal associate of James V of Scotland and it was for the king that he wrote *The Dreme*, beginning with a kind of dantesque excursion into the other-worlds but developing into a picture of Scotland in its natural abundance contrasted with the deplorable state into which the nation had been brought by human vices and misgovernment. Lyndsay did not confine his reformatory zeal to exhortations on large matters of the general public welfare, but carried satire also into that lesser field of women's fashions which reformers in all generations have found it hard to ignore: *Ane Supplicatioun againis Syde Taillis* is an attack on long skirts, written with a combination of wit and obscenity more acceptable to contemporary taste than to the queasy modern palate.

Among Lyndsay's other works were poems on national and Court abuses put into the mouths of the king's parrot (*The Testament and Complaynt of our Soverane Lordis Papyngo*) and of one of his dogs (*Ane Publict Confessioun of the Kingis auld Hound callit Bagsche*), but these are of small account beside his play *Ane Pleasant Satire of the Thrie Estaitis in commendatioun of Vertew and Vituperatioun of Vyce* (*c.* 1540). This exceptionally long and complex work incorporates features from several types of early drama—chiefly the Morality and the Interlude. The playing time of the full text is said to have been about nine hours, almost as long as was taken by a whole cycle of Miracle plays in England. The 'three estates' are, of course, the Church, the Lords, and the Commoners, but it is impossible to indicate the range of subject matter treated in the play. The characters are legion: most are abstract personifications, but some were actual persons; and little that interested, amused, or outraged Lyndsay in contemporary life escapes some measure of sharp or bitter attention. The treatment roves from knockabout farce to a serious and extremely long sermon by John the Common Weill, who had already appeared in *The Dreme*. If it was Lyndsay's aim to put in something suited to the appetite of every part of his early sixteenth-century audience he surely succeeded beyond compare, though he must have been confident of powerful protection against the wrath that his play could not fail to excite among Catholics. As an inevitable consequence of its close concern with matters affecting the sixteenth-century Scots, large parts of *The Thrie Estaitis* can mean little or nothing to an unselected present-day audience, and only by shrewd editing has it been made acceptable as entertainment in the twentieth century.[1]

[1] The complete Works of Sir David Lyndsay, edited by Douglas Hamer, were published by the Scottish Text Society, 1931-6. Robert Kemp's 1948 'Edinburgh Festival Version', rendered into modern Scots and 'reduced to something near the conventional time of two hours' in performance, was also published in an English version, again by Mr. Kemp (Heinemann, London, 1951).

CHAPTER VI

ELIZABETHAN POETRY

THE writings of the Elizabethan age were so profuse and varied that even in our distant perspective view of the period we can avoid confusion only by grouping the literature according to accepted categories. Such categorizing is merely conventional, however, for Elizabethan literature was more closely inter-related than that of almost any other age. Elizabethan poetry, Elizabethan novels, Elizabethan pamphlets, Elizabethan trans-lations, Elizabethan chronicles, and Elizabethan plays were all operations of a common creative organism in which intellect and imagination were the equally vital motive forces. Moreover, Elizabethan literature was not precisely confined to the reign of Elizabeth (1558–1603); nor was the Jacobean literature which followed born at the accession of James I. Elizabethan and Jacobean were for the most part one literature, a number of the writers being active in both reigns. Nevertheless, as the Elizabethan impulse of imaginative freedom lessened, there developed that formal intellectualism which appears as the distinguishing Jacobean characteristic in literature. So far as such a distinction can be made, Shakespeare is the typical Elizabethan and Ben Jonson the typical Jacobean.

The subdivision of the whole body of sixteenth- and early seventeenth-century writings into several literary types must be regarded, then, as a mere convenience for the purpose of brief exposition. For a properly balanced appreciation of Elizabethan and Jacobean literature it is necessary to consider the frequently close relationship between diverse works and between diverse writers; and, more especially, between the writers and their works and that 'something in the air', that elusive yet irre-sistible 'spirit of the age', which served as a priming charge for the release of personal genius. It is conceivable that a *potential* Christopher Marlowe, even a *potential* Shakespeare, might be born in any age; but it is inconceivable that either a Shakespeare or a Marlowe could have written at any other time or in any other place as these wrote in Elizabethan England.

Renaissance Poetry

Two representative modern anthologies of sixteenth-century verse [1] include, between them, poems by nearly a hundred named writers, besides many anonymous pieces. While in our own day anthologies have come to be received with some critical contempt because of their often stale contents, the numerous anthologies brought out in the sixteenth century were for the most part invaluable repositories of poems not previously published. While professional writers—playwrights and others—became a familiar type as the century progressed, amateur poets were numerous and important. Making poems was a fashionable pastime among young gentlemen of fortune (who were not, however, always of good fortune; imprisonment or execution were frequently their lot) and it was customary for such poetry to circulate in manuscript within the writer's personal circle. Publication was not sought, even if it was not forbidden when printers and bookseller-publishers grew more enterprising and the book trade developed. It is known from Francis Meres's reference in *Palladis Tamia* (1598) that Shakespeare's 'sugred sonnets among his friends' were circulating in manuscript more than ten years before the first printed edition came out in 1609; and that good poetry was written for poetry's sake rather than in hope of personal fame is evident from the large number of anonymous poems that have survived more or less by chance. How much sixteenth-century poetry was destroyed in manuscript cannot be known, though our meagre harvest of Ralegh's poems suggests something of the seriousness of the loss.

The facts that poetry was a gentlemanly avocation and that continental travel for pleasure or business was habitual in the same circles would have enabled a deductive literary critic round about 1550 to forecast the immediate future of English poetry. For a century or more Italy had been excitedly absorbing classical culture, and this fortunate craze communicated its æsthetic consequences to other parts of continental Europe while England was preoccupied with those sterner aspects of scholarship which engaged More and his circle. Not

[1] *A Pageant of Elizabethan Poetry,* arranged by Arthur Symons (Blackie, London, 1906) and *The Oxford Book of Sixteenth Century Verse,* chosen by E. K. Chambers (Clarendon Press, 1932).

until 1557 (the year before Elizabeth succeeded to the throne), when Richard Tottel, a London printer, issued *Songes and Sonnets, written by the ryght honorable Lorde Henry Howard and others* did the conscious *art* of poetry as part of the Renaissance heritage invade England, though one of Tottel's principal contributors, Wyatt, had published a metrical translation of certain Psalms in 1549.

This anthology, commonly called *Tottel's Miscellany*, assembled 40 poems by Howard (the Earl of Surrey), 96 by Sir Thomas Wyatt, 40 by Nicholas Grimald, and 95 by 'Uncertain Authors' (including Thomas Churchyard, John Heywood, Sir Francis Bryan, Edward, Duke of Somerset, and Thomas, Lord Vaux). Apart from the high poetic worth of many of the pieces, the book had two features of special importance in the history of English poetry: (1) that among Wyatt's and Surrey's poems were the first sonnets printed in English; (2) that Surrey's pieces included the first specimens of blank verse, a form invented by him. Both the sonnet and blank verse were destined to fascinate not only Elizabethan poets but also innumerable successors down to the present century. In the Elizabethan period the consequences were fortunate in both kinds. After Marlowe had energized blank verse with rhetorical fire it became the perfect instrument for all Shakespeare's purposes in tragedy and comedy; while the sonnet form was used by Shakespeare to produce the greatest non-dramatic poetry of his age, as well as by many of his contemporaries for exceptionally graceful if not profound work.

Wyatt's rank as a poet has been contradictorily estimated. He took over the sonnet from the Italian Petrarch, but usually departed from the strict Petrarchan rhyme-pattern, which follows the order *abbaabba* in the octave and allows the alternative of two or three new rhymes in the remaining six lines (sestette): e.g. *cdecde, cdcdcd, cdedce,* etc. And whereas the Petrarchan sonnets never close with a rhyming couplet, Wyatt's always do. He was largely responsible for diverting the Elizabethan sonneteers, including Shakespeare, from the Italian form to which Milton and some later poets were to return, though Milton often ignored Petrarchan practice (a complete octave with a complete sestette as its pendant) by running the eighth line into the ninth without a break. The movement of a strict-pattern sonnet has been likened to that of a wave, rising to its crest at the end of line 8 and quietly receding in the remaining six lines. The Elizabethan preference for ending with a rhyming couplet produces a more emphatic close than the Italian pattern gives. Indeed, the sixteenth-century English passion for freedom in literary forms led the Elizabethans to preserve little from the Italian sonnet but its fourteen ten-syllable lines.

Whatever departures Wyatt made from the sonnet form as he found it in Petrarch were a matter of preference; but there are also marked irregularities in the metrical flow of a good deal of his poetry. This was formerly assumed to be a fault due to the poet's lack of skill in verse-craft, and he was compared unfavourably with Surrey on that account. More recently a shift in critical attitude has elevated Wyatt above Surrey for poetic merit [1] and has favoured the view that his roughnesses are due to deliberate metrical experimentation and are not mere signs of incapacity. This more favourable opinion of Wyatt may well be due in part to the preference for less rigid metrical forms which marks mid twentieth-century poetry and which has minimized the importance of Surrey's innovation by transferring to free verse much of the importance formerly attached to blank verse. [2]

There is no call to debate the relative merits of Wyatt and Surrey, however, in order to establish that Wyatt is a notable poet in his own right and often an accomplished metrist. Some of his lyrics in other than sonnet form are original poetry of a high order. Though Wyatt was dead some sixteen years before the great age began, none of the Elizabethans wrote a technically more accomplished, a more musically effective, or a more moving lyric than this best-known of Wyatt's:

> Fforget not yet the tryde entent
> Of suche a truthe as I haue ment,
> My gret travayle so gladly spent
> Fforget not yet.

[1] See *Collected Poems of Sir Thomas Wyatt*, edited with an introduction by Kenneth Muir (The Muses' Library, Routledge, London, 1949).

[2] The free-verse mode in twentieth-century English poetry is chiefly American in origin, from T. S. Eliot out of Walt Whitman, though Milton's (and in some degree Shakespeare's) later blank verse was veering away from metrical regularity.

Fforget not yet when fyrst began
The wery lyffe ye know syns whan,
The sute, the seruys none tell can,
    Fforget not yett.

Fforget not yet the gret assays,
The cruell wrong, the skornfull ways,
The paynfull pacyence in denays,
    Fforget not yet.

Fforget not yet, forget not thys,
How long ago hathe ben and ys
The mynd that neuer ment amys,
    Fforget not yet.

Fforget not then thyn owne aprovyd,
The whyche so long hathe the so lovyd,
Whose stedfast faythe yet neuer movyd,
    Fforget not thys.

Since Wyatt was the forerunner of the many sonneteers and lyrists who followed in the reign of Elizabeth, it is well to face at this point the much-discussed question of the 'sincerity' or otherwise of Elizabethan lyric poetry.

The expression of subjective emotion, rare in earlier poetry, grew common among sixteenth-century writers, and it has since been almost equally common for literary historians to submit that this subjective element was a literary convention, a verbal game, not the product of direct personal feeling. The 'problem', in so far as it is not in itself part of an academic game, arises from critics' inability to understand the creative process. No line can be drawn between what is 'genuine' and what is 'false' in literature until it is conceded that the creative imagination is as genuine a source of experience, and by its nature a more profound source, than any personal emotional relationship can be. Jack who loves Jill, with whatever intensity of passion or whatever torment of frustration, is not thereby qualified to write more 'genuinely' of love's delights and distresses than a poet who, while possibly knowing little of any individual Jill, comprehends utterly the universal Jill and the whole tangle of Jack-and-Jillery. It is as nonsensical to ask if Elizabethan love poetry was written by actual lovers as it would be to ask if the Elizabethan tragedies of blood (including *Macbeth*) were written by actual murderers. The genuineness consists in the quality of the work, that quality being determined (apart from such factors as form and style) by the degree of conviction communicated to readers and audiences; and this quality of the product is determined by the quality of the originating imagination and mind. Insincerity and sentimentality and all falsity in literature come from inferior or perverted or misapplied imaginative and mental faculties, not from simple limitation of individual experience.

Thus, though there is an historical interest in the inquiry as to whether certain allusions in Wyatt's poems relate to his having been Anne Boleyn's lover before she became Henry VIII's wife—whether she is Brunet (in the sonnet beginning 'If waker care, if sodayne pale Coulor') and whether it is to her that he refers in another sonnet:

> There is written her faier neck rounde abowte:
> *Noli me tangere*, for Cesars I ame—

it is irrelevant to the poetry as such. It has been supposed that the first of Wyatt's two short spells of imprisonment in the Tower of London (1536 and 1541) was on account of his association with Anne, but there is no certain evidence. His life was marked by periods of royal favour offset by periods in which he was accused by influential enemies of offences ranging from adultery to high treason. He survived the attempts to secure his condemnation, however, though he was only thirty-nine when he died of fever in 1542.

Henry Howard, Earl of Surrey, less fortunate than Wyatt, was executed in 1547 on a baseless charge of treason, when he was twenty-nine. Like so many other poets of the century he was a man of action and affairs, serving with the army in France and commanding at Boulogne in 1545–6.

The impact of classical literature is more clearly seen in Surrey's poetry than in Wyatt's, though they were equally indebted to Italian sources for the Renaissance influences dominant in their writings. Whatever they owed to foreign sources, ancient and modern, however, their knowledge of Chaucer and their feeling for his poetry is not to be ignored. It was in his translations from Virgil's *Æneid* that Surrey mainly employed the iambic pentameter decasyllabic unrhymed line which he

had devised and which we know as blank verse. When used by
minor poets blank verse becomes as monotonous as inferior
rhyming couplets, and some early users of blank verse appear
to make a conscious effort to avoid the rhymes which would
come pat at the end of their too regularly accented lines. A brief
passage (spelling modernized) from the description of Dido in
Surrey's translation will indicate both the regularity of much
of his blank verse and also the occasional shifts of stress and
voice-pause which act as a safeguard against monotony:

> The Carthage lords did on their queen await;
> The trampling steed, with gold and purple decked,
> Fiercely stood chawing on the foaming bit.
> Then issued she, awaited with a train,
> Clad in a cloak of Tyre bordered full rich.
> Her quiver being behind her back, her tress
> Knotted in gold, her purple vesture eke
> Buttoned with gold . . .

Here, lines 1, 2, 4 and 6 have the stress on the second and
following alternate syllables (i.e. the regular iambic foot ⌣—)
while in the rest of the passage the beat is varied without break-
ing away from the standard five-stress blank-verse line. Furthermore, Surrey varies (as the less skilful among later users did not)
the position of the natural voice-pause (*cæsura*) in his lines. In
his blank verse this commonly falls after the second foot (fourth
syllable), as in lines 1, 2, 4, 7 and 8 above; but it falls after
the fifth syllable in line 3, after the sixth in line 5, and after the
eighth in line 6. Already, in the hands of its inventor, blank
verse was demonstrating its capacity for flexible movement
within formal bounds. On the whole, however, Surrey was a less
adventurous metrist than Wyatt (some would say, on the contrary, that Wyatt was clumsier and Surrey more skilful) and
his sonnets run more smoothly, perhaps because he paid even
less heed to his model, Petrarch. It was Surrey, indeed, who did
most to establish the Elizabethan type of sonnet as a poem of
four quatrains and a rhyming couplet: *abab cdcd efef gg*.

Classical literature, with its wealth of legendary material,
provided the sixteenth-century English poets with an inex-
haustible source of reference and allusion. Whether they were
aristocrats or plebeians, all of them were in some measure

scholars, and even those who did not qualify to be ranked with the 'university wits' managed to acquire some familiarity with classical themes. These were among the things in the air that the writers breathed, and which became part of themselves. Nevertheless, there was an ever-present tendency to use learning —classical and other—for barren dialectical display. There is more than the particular stage-occasion warrants in Moth's remark (*Love's Labour's Lost*, V. i, 37–8): 'They have been at a great feast of languages, and stolen the scraps.' Intellectual 'conceits' were part of the stock-in-trade of writers in the sixteenth and seventeenth centuries and they passed into metaphysical literature in their most exaggerated development, which was also their decline.

The skill with which the earlier poets could use and sustain a classical reference cogently and with conviction as well as literary charm is seen in Surrey's poem *The Lover Comforteth Himself with the Worthiness of his Love:*

> When ragyng loue with extreme payne
> Most cruelly distrains my hart:
> When that my teares, as floudes of rayne,
> Beare witnes of my wofull smart:
> When sighes haue wasted so my breath,
> That I lye at the poynte of death:
> I call to minde the nauye greate,
> That the Greekes brought to Troye towne:
> And how the boysterous windes did beate
> Their shyps, and rente their sayles adowne,
> Till Agamemnons daughters bloode
> Appeasde the goddes, that them withstode.
> And how that in those ten years warre,
> Full many a bloudye dede was done,
> And many a lord, that came full farre,
> There caught his bane (alas) to sone:
> And many a good knight ouerronne,
> Before the Grekes had Helene wonne.
> Then thinke I thus: sithe suche repayre,
> So longe time warre of valiant men,
> Was all to winne a layde fayre:
> Shall I not learne to suffer then,
> And thinke my life well spent to be,
> Seruyng a worthier wight than she?

Therefore I neuer will repent,
But paynes contented stil endure.
For like as when, rough winter spent,
The pleasant spring straight draweth in vre:
So after ragyng stormes of care
Joyful at length may be my fare.

Other anthologies of the period were more enchantingly named than Tottel's (*The Paradyse of Daynty Devises*, 1576; *A Gorgious Gallery of Gallant Inventions*, 1578; *Posie of Gilloflowers*, 1580), but no other matched his in poetic interest or equalled its importance in literary history. Among the contemporary miscellanies of a specialized kind by a single hand, none has retained so much curious interest for later generations as Thomas Tusser's *Hundredth good pointes of husbandrie* (1557) which went through several editions and became *Five hundredth pointes of good husbandrie* in 1573. Tusser (*c.* 1524–80) was a scholar, though his verse often suggests an unsophisticated mind. After being a St. Paul's chorister, he went to Eton and Cambridge, and was later in the Paget household in some musical capacity until about 1553. Then he settled for several years on a Suffolk farm, and was there the first to introduce barley into England. His book is an amusing and for the most part sententious rhymed guide to farming, horticulture, household management, frugality, moral conduct, religion, and things in general. Numerous proverbial sayings were either invented or first put into print in Tusser's writings: e.g. 'Christmas comes but once a year', 'pig in a poke', 'dog in the manger', 'Feb[ruary] fill the dyke', 'Sweet April showers Do spring May flowers', 'Look ere thou leap',

The stone that is rolling can gather no moss,
For master and servant, oft changing is loss.

The solider purposes of Tusser's book are presented thus:

Hops hate the land
With gravel and sand.
The rotten mould
For hop is worth gold.
The sun south-west
For hop-yard is best.
Hop-plot once found
Now dig the ground.

In its own time no compilation equalled in immediate importance *A Myrroure for Magistrates: Wherein may be seen by example of other[s], with how grevous [plagues] vices are punished: and how frayle and mistakable worldly prosperitie is founde, even of those, whom Fortune seemeth most highly to favour.* This now almost unreadable work was at one time thought to have been planned by Thomas Sackville, Earl of Dorset, part author of the first regular English tragedy, *Gorboduc (see below*, p. 177). That he had a special interest in the *Mirror* is proved by his famous induction, the only portion with real merit as poetry. The book was intended to serve for the sixteenth century as Lydgate's *Falls of Princes (see above*, p. 35) had for the fifteenth, and it was first published in 1559 with William Baldwin as its editor, a Court functionary George Ferrers being named as its planner. The first edition told in pedestrian rhyming verse some twenty cautionary tales of the eminent or notorious (Richard II, Owen Glendower, Jack Cade, Henry VI, and Edward IV among them) whose misspent lives had received due reward. Sackville's Induction did not appear until the second edition (1563), to which he also contributed 'The Complaynt of Henry Duke of Buckingham.' Whether the *Mirror* served virtue by persuading any of its readers to lead good lives must remain unknown, but it became invaluable as a source book for sixteenth-century playwrights and other poets who proposed to write on historical personages. It proved to be little more than a literary rocket, however, apart from the Induction, a work of nearly four-score stanzas in rhyme-royal which begins with a beautiful passage of nature poetry, before proceeding to its allegorical purpose with the introduction of Sorrow,

> A piteous wight, whom woe had all forwaste;
> Forth from her eyne the crystal tears outbrast,
>   And sighing sore, her hands she wrung and fold,
>   Tare all her hair, that ruth was to behold.
>
>   .   .   .   .   .
>
> 'Come, come,' quod she, 'and see what I shall show;
> Come hear the plaining and the bitter bale
>   Of worthy men by Fortune's overthrow;
>   Come then and see them rueing all in row. . . .'

She leads the poet into Avernus, where they see Remorse, Dread, Revenge, Misery, Old Age, Malady, Famine, War, and then Darius, Hannibal, Pompey, Cæsar, Xerxes, Cassandra, Charon, Cerberus, and other monstrous phantoms. The subject matter used by Sackville had long before been staled by allegorizing poets, but here it is magnificently reinvigorated and transformed. Almost for the first time in English, at any rate since Chaucer, allegory becomes true, vivid, and rousing poetry. Yet the brilliant imaginative quality of the Avernus descriptions does not dim the beauty of the English winter pictures in the opening stanzas:

> The wrathful winter prochinge on a pace,
> With blustring blastes had all ybared the treen,
> And olde Saturnus with his frosty face
> With chilling colde had pearst the tender green:
> The mantels rent, wherein enwrapped been
> The gladsom groves that nowe laye ouerthrowen,
> The tapets torne, and euery blome downe blowen.[1]

> The soil, that erst so seemly was to seen,
> Was all despoiled of her beauty's hue;
> And sweet fresh flowers, wherewith the summer's queen
> Had clad the earth, now Boreas' blasts down blew;
> And small fowls flocking in their song did rue
> The winter's wrath, wherewith each thing defaced
> In woeful wise bewailed the summer past.

> Hawthorn had lost his motley livery,
> The naked twigs were shivering all for cold,
> And dropping down the tears abundantly;
> Each thing, methought, with weeping eye me told
> The cruel season, bidding me withhold
> Myself within; for I was gotten out
> Into the fields, wherein I walked about.

Edmund Spenser

From the year 1579 in which Spenser published the *Shepheardes Calender* down to the death of Thomas Hardy in 1928 England was never without a great poet: Spenser, Shakespeare, Donne, George Herbert, Milton, Dryden, Pope, Gray, Blake, Wordsworth, Shelley, Keats, Tennyson, Browning, Hardy—without calling in lesser poets the line is unbroken. For intrinsic worth Spenser's poetry is surpassed only by Shakespeare's, Milton's,

[1] Original spelling; following stanzas modernized.

and Chaucer's; while as the cause of poetry in others no one but Chaucer has equalled him, and certainly the fifteenth-century Chaucerians were a less illustrious band than the Spenserians of the Romantic period at the turn of the eighteenth-nineteenth century. Yet Spenser has never taken a secure hold of the affections of lay readers of poetry. A few of his shorter poems are genuinely liked, but his greatest work, *The Faerie Queene*, is more read about and praised than read and loved. It is not difficult to account for this. Though it is only a fragment of what it was intended to be, there is nevertheless too much of *The Faerie Queene*. Even if to modern taste it were not dulled by the extremely involved and often confusing allegory, it would cloy by excess of poetic splendour. If Spenser had been less profusely great he would have been greater, for nothing repels like excess.

A contributory hindrance is that none but a handful of readers now meet Spenser's poetry attractively printed and set out. All but experienced and determined readers are likely to be deterred by poetry in small type on double-column pages. The beauty of great poetry needs to receive its preliminary declaration through seemly typography on a generous page. Spenser, in particular, should be offered to beginners in an attractively printed brief selection, before they are faced with his whole works in the utility dress imposed by the economics of publishing.

Spenser's *Prothalamion* tells that he was born in London (*c.* 1552). The locality is not specified but it was probably East Smithfield. He was related to the Spencer family of Althorp, Northants, and to his cousins the three daughters of Sir John Spencer he dedicated, respectively, *The Teares of the Muses*, *Prosopopoia* (*Mother Hubberds Tale*), and *Muiopotmos*, besides addressing them by pastoral names in *Colin Clouts Come Home Again* as

> *Phyllis, Charillis*, and sweet *Amaryllis*,
> *Phillis* the faire, is eldest of the three:
> The next to her, is bountifull *Charillis*.
> But th'youngest is the highest in degree.

His father, John Spenser, migrated from Lancashire to London, where he engaged in the cloth-making industry and became a member of the Merchant Taylors' Company. Edmund's education began at the Merchant Taylors' School and continued at Pembroke Hall, Cambridge.

The poet was fortunate in his school. Mulcaster, its first head master, was a keen scholar with a generous conception of the aims of education. 'It is not a mind,' he wrote, 'not a body, that we have to educate, but a man; and we cannot divide him.' The conception derives from the enthusiastic culture of the Renaissance, and something both of the ideal and the practice of the perfect courtier, which Spenser was later to emulate and to portray, must have been instilled into him in early youth.[1]

Spenser had a wide if not remarkably deep knowledge of ancient and modern languages, and up to that time no English poet had equalled the general range of his learning. His own poetry was moulded chiefly by Virgil and Plato, his technical artistry through the former and his inclination towards mystical thought through the Platonic dialogues. But however much he was affected by æsthetic and philosophic ideas from the ancient world, an innate strain of asceticism controlled him and at times made him, through moral excess, strangely insensitive to ugliness, as in the description of the monster Errour and her brood in Book I (Canto I, 14–26). This conflict or confusion of Platonism and Puritanism in Spenser blurred his vision of the universe and, as Caroline Spurgeon suggested, in her references to *An Hymne of Heavenly Beautie*,[2] made 'the dominating feature in Spenser's poetry ... a curious blending of Puritanism of spirit with the Platonic mind'. It was less a blending, however, than an unresolved contradiction, as Dr. Spurgeon's quotations show; for whereas in lines 127–9 the poet says that the means whereby we behold the Creator is by looking on his works 'Which he hath made in beauty excellent', in the final lines of the *Hymne* he speaks of the love of God as bringing 'loathing ... of this vile world, and these gay seeming things'. It is perhaps a subconscious awareness of this loathing, this nausea to which many Christian stomachs besides Spenser's are unbecomingly prone, that has been in part responsible for the failure of Spenser to win the full confidence and affection of non-scholastic readers.

[1] E. de Selincourt: Introduction to *The Poetical Works of Edmund Spenser* (Oxford Standard Authors edition, 1912).
[2] *Mysticism in English Literature* by Caroline E. Spurgeon (Cambridge, 1913).

At Cambridge Spenser became acquainted with Gabriel Harvey (*c.* 1545–1630), who was a respectable scholar, a bit of a poet, a bit of a satirist, a bit of a pamphleteer, a good deal of a controversialist, much of a pedant, and still a stubbornly unattractive figure in the Elizabethan landscape in spite of attempts in this century to present a more engaging portrait of him. Harvey became a Fellow of Pembroke College while Spenser was at Cambridge, and although his talent for earning dislike amounted almost to genius, he also had reputable friends, among whom Spenser was as important and devoted as any. Since Harvey held rigid puritanical convictions it is likely that he coloured Spenser's religious outlook; but it is on account of his endeavours to persuade, if not to browbeat, Spenser into using classical metres that Harvey keeps a place in literary history. His aim was to establish *quantity* as the ruling principle of English versification as well as to abolish rhyme, and his arguments are presented long-windedly in the letters to Spenser published during their lifetime. Since Spenser was to prove himself the great reformer of English verse structure and a supreme poetic artist, it would have been a calamity of the first order to English poetry if Harvey had succeeded in imposing a prosodic system which could only have fettered our language and destroyed its flexibility and freedom of movement.

Spenser's doings immediately after leaving Cambridge in 1576 are uncertain. The fact that he uses in his poetry dialect words belonging to northern England makes it likely that he was for a while in his father's county, Lancashire; but two years later he obtained through Harvey an appointment in the household of the Earl of Leicester, and about the same time began his friendship with Philip Sidney, to whom he dedicated *The Shepheardes Calender* (1579), his first important work. There was much mentally in common between Spenser and Sidney, who were near in age, but the difference in their social standing and the exceptional fineness of mind and character of the brilliant young aristocrat led Spenser to look up to Sidney as the ideal pattern of mankind. The terms of his dedication have less verbal rotundity than Spenser was accustomed to use for that purpose, and what he wrote was genuinely felt: 'To the noble and virtuous Gentleman most worthy of all titles both of learning and chivalry M. Philip Sidney'. Strong though

Spenser's regard was, he withstood Sidney's preference for classical metres as firmly as he had Harvey's importunity in the same matter; but Sidney, unlike Harvey, recognized the excellences of the new poetry which Spenser was raising to so high a level.

As a member of Leicester's household Spenser obtained his first glimpses of Court life and his first personal contact with Queen Elizabeth. The heady atmosphere appears to have stirred ambition in him and the expectation of worldly success in those circles; but he lacked the moral pliancy necessary for advancement as a courtier. If, as is probable, his poems circulated in manuscript before publication, the disfavour into which he fell among the powerful may have been due to his major impudence in *Prosopopoia: or Mother Hubberds Tale*, which, in the guise of a fable of the ape and the fox, delivers a mordant satirical attack on current political and religious standards, particularly on a scheme, alarming to the Protestants, for marrying the Queen to the Duke of Alençon. But whatever the cause, Spenser's hopes of employment at Court were unfulfilled, and towards the end of 1580 he went to Ireland as private secretary to Lord Grey de Wilton, the newly appointed Lord Deputy. Grey conceived it to be his duty to deal ruthlessly with the turbulent Irish and his period of office was one of the many ugly chapters in their history. Spenser nevertheless believed Grey's actions to be justified in the circumstances and defended his policy in a prose *View of the Present State of Ireland*, written in 1596. Book V of *The Faerie Queene* praises Grey under the chivalric name Sir Artegall, figuring him as the champion of Justice sent to rescue Irena (Ireland) from the 'strong tyrant' Grantorto (anarchy).

After two years Grey was recalled but Spenser stayed on, being in turn Clerk of Decrees in Dublin (1581), Clerk of the Council of Munster (1589), and finally Sheriff of Cork (1598). In 1586 he was granted an estate of some 3,000 acres with a castle at Kilcolman, county Cork, which was his home until the castle was set on fire and completely destroyed in the revolt of 1598. Spenser had married Elizabeth Boyle (related to Sir Richard Boyle, afterwards 1st Earl of Cork) in 1594 when he was over forty, and it was for their marriage that he wrote his most exquisite and perfect poem *Epithalamion*. His service in

Ireland was interrupted by periods of residence in London in 1589–91 and 1595–6. After the burning of Kilcolman Castle he reached London on Christmas Eve and died at Westminster less than a month later (16 January 1599). He was buried in the Abbey. There is little to support the story that he died in utter poverty. The sudden loss of his home, and no doubt of his personal belongings also, may have plunged him into temporary need; but he was well liked by a large circle of influential friends who would have been as ready to succour him in need as they were to pay the most impressive memorial tribute ever offered to a poet, writing elegies in his honour and casting them and the pens that wrote them into his grave.

The position which Spenser has held for some four centuries among the English poets is a triumph of art. His genius was recognized immediately by his contemporaries, who were better qualified to grasp the implications of his religious and political subject-matter than readers in later ages could be; but, also, their admiration of him as a poetic artist was as deep as ours. In the present century his admirers are separated into two camps which, while not necessarily opposed, are certainly aloof from each other. There are those who claim that it is enough to enjoy Spenser's poetry æsthetically—for its beauty of form, its music, its colour and verbal pageantry—and that it gains nothing *as poetry* from close probing into its spiritual and philosophical significances. Others hold that his greatness lies at least as much in the complexities and (as they believe) in the profundities of allegory in *The Faerie Queene*. No doubt the satisfaction which comes from painstaking labour is an additional reward to those who probe the metaphysical depths and dredge the political shallows of Spenser's works; yet no doubt also, Spenser would remain an almost entirely closed book to the vast majority of modern readers of poetry if all were required to possess the scholarly *expertise* essential to an exhaustive appreciation of the whole content of his poetry, which is almost the whole content of the Renaissance mind and spirit moulded (and in certain respects misshapen) by the circumstances and events of the late sixteenth century. It is more sensible and profitable to get what we can from Spenser—and that is much—than to retire baffled from a great deal in him that, on first acquaintance, may appear wearisome, or distasteful, or unintelligible. Moreover, while being a man of the Renaissance, Spenser inherited a strain of medievalism which appears in the large in his addiction to allegory, and in fragmentary detail in his use of archaic words and his frequent recourse to alliteration. These latter features are an ineradicable part of his literary charm, and without the spell of Spenserian archaisms the poetry of Coleridge and Keats, at least, is unimaginable. The poetic magic and mystery which run through *The Ancient Mariner* echo from Spenser:

> Eftsoones her shallow ship away did slide,
> More swift, then swallow sheres the liquid skie,
> Withouten oare or Pilot it to guide,
> Or winged canvas with the wind to flie, . . .[1]

It is not a matter of indebtedness by the later poet to particular lines in the earlier, but of saturation in the romantic atmosphere of Spenser's poetry. The sensuous beauty which is strong in his work—and strange in one with his puritan sensibilities, for at times it is a pronounced sensual flush—communicated itself markedly to Keats, whose *Eve of St. Agnes* is recognizably descended from the imagination that conceived the following lines:

> Upon a bed of Roses she was layd,
> As faint through heat, or dight to pleasant sin,
> And was arayd, or rather disarayd,
> All in a vele of silke and silver thin,
> That hid no whit her alabaster skin,
> But rather shewd more white, if more might bee:
> More subtile web *Arachne* cannot spin,
> Nor the fine nets, which oft we woven see
> Of scorched deaw, do not in th'aire more lightly flee.
>
> Her snowie brest was bare to readie spoyle
> Of hungry eies, which n'ote therewith be fild,
> And yet through languour of her late sweet toyle,
> Few drops, more cleare than Nectar, forth distild,
> That like pure Orient perles adowne it trild,
> And her faire eyes sweet smyling in delight,
> Moystened their fierie beames, with which she thrild
> Fraile harts, yet quenched not; like starry light
> Which sparckling on the silent waves, does seeme more bright.[2]

[1] *The Faerie Queene*, II, vi, 5. In these quotations the use of u for v (canuas, siluer, etc.) or v for u (Vpon) is not retained.
[2] *Op. cit.*, II, xii, 77-8.

Of the many debts that later poetry owes to Spenser none has been more productive than the nine-line stanza he invented for *The Faerie Queene* and used throughout its immense length. Next to the sonnet and blank verse, the Spenserian stanza was to become for generations the most important of English verse forms, and a further medium of intoxication for the Romantic poets. Its rhyme-scheme (*ababbcbcc*) has a unifying effect, but the stroke of instinctive genius was in the lengthening of the final line from ten syllables to twelve. (In the technical language of prosody, the Spenserian stanza consists of eight iambic pentameter lines followed by an alexandrine.) It was a wonderfully happy invention, so ideally suited to the greater part of *The Faerie Queene* that any other verse form for the poem is unimaginable. But since the stanza has an inherent beauty of structure, its use appears incongruous when Spenser's stomach was turned with disgust, as in the Errour passages of Book I:

> Therewith she spewd out of her filthy maw
> A floud of poyson horrible and blacke,
> Full of great lumpes of flesh and gobbets raw,
> Which stuncke so vilely, that it forst him slacke
> His grasping hold. . . .

Spenser set out with the intention that *The Faerie Queene* should be 'disposed into twelve bookes, fashioning XII Morall vertues'. He began it in London in 1579, the year before he went to Ireland, where he continued it at intervals during the following twenty years of his life, but completed little more than half of the undertaking. Books I–III were published in London in 1590, Books IV–VI in 1596. Book VII was uncompleted at his death, and the remaining five books unwritten. The work was dedicated 'To the most high, mightie and magnificent Empresse renowned for pietie, vertue, and all gracious government Elizabeth by the Grace of God Queene of England France and Ireland and of Virginia, Defendour of the Faith, etc.'. In a letter written to Sir Walter Ralegh on 23 January 1589 and appended to *The Faerie Queene*, Spenser (who was an industrious explainer of his own works) expounds his intention in writing this 'continued Allegory or darke conceit', saying that 'The generall end . . . of all the booke is to fashion a gentleman or noble person in vertuous and gentle discipline'. He chose the history of Arthur as a framework and wrote of himself as in method a follower of Homer, Virgil, Ariosto, and Tasso. Ariosto's Italian romantic epic, *Orlando Furioso,* published in complete form in 1532, greatly impressed the men of the Renaissance and by command of Elizabeth Sir John Harrington made an English version, published in 1591. Tasso's *Jerusalem Delivered (Gerusalemme Liberata)* was issued in its final shape in 1593 (first unauthorized version 1576) and first translated into English by R. Carey in 1594. But whatever *The Faerie Queene* owes to the ancient and modern poets named, its main purpose was to portray 'the twelve private morall vertues, as Aristotle hath devised'. Aristotle was Spenser's chief mentor. Ambitious though the initial scheme was, and imposing though the completed portion is, Spenser told Ralegh that if the projected twelve books were 'well accepted' he might 'be perhaps encoraged' to frame a second work to show the 'politicke vertues' in the person of Arthur after he became king, as in the first he essayed to show the private virtues associated with Prince Arthur. As his letter to Ralegh shows, the Arthurian material is extended by Spenser's further purpose of representing the Faery Queene (seen by Arthur in a dream or vision) as 'glory in my generall intention, but in my particular I conceive [her as] the most excellent and glorious person of our soveraine the Queene [i.e. Elizabeth], and her kingdome in Faery land. And yet in some places els, I doe otherwise shadow her. For considering she beareth two persons, the one of a most royall Queene or Empresse, the other of a most vertuous and beautifull Lady, this latter part in some places I doe expresse in Belphœbe, fashioning her name according to your owne excellent conceipt of Cynthia (Phœbe and Cynthia being both names of Diana.) . . .' The letter to Ralegh also summarizes the large part of the story that transpired in Spenser's imagination before he set pen to paper far on in the narrative, with the Red Cross Knight representing Holiness (identified with the Church of England) riding on his 'great adventure . . . That greatest Gloriana to him gave', accompanied by the 'lovely Ladie' Una (true religion) on her snow-white ass to combat with Errour (as a monster, half serpent, half woman), the evil magician Archimago (representing Hypocrisy and the Pope), and Duessa (Falsehood and the Roman Church in Book I, Mary Queen of Scots in Book V).

After the private virtue of Holiness has been celebrated in this first book in the character of the Red Cross Knight, Book II brings in Sir Guyon to stand for Temperance, Book III Brito-mart and Belphœbe for Chastity, Book IV Cambel and Tria-

Februarie.

Ægloga Secunda.

The Shepheardes Calender

mond for Friendship, Book V Sir Artegall for Justice, Book VI Sir Calidore for Courtesy; while Book VII of which only a fragment exists (Cantos vi and vii and two stanzas of Canto viii) was to show Constancy opposing Mutability.

That last fragment of *The Faerie Queene* includes in stanzas 28–43 of Canto vii a procession of the four seasons followed by the twelve months. Spenser had previously gone the round of the year at greater length in *The Shepheardes Calender* 'conteyning twelve Æglogues proportionable to the twelve monethes' and prefaced with an epistle to Gabriel Harvey and a statement of 'the generall argument of the whole booke'. The twelve ec-logues are written in varying metres and in subject they range from genuine pastoral to moral allegory. January is devoted to the shepherd boy Colin Clout's complaint of his unrequited love for Rosalind, and this poem is considered to have an autobiographical background, though the Rosalind has not been identified with certainty. The *February* eclogue 'is rather moral and generall, than bent to any secrete or particular purpose' and contains one of Spenser's notable pieces, the tale of the old oak tree and the young boastful brier who complains to the husbandman that the oak hides the sun and does damage with his swaying branches; but when the tree is cut down the briar is left unprotected. When winter comes

> The blustring Boreas did encroche
> And beate upon the solitarie Brere:
>
> . . . . .
>
> The byting frost nipt his stalke dead,
> And watrie wette weighed downe his head,
> And heaped snowe burdned him so sore,
> That nowe upright he can stand no more:
> And being downe, is trodde in the durt
> Of cattell, and brouzed, and sorely hurt.
> Such was thend of this Ambitious brere,
> For scorning Eld . . .

April begins with a shepherds' dialogue, again concerned with the heartless Rosalind, and proceeds with a poem to 'fayre Eliza, Queene of shepheardes all'. *May* has a Protestant versus Catholic theme; Rosalind comes up again in *June*; *July* is concerned with good shepherds and proud and ambitious pastors; *August* sets forth 'a delectable controversie, made in imitation of that in Theocritus'; *September* is mainly a discourse on 'the loose living of Popish prelates'; *October* complains against the contempt in which poetry is held; *November* laments the death of Dido, whose real identity is unrevealed, though the gloss to the poem declares she is not the Rosalind to whom the *December* poem is a farewell complaint:

> My boughes with bloosmes that crowned were at firste,
> And promised of timely fruite such store,
> Are left both bare and barrein now at erst
> The flattring fruite is fallen to grownd before,
>   And rotted, ere they were halfe mellow ripe:
>   My harvest wast, my hope away dyd wipe.

> The fragrant flowres, that in my garden grewe,
> Bene withered, as they had bene gathered long.
> Theyr rootes bene dryed up for lacke of dewe,
> Yet dewed with teares they han be ever among.
> Ah who has wrought my *Rosalind* this spight
> To spil the flowres, that should her girlond dight?

Appended to each of the twelve poems in *The Shepheardes
Calender* is a gloss attributed to E. K. (perhaps Spenser's Cambridge friend Edward Kirke)[1] who either acted as editor of the
poem or served as a mask for Spenser himself. The gloss contains, besides definitions of Spenser's archaic words, much miscellaneous lore, often set down with sly humour: e.g. of a phrase
in the October eclogue—'He [the poet] seemeth here to be
ravished with a Poetical furie. For (if one rightly mark) the
numbers rise so ful, and the verse groweth so big, that he
seemeth he hath forgot the meanenesse of shepheards state and
stile.' Also in these glossarial notes are numerous references to
Chaucer. Explaining the feigned name Tityrus in *February*: 'I
suppose he meane Chaucer, whose prayse for pleasaunt tales
cannot dye, so long as the memorie of hys name shal live, and
the name of Poetrie shal endure'. It is hard to believe that
Spenser did not collaborate with E. K., even if the glosses are
not wholly his own.

Besides *Mother Hubberds Tale*, to which reference has been
made above, Spenser's other principal works were *Colin Clouts
Come Home Againe*, an after-product of his first return to London.
It describes, allegorically, Ralegh's visit to him in Ireland,
refers to the Queen, and satirizes the abuses of life at Court:

> For sooth to say, it is no sort of life,
> For shepheard fit to lead in that same place,
> Where each one seeks with malice and with strife,
> To thrust downe other into foul disgrace,
> Himselfe to raise. . . .

Astrophel is an elegy upon the death of Sir Philip Sidney, and
Amoretti a sequence of love sonnets possibly written to Elizabeth
Boyle before their marriage, though they may be of earlier date.

---

[1] A writer in *Notes and Queries*, 2 Aug. 1952, argues persuasively that
'E. K.' is a mystification covering the identity of Spenser's schoolmaster,
Richard Mulcaster.

They were published in 1595 in the same volume as his marriage song, *Epithalamion*, while in the next year *Prothalamion* was issued 'in honour of the double mariage of the two Honorable and vertuous Ladies, the Ladie Elizabeth and the Ladie Katherine Somerset', daughters of the Earl of Worcester. The memorable feature of *Prothalamion* is the refrain 'Sweet Themmes runne softly, till I end my Song', but *Epithalamion* is pure poetry from first to last and has its own lovely but more subtle refrain, used with slight variations of phrasing. There is little reason for selecting one stanza before any other, but this which follows is as excellently Elizabethan as it is Spenserian:

> Tell me ye merchants daughters did ye see
> So fayre a creature in your towne before,
> So sweet, so lovely, and so mild as she,
> Adornd with beautyes grace and vertues store,
> Her goodly eyes lyke Saphyres shining bright,
> Her forehead yvory white,
> Her cheekes lyke apples which the sun hath rudded,
> Her lips lyke cherryes charming men to byte,
> Her breast like to a bowle of cream uncrudded,
> Her paps lyke lyllies budded,
> Her snowie necke lyke to a marble towre,
> And all her body like a pallace fayre,
> Ascending uppe with many a stately stayre,
> To honors seat and chastities sweet bowre.
> Why stand ye still ye virgins in amaze,
> Upon her so to gaze,
> Whiles ye forget your former lay to sing,
> To which the woods did answer and your eccho ring.

Later Poetry

Among the more commonplace clichés of criticism used against lesser contemporary poets at the middle of the twentieth century is the complaint that they speak with a uniform voice and are indistinguishable from each other. This is not the singular reproach it is often assumed to be, for in other periods marked by a large output of verse the voices of minor writers also tended to share a common tone. This was so in the Elizabethan age, but the sameness is less remarked, partly because we are accustomed to a romantical kindly view of most things Elizabethan without too precise an examination of their quality, and partly also because the Elizabethan voice was more tuneful than the twentieth-century voice: much singing of larks pleases more than much cawing of rooks.

No useful purpose could be served here by more than passing comment on a few of the lesser poets who swarmed in the second half of the sixteenth century: e.g. Anthony Munday, Thomas Watson, William Warner, Robert Southwell, Henry Constable, Barnabe Barnes, Richard Barnfield, leaving out of account until the next chapters those (such as Dekker, Greene, Lodge, Lyly, Nashe, and Peele) whose verse was secondary to their prose writings and plays. This list is very far from exhaustive, but no important difference of character would be detectable in the lesser Elizabethan poetry if a score or so of other writers were added. It is significant that so much Elizabethan poetry remains anonymous—melodious, charming, and in every way attractive, but with no marked individuality such as might point to the authors' identity.

This factor of similarity was largely dictated by submission to the pastoral convention. The pervasion of pastoral poetry in sixteenth-century England was among the specifically Renaissance characteristics which derived from the interest in the literature of antiquity—mainly, in this connection, the *Idylls* of Theocritus (third century B.C.) but distilled through Italian channels and, later, Spanish also. The pastoral theme pervaded the Elizabethan novels and some plays also: for example, *Arcadia* by Sir Philip Sidney and *Rosalynde* by Thomas Lodge, *As You Like It* and the country scenes in *The Winter's Tale*, as well as in numerous masques by Ben Jonson and others. The essence of pure pastoral as it appears in lyric poetry is in the delicious artificiality and dainty make-believe of fancy-dress shepherds and shepherdesses toying and languishing in the eternal summer of a Dresden porcelain never-never land. One of the last and most pleasing of the Elizabethan anthologies, *England's Helicon*[1] (1600), is almost wholly pastoral and shows that many minute variations could be played upon the single small-scale theme without moving out of its narrowly restricted conventions. These Phyllises and Coridons, Astrophels and Daphnises, Damons and Amaryllises, inhabit a world no bigger than a

---

[1] Reissued in The Muses' Library and edited by Hugh Macdonald (Routledge, London, 1949).

40. St. George and the Dragon from Spenser's *The Faerie Queene*

Oh that my wayes were directed
to keepe thy ſtatutes. Ps: 119. 5.

W. Simpſon Sculp:

TO the worthie Ladie the L: E: W

T H E feircest natures; wheeme in youthfull prime,
  Nor counſel good, nor reaſons rule, could tame,
Are by their owne experience, and in time;
To order brought, and * taught themſelues to frame,
  To honeſt courſes, and to loath the waies;
  So well they liked, in their youthfull daies.

Why then diſpaire yee Madame, of your ſonne,
  Whoſe wit, as in the ſappe, doth but abound:
* Theſe braunches prun'd, that over rancklie runne,
  You'le find in time, the bodie inward found:
  When Dullard ſprightes, like fenny flagges belowe,
  Or fruitles beene, or rot while they do grow.

Eximit ipſa dies omnes de corpore mendas,
Quodſ fuit vitium, deſinit eſſe, morus.

* Ingenia noſtra vt nobiles et generoſi equi, mre-lius facili freno reguntur. Seneca de clementia.

* Vellem in adoleſcente quod amputem. Cicero 1 de oratore.

Ovid. 2. de arte amandi.

Labor

43. Queen Elizabeth confounding Juno, Minerva, and Venus, by Hans Eworth

44. Sir Philip Sidney, attributed to Federigo Zucchero

45. Scene from Sidney's *Arcadia* at Wilton by Emanuel de Critz

46. Title-page of *Poly-Olbion* by Michael Drayton

47. Sir Walter Ralegh, after Marc Gheeraedts

48. Title-page of Ralegh's *The History of the World*

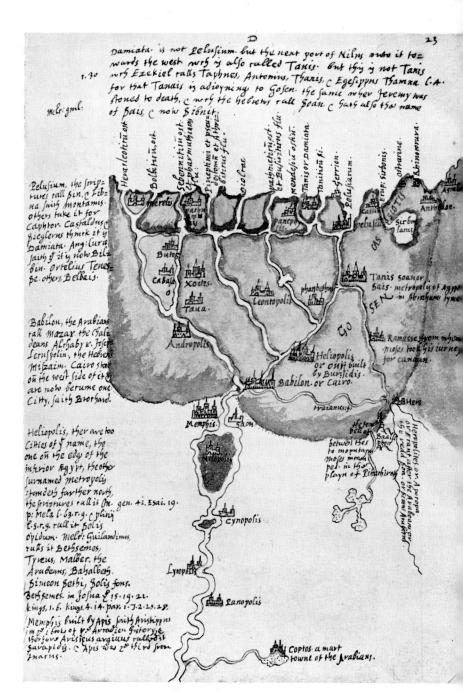

49. Map of the Nile Delta, by Sir Walter Ralegh

pocket handkerchief, while their pleadings and refusings, their sighs and tears, are on a correspondingly miniature scale. Nicholas Breton (*c.* 1545–1626), whose works include *The Passionate Shepheard* and *A Mad World my Masters*, contributed several pieces to *England's Helicon*, and these lines from 'Corridons *supplication to* Phillis' are a fair sample of English pastoral verse:

> Sweete *Phillis*, if a silly Swaine,
>> may sue to thee for grace:
> See not thy loving Sheephearde slaine,
>> with looking on thy face.
> But thinke what power thou hast got,
>> upon my Flock and mee:
> Thou seest they now regard me not,
>> but all do follow thee.
> And if I have so farre presum'd,
>> with prying in thine eyes:
> Yet let not comfort be consum'd,
>> that in thy pitty lyes.
> But as thou art that *Phillis* faire,
>> that Fortune favour gives:
> So let not Love dye in despaire,
>> that in thy favour lives. . . .

This same anthology also includes poems by three of the writers named above: Munday, Watson, and Barnfield, as well as Michael Drayton, Sir Walter Ralegh, and Sir Philip Sidney.

Anthony Munday (1553–1633) was a jack of all trades— ballad-monger, hack playwright, actor, anti-Catholic propagandist, translator, and for many years the pageant master of the annual Lord Mayor's Show in London. He was a butt for satirists, among them Ben Jonson, who put Munday into *The Case is Altered* as Antonio Balladino. If it could be indisputably established that the poems signed Sheepheard Tonie in *England's Helicon* are Munday's, as many believe them to be, his reputation would be higher, if only for one poem—'Beautie sate bathing by a Spring' (included in many anthologies)—than for the whole of the miscellaneous and mostly indifferent longer writings known to be his. That some of his contemporaries thought well of him is evident from the reference in William

Webbe's *Discourse of English Poetrie* to Munday's '*sweete sobs of Sheepheardes and Nymphes*' as 'very rare Poetrie'.[1]

Since he was hailed in his lifetime as the equal of Theocritus, Virgil, Petrarch, and Ronsard, it is disappointing to find little more than a few moderately good lyrics among the works of Thomas Watson (*c.* 1557–92), which include *The Hekatompathia, or Passionate Centurie of Love* (1582) and *The Teares of Fancie, or Love Disdained* (1593). The contents of both volumes were called sonnets, though the first was chiefly made up of 18-line poems having three stanzas of six lines each. The other book consists of sonnets in the typical Elizabethan form, which Watson did as much as anyone to establish, and in that limited respect Shakespeare's sonnets may owe something to his.

The ambitions of authors and the praises of contemporary critics are often remarkably unimpressive to posterity, and no one could now recover the enthusiasm with which *Albion's England* by William Warner (*c.* 1558–1609) was received during two decades or more after the first part came out in 1586. This immensely long narrative poem is a rhyming chronicle of history and legend from the Flood onward to Warner's own time. Greek myths are taken in, no less than such current events as the execution of Mary Queen of Scots and the defeat of the Spanish Armada, but the interest of *Albion's England* in retrospect is chiefly that belonging to a once-popular type of chronicle literature which, in differing forms in prose and verse by several writers, stirred the national imagination and not seldom suggested themes to contemporary playwrights. In its own kind Warner's poem was surpassed by those of Samuel Daniel and Michael Drayton (*see below*, p. 137).

From these writers it is invigorating to turn again to a true poet, Robert Southwell (*c.* 1561–95), who belonged to one of the Old Catholic families. His birthplace was probably near Norwich, and while still young he went to the Jesuit College at Douay, where he conceived a passionate desire to become himself a Jesuit. He was admitted as a novice in Rome about 1578, and later served as prefect of studies in the English College there. In 1586 he was sent back to England as a member of the

---

[1] See *Elizabethan Critical Essays*, edited by G. Gregory Smith, vol. I, pp. 244-5 (2 vols. Oxford University Press, London, 1904).

English Mission whose function it was to serve as the spearhead of the surreptitious crusade to recover England for the Catholic faith. The Mission was a glorious undertaking to those engaged in it, but an infamous conspiracy in the eyes of the Protestants, who adopted every possible means to hunt down and punish as spies and traitors the members of the Mission and those who sheltered or aided them. Since imprisonment, torture, and death were the rewards to be looked for if they were captured, men with a fanatical longing for martyrdom sought eagerly to join the English Mission. Southwell was inspired by that longing, though he succeeded in avoiding arrest for six years, and became domestic chaplain to the Countess of Arundel, before he was betrayed in 1592. He was repeatedly tortured in prison, where he remained until his execution in 1595. Most of his poems were written in prison and his purpose in them was to combat what he considered to be the godless sensuality of most of the poetry then being produced. He was a religious poet, a didactic poet; but he was also a poet without qualification, and it is upon the poetic quality of his writings that his reputation rests, and more upon the lyrics than upon *Saint Peters Complaint*, his longest work. The fact that this poem is written in the same metre as *Venus and Adonis* has led to the theory [1] that Southwell intended it in some measure as a spiritual antidote to Shakespeare's poem. *Saint Peters Complaint* (1595) is concerned with Peter's self-condemnatory communings after the betrayal and with events in the closing phase of Christ's life. It struck some of Southwell's contemporaries that his poetry was excessively poetical for its sacred and solemn theme, and so in truth it is:

> O bird, the just rebuker of my crime,
>   The faithful waker of my sleeping fears,
> Be now the daily clock to strike the time,
>   When stinted eyes shall pay their task of tears;
> Upbraid my ears with thine accusing crow,
> To make me rue that first it made me know.

The movement and the music overweigh the spirit and at times the poem becomes almost voluptuous in its verbal languor.

---

[1] See *Cambridge History of English Literature*, vol. IV, ch. vii (Cambridge University Press, 1909), where it is also indicated that Shakespeare was familiar with Southwell's poems.

Furthermore, it is loaded with ingenuities of imagery and with those artifices of wit and intellectual contrivance which are the very stuff of Elizabethan secular poetry and the substance of its conceits. Southwell, however, by employing these devices in religious poetry became a precursor of the seventeenth-century metaphysical poets. It is in this aspect that he appears in the finest of his lyrics 'The Burning Babe':

> '. . . My faultless breast the furnace is, the fuel wounding thorns;
> Love is the fire, and sighs the smoke, the ashes shame and scorns;
> The fuel justice layeth on, and mercy blows the coals; . . .'

while in 'New Prince, New Pomp' he remains an Elizabethan lyrist:

> Behold, a silly tender Babe
> In freezing winter night
> In homely manger trembling lies,
> Alas, a piteous sight! . . .

Henry Constable (1562–1613), educated at Cambridge, became a Roman Catholic, settled in Paris, and in 1599 was appointed papal envoy in Edinburgh. He moved to London in 1603, in the next year was imprisoned but soon released, and died at Liége. He was a sonneteer of some merit, though of little originality, his chief work, *Diana, The praises of his Mistress, In certaine sweete Sonnets* (1592; enlarged 1594 with poems by others), following closely his Italian and French sources. Barnabe Barnes (*c.* 1569–1609), who wrote against the papacy in his tragedy *The Divils Charter*, taking Alexander VI for villain, is better known for his sonnets and lyrics published in *Parthenophil and Parthenophe* (1593) and *A Divine Centurie of Spirituall Sonnets* (1595). But he composed no such memorable pieces as Richard Barnfield's 'A Shepheards Complaint' ('My flocks feed not, My ewes breed not, My rams speed not, All is amiss . . .') and the *Ode*

> As it fell upon a day
> In the merry month of May,
> Sitting in a pleasant shade
> Which a grove of myrtles made,
> Beasts did leap and birds did sing,
> Trees did grow and plants did spring; . . .

Barnfield (1574–1627) is, indeed, distinguished by having these poems attributed to Shakespeare, in some editions of whose works they continue to appear as part of the group of lyrics called *The Passionate Pilgrim*. Included with them is the sonnet 'If music and sweet poetry agree', also by Barnfield.

Ralegh and Sidney

From among those who, by the highest standards of Elizabethan achievement, have to be ranked as lesser poets, four stand apart from the rest: Ralegh and Sidney for the intrinsic quality of their writings hardly less than for that magic of personality which is still undimmed after nearly four centuries; Daniel and Drayton for their industrious, wide-ranging literary diligence and contemporary reputation.

Walter Ralegh (*c.* 1552–1618) has come repeatedly under the investigating light of historical and biographical research and speculation, but he remains baffling and contradictory. The son of one who is usually described vaguely as 'a Devonshire gentleman', he was born in the southern part of that county, at Hayes Barton, and went as a youth to Oriel College, Oxford. He appears to have had little money and he may not have taken a degree. Like many other young men of the time, he fought in France and Ireland, achieving nothing more imposing than a captaincy. Then, to all appearances suddenly, he became a great figure in Elizabeth's close circle at Court in 1582, and as suddenly, ten years later, fell into disgrace. Though during that decade he experienced the mutability of royal favour, his position as a friend and personal counsellor of the Queen was never seriously shaken until he was arrested and sent to the Tower of London in 1582. The only reason that has been suggested for his downfall is that he seduced one of the Queen's maids of honour, Elizabeth Throckmorton, and was commanded to marry her. Unless it can be supposed that the Queen's anger was due to jealousy, Ralegh's irregularity hardly accounts for the severity of his punishment; and the genuine affection and devotion known to have existed between himself and his wife until his death does not suggest the bondage of an enforced marriage. He was abroad commanding an expedition to Panama when he was recalled and imprisoned. He remained in the Tower only a few months, buying himself out—but not back into the Queen's good books—at the end of 1592. There-after he sought relief from disgrace in his several overseas adventures—to Guiana, Cadiz, and the Azores—colonizing, as well as harassing the Spaniards. Receiving him back into favour again, Elizabeth made him Governor of Jersey in 1601, but her death two years later was fatal to Ralegh, though he survived for another fifteen years. He was charged in November 1603 with joining a Spanish plot to overthrow James I and restore Catholic rule. The accusation was a barefaced invention and totally false; nevertheless he was condemned to death, but respited a day or two before the date fixed for his execution. He was kept in the Tower for nearly thirteen years, during which he began his *History of the World*, never carried beyond the first volume. Ralegh was released in 1616 in order to lead a gold-mining expedition to Orinoco which set out in the next year but failed. On returning to England in 1618 Ralegh (who, against James's orders, had fought the Spaniards in America) was rearrested—ostensibly on the old charge of plotting with Spain but, in cold fact, to placate the Spaniards—and be-headed on 29 October 1618, being buried in St. Margaret's, Westminster.

Not only is there much that is unexplained in Ralegh's life-story, but his poems also are puzzling in more ways than one. In the first place, only a few fragments have survived directly: it is reasonably certain that, apart from those fragments, all the manuscripts were destroyed before his death. He published no poems in books of his own, though in this he was only con-forming with Elizabethan custom, which did not favour print for the poems of gentlemen; those of Ralegh's that have come down to us are gathered from anthologies and other indirect sources. Secondly, Ralegh's verse is puzzling because its mood and temper are out of harmony with the common mood and temper of the age. It was a buoyant and expansive age, ebullient and extroverted, and in general its poetry reflects those charac-teristics. Ralegh's poetry, however, is in a sustained minor key, reflective and introspective; even his love poems have a remote air, tinged with melancholy, quite unlike anything found e.g. in the pretty despairs of pastoral verse. Among the poems attri-buted pseudonymously to Ralegh in *England's Helicon* only one is probably his—the famous rejoinder to Marlowe's 'The passionate Sheepheard to his love'—and that one, 'The Nimphs reply to the Sheepheard', is emphatically anti-pastoral in its outlook. It answers the invitation

> Come live with mee, and be my love,
> And we will all the pleasures prove, . . .

with:

> If all the world and love were young,
> And truth in every Sheepheards tongue,
> These pretty pleasures might me move,
> To live with thee, and be thy love.
>
> . . . . .
>
> But could youth last, and love still breede,
> Had joyes no date, nor age no neede,
> Then these delights my minde might move,
> To live with thee, and be thy love.[1]

While it is obvious that Ralegh had much occasion for melancholy, scepticism, and despair, all of which we should expect to find mirrored in his poems, it is not less obvious that during the years of his triumphs at Court—when he was all men's envy and the observed of all observers—he had reason to be sanguine, confident, and well content. No extant poem by him registers such an outlook, and it would be fantastic to suppose that Ralegh wrote such poems but that they have all perished while those that have survived happen to show only the darker side. It is safe to assume then, that although Ralegh was the friend of Spenser (with whom he spent some time in Ireland and elsewhere), Sidney, and other poets, he preserved an innate peculiarity of disposition fairly represented by the small body of about fifty poems and fragments which have been preserved. The longest is the curiously titled 'The 11th: and last booke of the Ocean to Scinthia', containing 522 lines in the metre of Spenser's *Colin Clouts Come Home Again*. The MS. of this at Hatfield House is accompanied by a fragment (it breaks off in the middle of the twenty-second line), called 'The end of the bookes, of the Oceans love to Scinthia, and the beginninge of the 12 Boock, entreatinge of Sorrow'. It is known that while Ralegh was in Ireland in 1589 he read to Spenser a poem (or

[1] *The Poems of Sir Walter Ralegh*, edited with an Introduction by Agnes M. C. Latham (The Muses Library, Routledge, London, 1951). I have not retained u for v, nor i for j in the quotations.

part of a poem) named *Cynthia* (i.e. Scinthia). Whether any part of *Cynthia* before Book XI was written is unknown, though it has been conjectured that Ralegh began at that point and did not proceed with this plan for a poem in twelve Books in honour of Queen Elizabeth. If Book XI was written by 1589 it is difficult to account for its references to the Queen as though she were dead. There can be little doubt, however, that it is autobiographical, a lament relating to the poet's loss of the Queen's affection and ending on a note of resignation:

> To God I leve it, who first gave it me,
> And her I gave, and she returnd agayne,
> As it was herrs. So lett his mercies bee,
> Of my last cumforts, the essentiall meane.
> But be it so, or not, th'effects, ar past.
> Her love hath end; my woe must ever last.

Amid his worst trials, Ralegh never lacked physical or spiritual fortitude. The letter written to his wife at the time he was first on the eve of execution is a dignified and touching document, while the verses made 'the night before he dyed and left at the Gate howse' are a perfect epitaph:

> Even such is tyme which takes in trust
> Our yowth, our joyes, and all we have,
> And payes us butt with age and dust:
> Who in the darke and silent grave
> When we have wandered all our wayes
> Shutts up the storye of our dayes.
> And from which earth and grave and dust
> The Lord shall rayse me up I trust.

There is less to say about Philip Sidney (1554–86), inasmuch as he was built more nearly to the Elizabethan pattern than was Ralegh. He had the fullest advantages of high birth as the son of Sir Henry Sidney (Lord Deputy of Ireland) and Lady Sidney, sister to the Earl of Leicester; he was educated at Shrewsbury and Oxford; his friends were among the greatest in the land; and on the Grand Tour through France, Austria, and Italy he met in Venice the great painters Tintoretto and Veronese. Before he was twenty he married the daughter of Sir Francis Walsingham, and in 1584 was made Governor of Flushing. His immortality arises from the story of his forgoing for the benefit of a wounded soldier a cup of water offered to him while he himself lay dying of a wound received in the battle of Zutphen.

His sonnet sequence *Astrophel and Stella* was written for, though probably not *to*, Lady Penelope Rich, the married daughter of the first Earl of Essex. These sonnets are graceful, accomplished, and pleasing, but more praiseworthy as a finished technical and complimentary exercise than for any implicit depth of feeling or compulsive poetic energy. There is no external means of knowing whether Sidney loved Penelope Rich (that she was not more than conventionally enamoured of him appears from her marrying an earlier lover, the Earl of Devonshire, after she was divorced from Lord Rich), nor is there any convincing internal evidence. *Astrophel and Stella* is perhaps the best of all examples of a cultured Elizabethan *gentleman's* poetry, written by one who had mastered all the rules; but by contrast it emphasizes that the true Elizabethan *poets'* poetry has some driving force which is missing from Sidney's. (For his prose, *see below*, p. 158.)

Daniel and Drayton

In *Colin Clouts Come Home Again* Spenser alludes to Samuel Daniel (1562–1619) as a 'new shepherd late up sprong', and he is always treated with respect both in histories of literature and in anthologies. Almost the only one of his pieces that has taken firm root, however, is the delightful lyric beginning:

> Love is a sickness full of woes,
>   All remedies refusing;
> A plant that with most cutting grows,
>   Most barren with best using.
>   Why so?
>
> More we enjoy it, more it dies;
> If not enjoyed, it sighing cries,
>   Hey ho.

His formal reputation is linked principally with the sonnet sequence *Delia* and with *The Civill Warres* (i.e. the Wars of the Roses), a poem in eight books, published in part in 1595 and complete in 1609. *Delia* leans heavily upon foreign sources, and only occasionally does such a line as 'Short is the glory of the blushing rose' appear felicitously as a natural touch amid the smooth conventionalities of 'sable hairs', 'sable night', 'sable clouds', 'care-charmer Sleep', 'Elysian ghosts', and similar verbal bric-à-brac. But it is all too easy to be contemptuous of Daniel if he is judged inappropriately from a twentieth-century angle. He counted for a great deal among contemporary men of intelligence and taste, even though he displeased Ben Jonson. He took poetry, as well as himself, seriously; hoped for at least a small immortality, but recognized that it was unlikely to be other than small. There is mental and even philosophical substance in his work, and if he went astray in thinking that epic poetry had a closer affinity with the English genius than time has proved, his own epic performance in the *Civill Warres* impressed his generation and deservedly, however little it may please us.

Michael Drayton (1563–1631), like Daniel, was a devoted lover of his country, and in *Poly-Olbion* (1613 and later) he conducts the reader over most of England in thousands of 12-syllable rhyming couplets. Daniel dealt in patriotic history, Drayton in patriotic geography:

> Of Albion's glorious isle the wonders whilst I write,
> The sundry varying soils, the pleasures infinite, . . .
> Direct my course so right, as with thy [1] hand to show
> Which way thy forests range, which way thy rivers flow;
> Wise genius, by thy help that so I may descry
> How thy fair mountains stand, and how thy valleys lie.

Drayton's verse output was enormous and of extraordinary variety: religious and secular, historical and satirical, solemn and playful, critical and autobiographical, lyrical and pastoral. He handled all with skill and most with attraction, and could use even doggerel verse with charm, as in 'Cassamen and Dowsabell' (from *The Shepheards Garland*, 1593), where Dowsabell is described at length in such lines as these:

> Her features all as fresh above,
> As is the grass that grows by Dove,
>   And lithe as lass of Kent:
> Her skin is soft as Lemster wool,
> As white as snow on Peakish hull,
>   Or swan that swims in Trent.

[1] He is here addressing The Genius of England.

His sonnet sequence, *Idea* (1593, with later additions), contains
some of the best Elizabethan sonnets below the very first rank.
In one of them Drayton rises to the level of the greatest, technically and emotionally:

> Since there's no help, come let us kiss and part.
>   Nay, I have done; you get no more of me,
>   And I am glad, yea, glad with all my heart,
>   That thus so cleanly I myself can free;
> Shake hands for ever, cancel all our vows,
>   And when we meet at any time again,
> Be it not seen in either of our brows
>   That we one jot of former love retain.
> Now at the last gasp of Love's latest breath,
>   When, his pulse failing, Passion speechless lies,
> When Faith is kneeling by his bed of death,
>   And Innocence is closing up his eyes,
>   Now if thou wouldst, when all have given him over,
>   From death to life thou mightst him yet recover.

Song Books and Emblem Books

If one were compelled to select from the unparalleled riches of
the Elizabethan-Jacobean period a body of literary work more
precious to the English than any other, apart from Shakespeare
and the translated Bible, the choice could hardly fall upon anything finer than the Song Books. Not only did English poetry
touch the highest level at that time, but English music, both
secular music and church music, was in standard and variety
the most remarkable England has produced. For a generation
or so the English composers were second to none, and William
Byrd and Henry Purcell, at least, are among the world's masters
of music.

Samuel Johnson's phrase, 'Sir, we are a nest of singing birds',
is often borrowed to describe Elizabethan England, and even if
in that connection it long since became a cliché it nevertheless
still conveys a truth. Never before or since was part-singing for
small family groups so much practised; never before or since
was so much good poetry married so suitably to music. The
marriage was a love match, moreover, in which it was often
impossible to say from which side the first advances came.
There is no feeling that the composers were using poems as

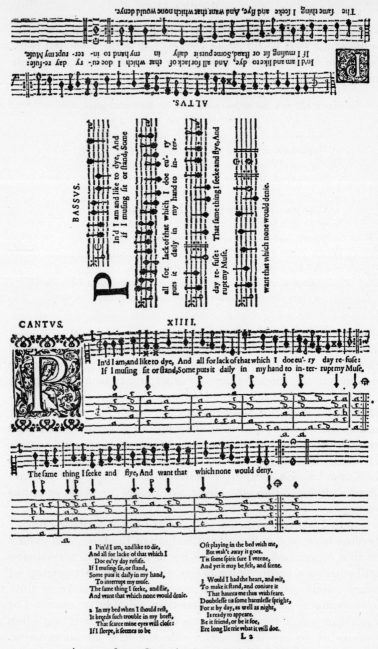

A page from Campion's second *Book of Ayres*

mere words, artificially and forcibly 'set to music' and suffering distortion in the process, as often appears in nineteenth- and twentieth-century settings. It is true that, in the sixteenth-seventeenth century, song-book composers frequently made verbal changes to fit their music; but the finished product almost invariably appears a perfect match, ideal and inevitable.

Several hundreds of poems—by some fifty named poets, besides many unidentified—are represented in Canon Fellowes's[1] garnering from song books of the years 1588–1632. A small proportion of the poems are repeated, when they were used by more than one composer, occasionally with small textual differences. Most of the poets already referred to in the present chapter appear in the song books, together with a small number who will be mentioned later (Donne, Ben Jonson, George Wither, Thomas Carew, in particular). Of them all, the poet most intimately associated with the song books is Thomas Campion (1567–1619), himself also the composer of four *Bookes of Ayres* (1610–17). In addition to the scores of poems set to music by himself, several other composers used his verses, including his best-known piece, 'There is a garden in her face' (or 'Cherry ripe') set by Robert Jones and again by Richard Alison. Campion was a prolific writer of lyrics, his standard of poetic skill and grace was high, and his range of subjects and moods wide—from, e.g., 'Most sweet and pleasing are thy ways, O God' and other hymns, to the homely 'Jack and Joan they think no ill'; from songs of mourning to marriage songs; from moral gravity to amorous delight. He wrote a large number of the most pleasing rhymed poems that we have, yet his *Observations in the Art of English Poesie* (1602) is specifically an attack on 'the vulgar and unartificial custom of riming'. Campion, a doctor of medicine by profession, also wrote Court masques, and a treatise on music, *A New Way of Making Four Parts in Counterpoint* 'by a most familiar and infallible rule'. His lyrics are exceptionally rich in happy lines of which the final line of No. XIV in the first (1601) *Booke of Ayres* is among Campion's loveliest:

[1] *English Madrigal Verse 1588-1632*. Edited from the Original Song Books by E. H. Fellowes (2nd edn. Clarendon Press, 1929). Part I consists of poems set by the madrigalists, Part II those of the lutenists.

Blame not my cheeks, though pale with love they be;
The kindly heate unto my heart is flowne,
To cherish it that is dismaid by thee,
Who art so cruell and unsteadfast growne:
For nature, cald for by distressed harts,
Neglects and quite forsakes the outward partes.

But they whose cheekes with careles blood are stain'd,
Nurse not one sparke of love within their harts,
And when they woo, they speake with passion fain'd,
For their fat love lyes in their outward parts:
But in their brests, where love his court should hold,
Poore Cupid sits and blowes his nailes for cold.

While the song books contain much that equals the best in English lyrical verse, the Emblem Books are of no great poetic worth. They are literary and pictorial curiosities, yet also something more; for they helped, if only in a small way, to conduct the medieval allegorical impulse onward to the new metaphysical age in the seventeenth century. Allegories, emblems, and metaphysical poems all originate in man's reluctance to take the universe at sight value. He sees objects in the material world, but is not content with the object in itself; he is impelled to endow it with a subjective significance. It thus becomes emblematic. This symbolizing activity, tiresome to the materialist, is primitive, fundamental, and ineradicable. It begins in ancient ritual and art and culminates in Christianity (with the Cross as the sublime Emblem) and, on the intellectual and æsthetic plane, in *symbolisme*.

English emblem books began with *A Choice of Emblemes* by Geoffrey Whitney, published in 1586, continued in fashion until roughly the middle of the seventeenth century, and went almost completely out of fashion round about 1700. The best-known of the writers of emblematic verse are Henry Peacham (*Minerva Britanna*, 1612), Francis Quarles (*Emblemes*, 1635; *Hieroglyphikes of the Life of Man*, 1638), and George Wither (*A Collection of Emblemes*, 1635). In 1686 came Bunyan's *A Book for Boys and Girls; or Country Rhimes for Children*, which was not provided with pictures until 1724, by which time it had passed through several editions and changed its name, becoming *Divine Emblems; or Temporal Things Spiritualized*, with woodcuts.

Bunyan's volume was the only one of its kind especially for

children, and it was exceptional among the emblem books in having no illustrations in its early editions. Other authors were accustomed to writing verses which elucidated pictures. Peacham provided his own woodcuts, but it was common to use engravings by other hands, and sometimes foreign artists and publications were utilized. The essence of the matter is that 'emblem books are picture books made up of emblematic pictures and explanatory words. . . . The apologists of the emblem books, both the writers in their prefaces and the critics, write in one common critical formula . . . that poetry is a speaking picture and painting dumb poetry.'[1] To what extent emblem verses justified the claim that poetry is a speaking picture can be tested from Bunyan's book:

> What hast thou there, my Pretty Boy?
> Plumbs? How? Yes, Sir, a Paper full.
> I thought 'twas so, because with Joy
> Thou didst them out of thy Paper pull. . . .

COMPARISON

> This Boy an Emblem is of such
> Whose Lot in worldly things doth lie:
> Glory they in them ne'er so much,
> Their pleasant Springs will soon be dry,
>   Their Wealth, their Health, Honours and Life,
> Will quickly to a period come;
> If for these, is their only Strife,
> They soon will not be worth a Plumb.

When at length the naivety of the emblem books was swallowed up in the subtleties of metaphysical poetry, a relic or two survived, as in George Herbert's 'Wings', where the lines of verse are so devised that in print they take the shape of a pair of angel's wings; and similarly with his 'The Altar' (*see* Vol. II *of the present work*).

---

[1] *English Emblem Books*, by Rosemary Freeman (Chatto & Windus, London, 1948), pp. 9, 14.

CHAPTER VII

ELIZABETHAN PROSE

WHEREAS the greater part of Elizabethan verse belongs to the living heritage of English literature and is unlikely to be less cherished in the future than now, Elizabethan non-dramatic prose writings long ago ceased to be regarded as more than a closed chapter in literary history. While innumerable later writers have aimed to write poetry after the Elizabethan model, none but the perverse could wish to imitate the general run of Elizabethan prose. For students of literature and history the prose writings of the period are valuable and illuminating, but the interest is largely antiquarian and mainly confined to the curiosity aroused by any performance in a long discarded mode.

How far we may be justified in supposing that in the Elizabethan age poetry was closer than prose to current natural speech is a matter for speculation; yet in the light of the Elizabethans' widespread devotion to singing this is no fantastic supposition, for it has to be kept in mind that their songs were, so to say, fresh home-grown products. They did not, as modern vocalists and choirs do, put on their party frocks and dress-suits and sing 'standard works' (often from long ago and far away) in concert halls. They sang for the most part in their own and their neighbours' houses; they sang for pleasure and personal satisfaction, and not seldom for spiritual satisfaction. Much of their greatest music was liturgical, but this did not make it remote from common experience; the Church and its services had not then lost touch with the daily lives of the majority of English people.

Since the movement of musical sound was so familiar to Elizabethan ears, it is not surprising that their prose was too ready to conform to musical rhythms. This was a happy tendency in poetry, but for prose it was (at least to our drier minds) a misfortune. Our modern view of prose is strictly and perhaps too narrowly practical and utilitarian—or, using a favoured twentieth-century word, *functional*. Prose, we hold, has a job to do and should do it without fuss, nonsense, or æsthetic capers.

It should say what it has to say in the shortest and most time-saving manner, and there finish. That, at least, is what the manuals of instruction advise; and careful writers do in the main observe the advice, taking clarity and lucidity as the ideal. Before we turn to consider the character of Elizabethan prose, however, there are two points to acknowledge about ourselves. *First*, that our ideal is a self-conscious literary one, all too rarely followed outside the covers of books, and not invariably within them. *Second*, that while what has come to be known as Whitehall English (from its use in official documents and correspondence) has some superficial resemblance to Elizabethan prose in being indirect and convoluted, the motive in Whitehall English is the dread of personal responsibility for statements made, an enfeebling dread which fosters circumlocution and ambiguity. The governing factor is psychological, whereas in Elizabethan prose the governing factor was mainly æsthetic, though also partly physical.

The Elizabethan age was a 'young' age. It abounded with energy which made it thrustful and adventurous; its impulses were dominated by adolescent extravagance and impatience; its tastes were youthful and therefore often flamboyant and undisciplined—as can be seen in the dramatists' addiction to magnificos, murderers, and such monsters as Tamburlaine. The greatness of their poetry and the relative inferiority of their prose is no mystery; the qualities of each are interdependent and may be accounted for quite simply. The restrictive influence of verse-forms imposed the discipline required to bring their restlessness and flamboyance under control without quelling their natural energy. That so much poetry was written in strict stanzaic metres—the sonnet, the Spenserian stanza, etc.—in an age thus charactered, an age which might have been expected to shatter every formal mould, must be attributed to an instinctive and unconsciously felt need for a controlling instrument of expression. When the controlling instrument of verse was put temporarily aside, more than one accomplished poet showed himself to be a stumbling novice in dealing with prose rhythms. Prose is, in truth, far more difficult than verse, for the very reason that it has no written constitution beyond the grammatical rules, which have only an elementary bearing on good prose.

L

Yet the failures of Elizabethan prose-writers were due not so much to want of skill as to misconceived aims and methods. The musical underplay which was of such great service to poetry was otherwise a hindrance, since it forced upon prose a counterpointed, fugal style inimical to direct statement. If it were possible to separate sound from sense, much Elizabethan prose which irritates us would be found charming. But we cannot by any effort of goodwill read prose as a purely æsthetic exercise; it must mean, or signify, or suggest something directly to the mind; its primary purpose must be intellectual, not æsthetic. Elizabethan prose is, on the contrary, primarily æsthetic in intention, and it therefore gives precedence to sound over sense. For that reason the Elizabethans were excited by the elegances and artifices of style in John Lyly's *Euphues*, which represented the culmination of certain earlier English prose tendencies, however much it owed also to continental models.

Pamphleteers

Fickleness in love and constancy in hate are among the ruling characteristics of civilized man. That this should be so on the political plane is understandable enough, for politics is concerned with material possessions and the exercise of worldly power, but hatred as a lasting passion in Christian affairs is more baffling. In the sixteenth and seventeenth centuries England was more tormented by religious hatred than at any other time, and the controversial pamphlets of the period bear all too eloquent witness to the virulence of the passions aroused by theological differences and ecclesiastical greed and oppression.

Something has already been said above (pp. 63 ff.) of the sufferings of the Bible translators and others, including Tindale. It was one of Tindale's companions in exile who fired an early and weighty broadside in the pamphlet war [1] which raged for some two centuries from the Reformation period until the early years of the eighteenth century, when Defoe showed in *The Shortest Way with the Dissenters* (1702) the double-edged nature

---

[1] For some of the material in this section I have drawn on my *Miscellany of Tracts and Pamphlets XVI-XX Centuries*, edited with a Preface and Introductory Notes by A. C. Ward (World's Classics, Oxford University Press, 1927).

of irony. Before Simon Fish (? —— *c.* 1530) escaped to the
Continent to join Tindale he had been a gentleman of Gray's
Inn, and he offended by performing in a play which satirized
Cardinal Wolsey. While abroad, Fish wrote and had printed
a pamphlet called *A Supplicacyon for the Beggers* (*c.* 1529) which
was smuggled into England, where it circulated widely, even
being sold in the streets of London. Fish, championing the poor
of the realm, besought 'the King our Sovereign Lord' to rescue
his people from the exactions and lubricity of 'the ravening
wolves in sheep's clothing devouring the flocks'—the wolves
being catalogued as Bishops, Abbots, Priors, Deacons, Arch-
deacons, Suffragans, Priests, Monks, Canons, Friars, Pardoners,
and Summoners. He alleged that these had taken possession of
more than a third of the land in the kingdom, besides a tenth
of all the corn, pasture, grass, wool, colts, calves, lambs, pigs,
geese, chickens, milk, honey, wax, cheese, butter, eggs, and
servants' wages. He calculated that, in addition, the five orders
of begging friars drew fourpence each a year from every household, making £44,333 6s. 8d. sterling a year. Simon Fish was
nothing if not thoroughgoing and precise in his accusations,
concerning not only property and money, but also the debauchery of women and 'the felonies, rapes, murders, and
treasons committed by this sinfull generacion'. Fish's pamphlet
(which is among the important Reformation documents) is said
to have been brought to Henry VIII's notice by Anne Boleyn
and to have impressed him sufficiently to cause the author to
be recalled to England under a safe-conduct. (Fish died of
plague a few months later.) Sir Thomas More, reacting unfavourably, answered with another pamphlet, *The Supplication
of Souls.*

The fairness or otherwise of Fish's attack upon the Catholic
priesthood is of no present interest. It is his use of English prose
that concerns us here. Since he was not among the great masters
of invective—for he was deficient in irony—Fish was more adept
with a verbal axe than with a sword: for example, in a historical
aside referring to events in the reign of King John, he alludes
to the Pope as 'a cruel devilish bloodsupper drunken in the
blood of the saints and martyrs of Christ', bloodsupper being
his favourite term of abuse. *A Supplicacyon for the Beggers* was
written thirty years before the reign of Elizabeth began, and

its prose is consequently free from the calculated artifices of the later sixteenth-century writers, though already there are signs of that contrapuntal manner which was afterwards to become habitual. In the passage following (where his examples are not always tactfully chosen) Fish reflects upon how other states would have been handicapped if their revenues had been depleted as he alleged England's were by the bloodsuppers:

> The danes nether the saxons yn the time of the auncient Britons shulde neuer haue ben abill to haue brought theire armies from so farre hither ynto your lond to haue conquered it if they had had at that time suche a sort of idell glotons to finde at home. The nobill king Arthur had neuer ben abill to haue caried his armie to the fote of the mountaines to resist the coming downe of lucius the Emperoure if suche yerely exactions had ben taken of his people. The grekes had neuer ben abill to haue so long continued at the siege of Troie if they had had at home suche an idell sort of cormorauntes to finde. The auncient Romains had neuer ben abil to haue put all the hole worlde vnder theyre obeisaunce if theyre people had byn thus yerely oppressed. The Turke nowe yn youre tyme shulde neuer be abill to get so moche grounde of cristendome if he had yn his empire suche a sort of locustes to deuoure his substaunce.

In the year (1558) that Protestant Elizabeth succeeded her Catholic sister Mary, John Knox (1505–72) had printed at Geneva his famous tract *The First Blast of the Trumpet against the monstrous Regiment of Women*. It was probably written in Dieppe towards the end of 1557, at the time of the Marian persecutions in England, and fate played a scurvy trick on Knox by bringing a Protestant woman to the throne just as the tract began to circulate. Knox hastened to placate Elizabeth by exempting her from 'the monstrous Regiment of Women', calling her 'virtuous and godly' and recording his love and reverence towards her, though all this must have appeared singularly unpersuasive if Elizabeth had read and remembered his printed opinions, of which this is not the most forthright: 'To promote a woman to beare rule, superioritie, dominion or empire aboue any realme, nation, or citie, is repugnant to nature, contumelie to God, a thing most contrarious to his reueled Will and approued ordinance, and finallie it is the subuersion of good order, of all equitie and iustice.' There can be little doubt, however,

that Knox had been swayed less by misogyny than by im-
passioned religious dogmatism, for at the time he wrote the
tract not simply women but *Catholic* women were ruling in
England, Scotland, and France. There can be little doubt,
either, that less would have been heard of Knox's tract thereafter if he had not hit upon so memorable a phrase for its title.

The First Blast (he intended to follow it with two others which
did not come about) is obviously the work of a preacher. In
form it is a long-winded sermon; it calls upon an army of sup-
porting authorities, both scriptural and classical; and it thumps
away at a single proposition that would either be accepted with
alacrity well inside five minutes or be denied to all eternity
whatever authorities might be called to the witness box. But
Knox the preacher comes into his own in the prose style of the
pamphlet, for it is the direct and lucid prose of a speaker
accustomed to make himself understood immediately to the
listening ear and not expecting the indulgence of a reader's
lingering eye. The peroration, following a denunciation of
Mary I as 'that horrible monster Jezebel of England', runs:

> . . . And therfore let such as assist her, take hede what they do.
> For assuredlie her empire and reigne is a wall without founda-
> tion: I meane the same of the authoritie of all women. It hath
> bene vnderpropped this blind time that is past, with the fool-
> ishnes of people, and with the wicked lawes of ignorant and
> tyrannous princes. But the fier of Goddes worde is alredie laide
> to those rotten proppes (I include the Popes lawe with the rest)
> and presentlie they burn, albeit we espie not the flame: when
> they are consumed, (as shortlie they will be, for stuble and drie
> timbre can not long indure the fier) that rotten wall, the vsurped
> and vniust empire of women, shall fall by it self in despit of all
> man, to the destruction of so manie, as shall labor to vphold it.
> And therfore let all man be aduertised, for the trumpet hath
> ones blowen.

Because of its importance as a major battle in the pamphlet
war and for its circumstantial interest, a summary account of
the Martin Marprelate affair is due here. The tracts it directly
produced are of no great consequence as literature, though they
have been praised beyond their merits as 'the best prose satires
of the Elizabethan age'. In 1586 the Star Chamber, alarmed

by the flood of Puritan pamphlets then appearing, decreed that ecclesiastical approval must henceforward be sought for each publication. The consequent indignation of the Puritans moved the Dean of Salisbury (Dr. John Bridges) to issue in 1587 a *Defence of the Government established in the Church of England for Ecclesiastical Matters*, which only poured oil on what had been a relatively small blaze. Bridges was answered in 1588 by a tract with a sardonically verbose title-page beginning: *Oh read over Dr. John Bridges, for it is a worthy worke:* and saying lower down that the tract was 'Compiled for the behoofe and overthrow of the Parsons, Fyckers, and Currats [Vicars and Curates], that have lernt their Catechismes, and are past grace: By the reverend and worthie Martin Marprelate gentleman, . . . Printed oversea, in Europe, within two furlongs of a Bounsing Priest, at the cost and charges of M. Marprelate, gentleman'. Inasmuch as in the course of this titular preamble the tract is referred to as 'this learned Epistle' it is known as *The Epistle*. The statement that it was produced oversea was intended to mislead the authorities, for it was in fact printed at East Molesey, Surrey, in the house of an ardent Puritan, Mistress Crane. The type was provided by Robert Waldegrave, a printer who lived in London near Temple Bar, and who was rendered destitute when his house was raided and his plant destroyed for an earlier offence. The Marprelate Tracts numbered only seven, brought out from November 1588 to September 1589, but they maddened religious and secular rulers alike, and led to a heresy hunt and imprisonment, torture, and death to some who were implicated. The printing press was moved from place to place up and down the country, but the identity of Martin Marprelate was not discovered and is still not established with certainty, though a well-supported case has been made for Sir Roger Williams, Shakespeare's model for Fluellen in *Henry V*.

Hovering around the fringes of the Marprelate controversy were more than one of that curious class of Elizabethan writers who, though hardly to be named professional pamphleteers, seem to have been ever ready to throw off a pamphlet out of ungovernable pugnacity. Two at least of these, John Lyly and Thomas Nashe, wrote anti-Martin tracts which have small interest apart from their connection with the whole Elizabethan

Pappe with an hatchet.
Alias,
A figge for my God sonne.
Or
Cracke me this nut.
Or
A Countrie cuffe, that is, a sound boxe of the
eare, for the idiot *Martin* to hold his peace,
seeing the patch will take no
warning.

VVritten by one that dares call a dog, a dog,
and made to preuent *Martins* dog daies.

Imprinted by *Iohn Anoke,* and *Iohn Astile,* for the
Bayliue of Withernam, *cum priuilegio perennita-*
tis, and are to bee sold at the signe of the
crab tree cudgell in thwack-
coate lane.

A sentence.

Martin hangs fit for my mowing.

epidemic. Of this anti-Martin group only two are frequently recalled, for their titles not for their matter: these are *Pappe with an Hatchet* and *An Almond for a Parrat* (the former possibly by Lyly, the other by Nashe), titles which none but Elizabethans would have devised.

Among the secular pamphleteers, Robert Greene (?1560–92) has received far more attention from posterity than anyone else, on account of the posthumous *Greenes Groats-worth of Wit, Bought with a million of Repentance, Written before his Death and published at his Dying Request.* It was brought out in the year he died, 1592, edited by Henry Chettle (himself a playwright and controversialist) who refers in his own pamphlet *Kind-Harts Dreame* to his editorial dealings with Greene's last work. The *Groats-worth of Wit* is a pitiful and self-pitiful epilogue to a misspent life, telling of Greene's racketing in brothels and taverns, setting out rules for better living, introducing fables, tales, moral poems, and complaints against rivals, and ending with a letter of repentance to his ill-used wife. As a brief epitome of the life of one who was not unrepresentative of the generic Elizabethan literary man, the pamphlet has an interest much wider than that for which it is almost exclusively remembered—its oblique reference to Shakespeare, who was twenty-eight when the *Groats-worth of Wit* appeared. Greene addresses one section of his pamphlet to three fellow-playwrights (one of whom was no doubt Marlowe) and it is in this section that the famous allusion appears:

> . . . Base minded men all three of you, if by my miserie you be not warnd: for vnto none of you (like mee) sought those burres to cleaue: those Puppets (I meane) that spake from our mouths, those Anticks garnisht in our colours. Is it not strange, that I, to whom they all haue beene beholding; is it not like that you, to whome they all haue beene beholding, shall (were yee in that case as I am now) bee both at once of them forsaken? Yes trust them not: for there is an vpstart Crow, beautified with our feathers, that with his *Tygers hart wrapt in a Players hyde*, supposes he is as well able to bombast out a blanke verse as the best of you: and beeing an absolute *Iohannes fac totum*, is in his owne conceit the onely Shake-scene in a countrey.

This passage has occasioned great argument among modern scholars, who have seen in it more than it need suggest. Clearly

Greene had a grudge against Shakespeare, and affected to despise him as a jack-of-all-trades and a pretentious fellow ('upstart crow') who was not above taking credit for other men's work (if 'beautified with our feathers' means that; though it may mean only that Shakespeare added to or revised existing plays by Greene and others and was thus, in Greene's opinion, 'beautified' by the proximity of his verse to theirs). Greene was also sore with Shakespeare for something apparently having to do with *Henry VI*, in which (Part III, I, iv, 137) York, accusing the Queen, uses the line 'O Tygres Heart, wrapt in a Womans Hide'. In all, this passage in Greene's pamphlet may have no stranger or stronger significance than that a slightly older author was jealous and envious of a younger one who appeared likely to become more successful. To assume that Greene would not have made an unfounded charge on his death-bed and that Shakespeare must have acted shabbily or worse to Greene and his friends, is to take too simple a view: some men do nurse imaginary grievances to the end of their lives. Yet, though it may tell us nothing illuminating about Shakespeare, the whole passage throws a sidelight into a dark corner of the Elizabethan theatre with playwrights wrangling and backbiting, as authors have never ceased to do. In his pamphlets Greene is always most interesting when he is dealing with dark corners, whether in the theatre or among vagabonds elsewhere in the London scene, as in *A Notable Discovery of Cozenage* (1591), *The Defence of Conny-Catching* and *A Disputation between a He Conny-Catcher and a She Conny-Catcher* (both 1592), all three concerned with low life among the swindlers infesting the town.

Novelists

There is no fixed line of division between Elizabethan pamphlets and Elizabethan fiction: the one group shades off into the other, as appears more readily when such pieces as Greene's conny-catching pamphlets are compared with the realistic novels concerned with rascality and sordid living, such as Nashe's *The Unfortunate Traveller* (1594).

But the Elizabethan novel is bipolar, inclining in the one zone towards the murk and muck of 'realism' in the social underworld; in the other, towards the perpetual sunshine of pastoral romance, which has already been seen (*see above*, p. 128) as a factor in Elizabethan poetry. The English novel made, in fact, a false start in the sixteenth century, for the majority of writers who attempted it were not equipped with a prose style suitable for clear and progressive story-telling: their words could dance but not walk. Nor were they equipped with the ability to create and develop character, nor to handle credible human situations. Almost without exception the Elizabethan novelists give the impression of working under constraint in an alien medium. Again and again the reader has cause to reflect that the novel before him would be better as a poem or a play. Whole pages of Deloney's *Jacke of Newberie* (*see below*, p. 160) could be spoken as stage dialogue more naturally and more entertainingly than they can be read silently from the printed book.

Thomas Deloney (?1543–?1600) was probably by some ten years the eldest of the five—himself, Lyly, Sidney, Lodge, and Nashe—who made the principal contributions to that hybrid 'the Elizabethan novel'; but Deloney's books were among the latest of this group to be written. John Lyly (?1554–1606) was first in the field with *Euphues the Anatomy of Wit* (1578), followed by *Euphues and his England* (1580). Euphues, a young Athenian, while visiting Naples falls in love with his friend Philautus's betrothed Lucilla and is in turn discarded by her. In the later volume Euphues and Philautus are in England, where Philautus experiences more of the vagaries of love before he achieves a happy ending. Whereupon Euphues returns home to a bachelor cell. This small germ of plot is swollen into two large books by the accretion of what is (to modern taste) a tedious amount of moralizing and philosophizing: to the Elizabethan intellectual palate it was so acceptable that Lyly's mannered romances became immensely popular, mainly on account of the ornate language in which they were written—the style which came to be called *euphuism*. It is usual to say that Lyly developed this style through contemporary renderings from the Spanish of Antonio de Guevara (*The Dial of Princes*, translated by Sir Thomas North, 1557) and the Italian of Baldassare Castiglione (*The Courtier*, translated by Sir Thomas Hoby, 1561), and he certainly did draw directly from these; yet what we know as euphuism crept into the blood-stream of English prose long before *Euphues* was written. It can be detected faintly in Caxton, while in Skelton's prose it appears, considerably developed, at least half a century before *Euphues*.

Dictionaries define euphuism, slightingly, as an artificial, affected, high-flown style of writing, but this ignores the skill and resource which Lyly brought to his use of language in a genuine attempt to combine clarity, grace, and ornament. If it is difficult now to believe that prose so elaborated could have aimed at clarity, it may be equally hard for our descendants to believe that the excess of qualification in Henry James's prose was the outcome of his scrupulous attachment to precision. Lyly's intricate weaving of balanced phrases, antitheses, repetition, alliteration, and a range of other devices was even less simple than appears from a merely verbal examination, for behind this complex tapestry of words lay an impressive amount of classical learning, drawn both from Greek and from Latin sources and introduced with subtle skill into the web of the tapestry. Such prose was totally unsuited for narrative purposes; but as prose which aimed to be in itself a decorative art and the very focus of interest it was magnificent, however misconceived and monstrous it appears in an exclusively workaday view of writing. Lucilla addresses her father:

> . . . It is *Euphues* that lately arryued heere at *Naples*, that hath battered the bulwarke of my breste, and shall shortly enter as conquerour into my bosome; What his wealth is I neither know it nor waye it, what his wit is all *Naples* doth knowe it, and wonder at it, neyther haue I bene curious to enquire of his progenitors, for that I knowe so noble a mind could take no Originall but from a noble man, for as no birde can looke againe the Sunne, but those that bee bredde of the Eagle, neyther any Hawke soare so hie as the broode of the Hobbie, so no wight can haue suche excellent qualities excepte hee descend of a noble race, neyther be of so highe capacitie, vnlesse hee issue of a high progenie. . . .

Euphues soliloquizes:

> But seeinge I see mine owne impietie, I wyll endeuoure my selfe to amende all that is paste, and to be a myrrour of godlynes heereafter. The Rose though a lyttle it be eaten with the Canker yet beeing distilled yeeldeth sweete water, the yron thoughe fretted with the ruste yet beeing burnte in the fire shyneth

brighter, and witte although it hath beene eaten with the canker of his owne conceite, and fretted with the rust of vaine loue, yet beeinge purified in the stille of wisedome, and tryed in the fire of zeale, will shine bright and smell sweete in the nosethrilles of all young nouises.

Euphues writes a pamphlet called 'A cooling Carde for Philautus and all fond lovers', from which comes this illustration of the euphuistic affection for classical allusions:

Yet, although I wolde haue thee precise, in keeping these precepts, yet woulde I haue thee to auoyde sollytarinesse, that breedes melancholy, melancholy, madnesse, madnesse, mischiefe and vtter desolation: haue euer some faithfull pheere, with whome thou mayst communicate thy councells, some *Pilades* to encourage *Orestes*, some *Damon* to release *Pithias*, some *Scipio* to recure *Lælius*. *Phillis* in wandringe the woodes hanged hir selfe; *Asiarchus* forsakinge companye, spoyled himselfe with his own bodkin; *Biarus* a *Romaine*, more wise then fortunate, beeing alone destroyed himselfe with a potsherd.[1]

It will be seen from these extracts that a moralistic thread runs through the maze of ornament, and both these features —the moral as well as the ornamental—became fashionable among writers and readers alike. The easy divorce of personal conduct from literary precept has already been observed in the case of Sir Thomas Malory (*see above*, pp. 75 ff.) and, in a less spectacular way, it can be seen again in the writings (when compared with the life) of Robert Greene, whose several novels include *Pandosto* (1588), upon which Shakespeare drew to some extent for *The Winter's Tale*; *Menaphon* (1589); and *The Carde of Fancie* 'Wherein the Folly of those carpet Knights is deciphered, which guiding their course by the compase of Cupid, either dash their ship against most dangerous Rocks, or else attaine the haven with pain and peril. Wherein also is described in the person of Gwydonius a cruell Combate between Nature and Necessitie'. This was published within a decade of *Euphues* and reproduces its mannerisms of style, its elaborately artificial and voluble conversations, its classical embellishments, its images and comparisons from natural history (for Greene, like Lyly,

---

[1] *The Complete Works of John Lyly*, edited by R. Warwick Bond (3 vols. Clarendon Press, 1902), vol. I, pp. 231, 242, 256.

drew upon Pliny), its frequent and lengthy soliloquies. The considerable use of letters passing between the lovers, Gwydonius and Castania, makes *The Carde of Fancie* an early example of the epistolary novel, a type frequently experimented with in later centuries by Richardson and others but never comfortably established. Opposing families in which the fathers fight but the children love was a stock theme, raised by Shakespeare to its highest level in *Romeo and Juliet*. In Greene's novel the theme remains undeveloped for want of narrative skill and effective characterization. The lovers and everyone else in the book are puppets only. At the beginning the author draws up so imposing a catalogue of Gwydonius's vices that lively expectancy is stirred, only to be cheated by the young man's failure to achieve any impressive villainy in action. *The Carde of Fancie* is among the numerous examples of Elizabethan fiction which are more aptly described as love pamphlets than as novels. By far the most attractive feature in Greene's prose romances is the appearance in them of a number of his charming lyrics: e.g. in *Menaphon* the deservedly famous lullaby, 'Weepe not my wanton', sung by Sephestia.

The English Renaissance writers ransacked a large part of classical literature—though, very strangely, they appear to have been indifferent to the great Greek dramatists. The Elizabethan prose romances (or novels, or love pamphlets) as we have seen, are crammed with miscellaneous classical lore, and mention must be made of the Greek works of prose fiction which helped largely to shape the Elizabethan novel. Between 1569 and the end of the century appeared English translations of the *Æthiopica* of Heliodorus, the *Clitophon and Leucippe of* Achilles Tatius, and the *Daphnis and Chloe* of Longus. All three played a part in determining the character of Elizabethan fiction: the first two in their concentration on the adventures of far-travelling highborn lovers; the last in its cunning employment of sophisticated innocence and erotic charm in the sylvan atmosphere of pastoral. The most attractive specimen of the Elizabethan pastoral novel is *Rosalynde : Euphues Golden Legacie*, by Thomas Lodge (*c.* 1558–1625), which confesses an immediate derivation from Lyly in its sub-title. But the euphuistic factor consists mainly in the prose style of *Rosalynde*, while in other respects its ancestry is to be found in Greek pastoral romance. There is no need to dwell upon Lodge's novel, since its substance is familiar through *As You Like It*, in which Shakespeare borrowed much from *Rosalynde*, greatly bettering what he borrowed, not merely by turning prose into poetry but also by turning Lodge's character-less though engaging puppets into flesh and blood men and women, and by giving them a local habitation on English soil. Shakespeare's Forest of Arden is as genuinely English as the Ardennes of *Rosalynde* is manifestly not French but only the figment of a literary convention. Nevertheless, within the conventions of pastoral romance, Lodge's novel has at least some early-morning freshness to mitigate the hothouse airlessness common to that type of romance. It also enables Lodge to appear as a most attractive versifier in the incidental lyrics.

In the same year as *Rosalynde*, 1590, Sir Philip Sidney's *The Countess of Pembrokes Arcadia* was first published, though it was begun some years before and Sidney had died meanwhile. The Countess of Pembroke was Sidney's beloved sister, and the *Arcadia* was written for her. Sidney's noble character and heroic end have shed upon *Arcadia* a glory to which, on its own literary quality, it can make little claim. Nevertheless, although it follows the fashionable contemporary mode, it has surface beauties:

> There were hilles which garnished their proud heights with stately trees; humble valleis, whose base estate seemed comforted with the refreshing of silver rivers; meadows, enameld with al sorts of ey-pleasing floures; thickets, which being lined with most precious shade, were witnessed so to by the cherefull deposition of many wel-tuned birds; each pasture stored with sheep, feeding with sober security; while the prety lambs with bleting oratory craved the dams comfort; here a shepheards boy piping, as though he should never be old; there a yong shepherdesse knitting, and withall singing; and it seemed that her voice comforted her hands to work, and her hands kept time to her voices music.

To pass from *Arcadia* and *Rosalynde* to Nashe's *The Unfortunate Traveller, or The Life of Jacke Wilton* is to enter another world, a world of roistering rascality, of ugliness and horror. There is scarcely a trace of euphuism in Nashe's prose, which sweeps along like a river in spate and thick with human detritus. To give a semblance of verisimilitude to the tale, eminent contemporaries appear or flit by: Sir Thomas More, Erasmus, the Earl of Surrey (to whom Jack Wilton acts as part squire, part boon companion), and others. This device has caused Nashe's book to be described as the first English historical novel; it is also regarded as the first English picaresque novel, from the wanderings and vagabondage of the hero. Nashe was drunk with words, even besotted by them. In *The Unfortunate Traveller* he had a tale to tell, and told it; but except in the passages describing plague, rape, torture, and execution the incidents are drenched with words, sometimes in the vein of Rabelais, sometimes in that of James Joyce, who must either have been familiar with Nashe's work or have been his unconscious verbal descendant. At Wittenberg Wilton encounters

> A bursten belly inkhorne orator called *Vanderhulke*, they pickt out to present him with an oration, one that had a sulpherous big swolne large face, like a Saracen, eyes lyke two kentish oysters, a mouth that opened as wide euery time he spake, as one of those old knit trap doores, a beard as though it had ben made of a birds neast pluckt in peeces, which consisteth of strawe, haire, and durt mixt together. . . .

Vanderhulke delivers an oration to the Duke of Saxony:

> . . . Oratorie vncaske the bard hutch of thy complements, and with the triumphantest troupe in thy treasurie doe trewage vnto him. . . . Why should I gie gadding and fisgigging after firking flantando amfibologies, wit is wit, and good will is good will . . . The scholasticall squitter bookes clout you vp cannopies and foot-clothes of verses. We that are good fellowes, and liue as merry as cup and can, will not verse vpon you as they doe, but must do as we can, and entertaine you if it bee but with a plaine emptie Canne. . . .[1]

The naturalism and irony of Defoe, the corrosive satire and invective of Swift, appeared in the eighteenth century with an air of originality arising largely from the excellent plainness of Defoe's and Swift's prose style. The roots of their mental substance, however, are bedded deep in the soil and clay of language which clings about the clustering and tangled undergrowth of Elizabethan prose. The clearing of the undergrowth

---

[1] *The Vnfortvnate Traveller* by Thomas Nashe. Edited by H. F. B. Brett-Smith (Blackwell, Oxford, 1920).

began, or was at least attempted, before the sixteenth century ended, and in the novels of Thomas Deloney (*c.* 1543–1600) there is a distinct foreshadowing of Defoe, both in the direction of a clarified style and in the shifting of the focus of interest to a different social plane. In the Renaissance mind the persistent image of the Wheel of Fortune limited the types and worldly standing of the men and women suitable to appear as characters in creative writing. Tragic force depended upon a catastrophic fall from the pinnacle of success to the abyss of ruin and death; while in pastoral and romance the characters were pure idealizations. For the one purpose, therefore, none but exalted characters would serve; for the other, make-believe not actuality was the rule. In Nashe's *Unfortunate Traveller* some approach was made to the employment of characters from a wider social range, but the nature of the picaresque novel imposed swaggering extravagances of treatment which denied to that type of 'realistic' writing any true realism of character.

Lyly, Sidney, Lodge, and Nashe were all university men who had been fully exposed to the atmosphere of Renaissance learning at Oxford or Cambridge, but Deloney was a tradesman, a tramp, and a ballad-monger. When towards the end of his life he turned to novel-writing it was with the deliberate intention of giving a place in the literary sun to the tradesmen and artisans. *Jacke of Newberie* (1597) and *Thomas of Reading* (1600) are concerned with the clothiers (employers of 'spinners, carders, weavers, fullers, dyers, sheermen, and rowers'); *The Gentle Craft* (1597–8) with the shoemakers, and from that novel came *The Shoemaker's Holiday*, the better-known play by Thomas Dekker, who belonged to much the same social level as Deloney.

Deloney's novels are very loose in construction, and their democratic intention is sporadic. There is no unity of mood or even of subject; unrelated episodes are incongruously assembled and no chance is lost of introducing noble wooers or royal patrons. *Jacke of Newberie* is most in character in its opening chapter, which is a self-contained little comedy of the importunate wooing of Jack by his late master's widow, and of their squabblings after the hasty wedding. In Deloney's hands the novel became a kind of pedlar's pack holding descriptions of a pageant played before the king by workers' children, of the quips and tricks of the king's jester Will Sommers and of

50. Stage scene from *The Three Lords and Three Ladies of London*

51. Scene, with stage, from *Jack Jugler*

The labels visible in the drawing:

tectum

porticus

sedilia

orchestra

mimorum aedes

ingressus

proscænium

planities siue arena

quintum [...] apparei et [...], bestiarum [...]
[...] destinatum, in quo multi vrsi, tauri, et [...]
magnitudinis canes, distinctis caueis & septis aluntur, qui [...]
ad

52. Interior of the Swan Theatre in 1596, after Johannes de Witt

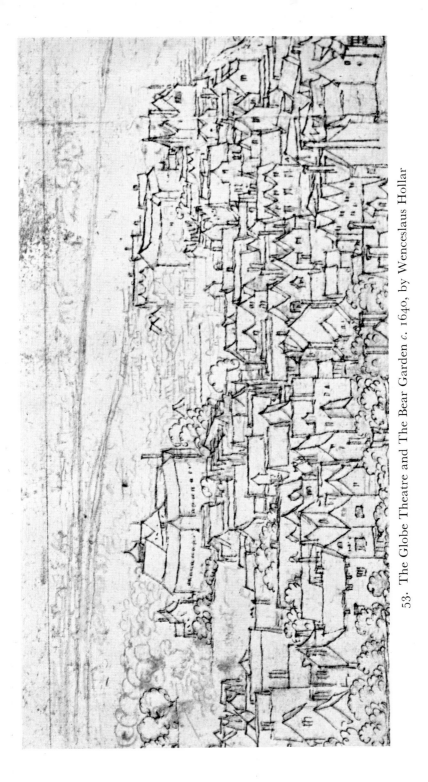

53. The Globe Theatre and The Bear Garden *c.* 1640, by Wenceslaus Hollar

54. Richard Burbage, possibly a self portrait

55. Edward Alleyn

56. William Shakespeare, from the First Folio

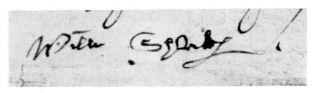

57. Part of a page from *The Booke of Sir Thomas More*, probably in Shakespeare's own hand

58. Shakespeare's signature from a deposition, 1612

59. Shakespeare's signature from his Will, 1616

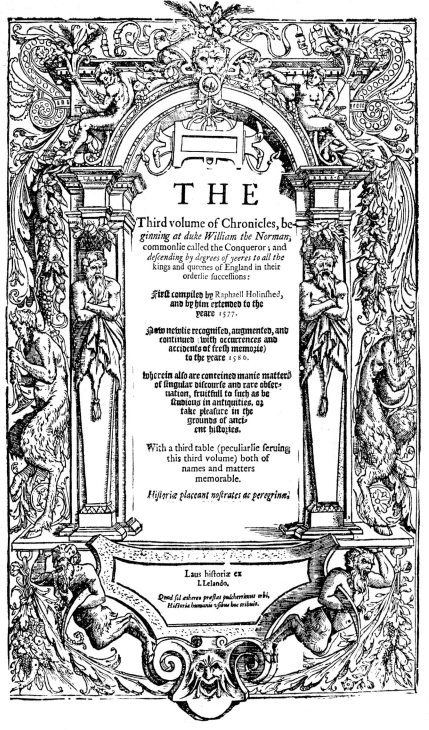

THE

Third volume of Chronicles, be-
ginning at duke William the Norman,
commonlie called the Conqueror ; and
descending by degrees of yeeres to all the
kings and queenes of England in their
orderlie succeſsions :

First compiled by Raphaell Holinſhed,
and by him extended to the
yeare 1577.

Now newlie recogniſed, augmented, and
continued (with occurrences and
accidents of freſh memorie)
to the yeare 1586.

wherein alſo are conteined manie matters
of ſingular diſcourſe and rare obſer-
uation, fruitfull to ſuch as be
ſtudious in antiquities, or
take pleaſure in the
grounds of anci-
ent hiſtories.

With a third table (peculiarlie ſeruing
this third volume) both of
names and matters
memorable.

Hiſtoriæ placeant noſtrates ac peregrinæ.

Laus hiſtoriæ ex
L.Lelando.

Quod ſol ætheræ præſtat pulcherrimus orbi,
Hiſtoria humanis vſibus hoc tribuit.

60. Title-page to the third volume of Holinshed's *Chronicles*

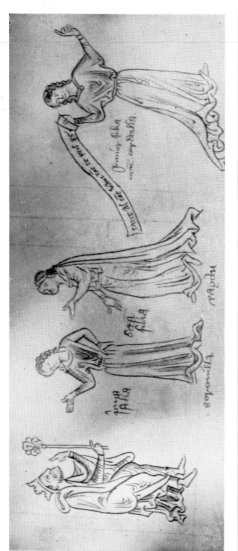

61. Lear with his daughters, from the *Historia Maior* of Matthew Paris

62. Illustration to *Titus Andronicus*, attributed to Henry Peacham

Wolsey's Patch, of a petition to the king on behalf of the un-
employed, of love scenes, of local gossipers and scandal-mongers,
of provincial tradesmen's wives tripping to London like any
modern Women's Institute party, of the putting out of eyes, of
London constables (catchpoles), of the murder of Thomas of
Reading in a remarkable chapter which smacks of both *Sweeney
Todd* and *Macbeth*. Moreover, Deloney interpolates ballads
cleverly varied in tone and metrical skill according to the
character and mental standing of the supposed author: e.g. a
servant's love-letter includes a poem of four verses in broken-
backed lines:

> O *Jenny* my joy, I die for thy love,
> And now I heare say that thou dost remove:
> And therefore, Jenny, I pray thee recite
> Where shall I meete thee soone at night.
> For why, with my Master no more will I stay,
> But for thy love I will runne away:
> O Jenny, Jenny, thou puttest me to paine,
> That thou no longer wilt here remaine. . . .[1]

Among the most curious features in Deloney's novels are his
attempts to reproduce phonetically the dialect of an old Ayles-
bury couple visiting Newbury and the broken English of a
young Italian merchant wooing a Newbury girl. But Deloney's
value to English literature lies in his demonstration that there
was a road of escape from the artificiality which academic
mannerisms had imposed upon the content and style of prose
literature. Wherever one reads in Deloney, the English is as
clear and direct as here:

> By means of the warres which our King had with other countries
> many Merchant strangers were prohibited for comming to
> *England*, as also our owne Merchants (in like sort) were forbidden
> to have dealings with *France* or the Low-countries: by meanes
> whereof the Clothiers had most of their cloath lying on their
> hands, and that which they sold was at so low a rate that the
> money scantly paid for the wooll and workemanship. Whereupon
> they sought to ease themselves by abating the poore workemens
> wages. And when that did not prevaile, they turned away many
> of their people, Weavers, Shearmen, Spinsters and Carders, so

[1] *Thomas of Reading*, ch. III (*Elizabethan and Jacobean Novels*, Everyman's
Library, Dent, London, 1929).

M

that where there was a hundred Looms kept in one towne, there was scarce fifty: and he that kept twenty put downe tenne. Many a poore man (for want of worke) was hereby undone, with his wife and children, and it made many a poore widow to sit with a hungry belly. This bred great woe in most places in *England*.[1]

Critics and Essayists

The characteristic roundaboutness of Elizabethan scholarly prose is nowhere more irritating to modern readers than in the critical writings of the period. This is the more unfortunate since English literary criticism began at that time and it would have been particularly valuable to possess succinct statements of critical principles from those who were either the begetters or the male midwives of the New Poetry. As it is, however, readers must press through a jungle of verbiage, sometimes with only small reward when the labour is ended. Certain Elizabethan writers who were themselves fully aware of the elaborations and affectations of contemporary prose uttered against it; yet even they were unable to achieve simplicity, and it is therefore proper to distinguish between those who were prolix because prolixity was an accepted fashionable proof of learning and wit and taste, and those who recognized the virtue of simplicity but failed to achieve it.

The chief causes of prolixity were (i) the passion for classical allusions aroused by the Renaissance rediscovery of the ancient authors; (ii) the snob adoption of foreign forms of expression, due to the rush of translations and to the aristocratic habit of Continental travel, especially in Italy—whence came that 'Italianate' manner complained of by the more austere writers; (iii) the persuasion among the learned that homely English was unbecoming except for groundlings; (iv) a genuine love of ornament, which imposed upon language a burden of excrescent decoration such as was to appear rather later in visual form in Baroque architecture, sculpture, and painting. In mitigation of what now seems a fault, it must be allowed that those who used the orotund style were writing for the like-minded who would approve the manner and could, presumably, follow the argument. Those who objected, often did so on non-literary grounds, for what has long since become labelled as

[1] *Jacke of Newberie*, ch. VI (*ibid.*).

Elizabethan literary criticism was originally one aspect of a moral and religious controversy started by the Puritans. But before turning to consider the case for the defence with which the poets and their friends met the Puritan attack, something more needs to be said about the difficulty of achieving simplicity even when simplicity was the aim.

As early as 1553 (five years before the Elizabethan age began) a Cambridge-educated man who became a privy councillor and secretary of state, Thomas Wilson (?1525–81), published his *Arte of Rhetorique*, a treatise urging the use of straightforward English, free from foreign and 'inkhorn' (i.e. pedantically archaic) terms. He wrote:

> . . . Some seeke so far for outlandish English, that they forget altogether their mothers language. And I dare sweare this, if some of their mothers were aliue, thei were not able to tell what they say: and yet these fine English clerkes will say, they speake in their mother tongue, if a man should charge them for counterfeiting the Kings English. Some farre iourneyed gentleman at their returne home, like as they loue to goe in forraine apparell, so thei wil pouder their talke with ouersea language. He that commeth lately out of Fraunce, will talke French English and neuer blush at the matter. An other chops in with English Italienated, and applieth the Italian phrase to our English speaking, the which is, as if an Oratour that professeth to vtter his mind in plaine Latine, would needes speake Poetrie, and farre fetched colours of straunge antiquitie. The Lawyer will store his stomacke with the prating of Pedlers. The Auditor in making his accompt and reckening, cometh in with *sise sould*, and *cater denere*, for vi.s. iiii.d. The fine courtier wil talke nothing but *Chaucer*. The misticall wiseman and Poeticall Clerkes, will speake nothing but quaint Prouerbes, and blinde Allegories, delighting much in their owne darkenesse, especially, when none can tell what they doe say. . . . I know them that thinke *Rhetorique* to stande wholie vpon darke wordes, and hee that can catche an ynke horne terme by the taile, him they coumpt to be a fine Englisheman, and a good *Rhetorician*. . . .[1]

Wilson proceeds to give an amusing letter in inkhorn terms written by a Lincolnshire man in application for a vacant benefice. Allowing for the inevitable differences in spelling as

---

[1] *Wilson's Arte of Rhetorique 1560*, edited by G. H. Mair (Clarendon Press, 1909).

between his time and ours his own English prose is admirably
direct. Where, then, is the difficulty—referred to above—which
the commenders of simplicity found in attaining it in their own
work? Wilson, it has to be remembered, was writing before the
mannerisms he deplored had taken a firm hold upon literature,
however much they were already affecting speech. His *Arte of
Rhetorique* preceded Lyly's *Euphues* by a quarter of a century.
When we turn from Wilson to a similar exhortation in *The Arte
of English Poesie* by George Puttenham (*d.* 1590), published in
1589, ten years after *Euphues*, an obvious and remarkable
change is seen:

> . . . Albeit peradventure some small admonition be not impert-
> inent, for we finde in our English writers many wordes and
> speaches amendable, & ye shall see in some many inkhorne
> termes so ill affected brought in by men of learning as preachers
> and schoolmasters, and many straunge termes of other languages
> by Secretaries and Marchaunts and travailours, and many darke
> wordes and not usuall nor well sounding, though they be dayly
> spoken in Court. Wherefore great heed must be taken by our
> maker in this point that his choise be good. And peradventure
> the writer hereof be in that behalfe no lesse faultie then any other,
> using many straunge and unaccustomed wordes and borrowed
> from other languages, and in that respect him selfe no meete
> Magistrate to reforme the same errours in any other person; but
> since he is not unwilling to acknowledge his owne fault, and can
> the better tell how to amend it, he may seem a more excusable
> correctour of other mens: he intendeth therefore for an indifferent
> way and universall benefite to taxe him selfe first and before
> any others.

It is as though the brain of the writer is fogged, or caught in
the kind of dream in which the dreamer moves but makes no
progress: his feet are gripped by some undetectable power.
Even though little difficulty be found in grasping the argument
advanced by Puttenham, the prose style wearies the reader's
mind and causes the protracted sentences to seem little better
than a mannered rigmarole. The contagion of euphuism had
spread to those who were crusaders against it. Nor must any
blame for this be placed solely upon Lyly. Euphuism was in the
air; *Euphues* deposited it.

In the same year as *Euphues* came *The Schoole of Abuse*, a pamphlet by a one-time Oxford scholar, Stephen Gosson (1554–1624), who had turned playwright and then been converted to Puritanism. His pamphlet attacked writers and actors of plays and enlarged upon the moral evils of playgoing. His prose is clogged with the names of classical characters and places and there are many of those references to natural history which it was the current fashion to draw from Aristotle and Pliny. At a single opening of a modern edition [1] of Gosson's booklet these names appear scattered over the two pages: Myrrha, the Syrens, the Harpies, Hyena, Danus, Epæus, Troy, Semyramis, Persia, Nero, Jupiter Capitolinus, Circe, Hippomenes, Atalanta, Plato, Cato, Marcus, Ennius, Tullie, Maximus Tyrius, Ajax, Ulysses, Nestor, Juno, Æsop, Hercules, Minerva, Venus, Vulcan, Lemnos, and Apollo. All the trappings of euphuism are present, with none of the pace imparted to them by Lyly. As an instance of academic exhibitionism at its grossest *The Schoole of Abuse* could hardly be surpassed. When it is also considered that Gosson's charges amounted to no more than the stereotyped Puritan objections to all secular entertainment, it appears improbable that this literary performance of his would be recalled at all if he had not dedicated it impertinently to Sir Philip Sidney, who thereupon wrote (1581) *An Apologie for Poetrie*, first published in 1595 and given its alternative title *The Defence of Poesie* in the edition of 1598. Before leaving *The Schoole of Abuse*, its own sole contribution to gaiety should be noted: it is subtitled 'Conteining a plesant invective against Poets, Pipers, Plaiers, Iesters and such like Caterpillers of a Commonwelth; Setting up the Flagge of Defiance to their mischievous exercise, and overthrowing their Bulwarkes, by Prophane Writers, Naturall reason, and common experience: A discourse as pleasaunt for Gentlemen that favour learning, as profitable for all that wyll follow vertue.'

There is no lack of displayed learning in Sidney's *Apologie*, but he has the advantage of most of his fellow prose-writers in having evidently assimilated his classical and other authorities, not merely hung them about his neck. If his prose occasionally serpentines to its point, at least its progress is elegant and the point is clear. He claims for poetry a superiority over philosophy and history, inasmuch as the philosopher is concerned with the

---

[1] In Edward Arber's 'English Reprints' series (London, 1895), pp. 20-1.

abstract and general, which are neither easily understood nor easily applied, while the historian is concerned with what is, not with what should be. The poet can better the functions of both, for 'whatsoever the Philosopher sayth shoulde be doone, [the poet] giveth a perfect picture of it in some one, by whom he presupposeth it was done'; and the historian is 'captived to the trueth of a foolish world' whereas poetry 'is more Philosophicall and more studiously serious then history . . . because Poesie dealeth with . . . the universall consideration'. The poet, that is to say, can create through images what is only a matter for speculation to the philosopher; and the poet, through his gift of vision, brings us to contemplate the ideal (or the Idea, in the Platonic sense) not only the actual. Sidney goes on to speak of the kinds of poetry—Pastoral, Elegiac, Comic ('Comedy is an imitation of the common errors of our life, which [the poet] representeth in the most ridiculous and scornefull sort that may be; so as it is impossible that any beholder can be content to be such a one'), Tragic, and Heroic— before defending the poet against the charges brought against him by the poet-haters. These were 'First, that there beeing many other more fruitefull knowledges, a man might better spend his tyme in them than in this. Secondly, that it is the mother of lyes. Thirdly, that it is the nurse of abuse, infecting us with many pestilent desires; with a Syrens sweetnes, drawing the mind to the Serpents tayle of sinfull fancy.'

Shakespeare is supposed to have read Wilson's *Arte of Rhetorique* and to have followed its precepts. If he also read the *Apologie* he paid little heed to Sidney's opinion of the kind of play in which Shakespeare himself triumphed. This passage in Sidney's pamphlet is among the most famous of all Elizabethan critical comments:

Our Tragedies and Comedies (not without cause cried out against), obseruing rules neyther of honest ciuilitie nor of skilfull Poetrie, excepting Gorboduck (againe, I say, of those that I haue seene), which notwithstanding, as it is full of stately speeches and well sounding Phrases, clyming to the height of Seneca his stile, and as full of notable moralitie, which it doth most delightfully teach, and so obtayne the very end of Poesie, yet in troth it is very defectious in the circumstaunces, which greeueth mee, because it might not remaine as an exact model of all Tragedies.

For it is faulty both in place and time, the two necessary companions of all corporall actions. For where the stage should alwaies represent but one place, and the vttermost time presupposed in it should be, both by *Aristotles* precept and common reason, but one day, there is both many dayes, and many places, inartificially imagined. But if it be so in *Gorboduck*, how much more in al the rest? where you shal haue *Asia* of the one side, and *Affrick* of the other, and so many other vnder-kingdoms, that the Player, when he commeth in, must euer begin with telling where he is, or els the tale wil not be conceiued. Now ye shal haue three Ladies walke to gather flowers, and then we must beleeue the stage to be a Garden. By and by, we heare newes of shipwracke in the same place, and then wee are to blame if we accept it not for a Rock. . . . Now, of time they are much more liberall, for ordinary it is that two young Princes fall in loue. After many trauerces, she is got with childe, deliuered of a faire boy; he is lost, groweth a man, falls in loue, and is ready to get another child; and all this in two hours space: which how absurd it is in sence euen sence many imagine, and Arte hath taught, and all auncient examples iustified, and, at this day, the ordinary Players in Italie wil not erre in.

There is nothing in the whole history of literature for which such heartfelt thanks should be given as that Sidney was no more successful in persuading English playwrights to accept the classical unities of time, place, and action than Gabriel Harvey and others were in trying to impose classical metres upon English poetry. Sidney was equally opposed to tragicomedy, without which the canon of Shakespeare would be vastly different and incomparably poorer:

. . . Theyr Playes be neither right Tragedies, nor right Comedies; mingling Kings and Clownes, not because the matter so carrieth it, but thrust in Clownes by head and shoulders, to play a part in maiesticall matters, with neither decencie nor discretion: So as neither the admiration and commiseration, nor the right sportfulnes, is by their mungrell Tragy-comedie obtained.

Among other critical writings of the Elizabethan period were Lodge's *A Defence of Poetry* (1579), replying energetically to Gosson's *School of Abuse*; William Webbe's *A Discourse of English Poetrie* (1586), which dwells not only on the nature and principles of poetry but also on Gower, Chaucer, Lydgate, Skelton,

Spenser (though Webbe was not sure that *The Shepheardes Calender*, published anonymously, was by him); and Francis Meres's *Palladis Tamia* (1598), a series of notes on poetry and poets, memorable for its reference to Shakespeare's sonnets (*see above*, p. 106) and the list of plays so far written by Shakespeare:

> As Plautus and Seneca are accounted the best for Comedy and Tragedy among the Latines: so Shakespeare among the English is the most excellent in both kinds for the stage. For Comedy, witnes his *Gentlemen of Verona*, his *Errors*, his *Loue Labors Lost*, his *Loue Labours Wonne*, his *Midsummers Night Dreame*, and his *Merchant of Venice*; For Tragedy, his *Richard the 2*, *Richard the 3*, *Henry the 4*, *King Iohn*, *Titus Andronicus*, and his *Romeo and Iuliet*.

Many attempts have been made to identify the mysterious *Loue Labours Wonne* with a play by Shakespeare under another title, but with no certainty.[1]

Though Roger Ascham (1515–68) is among the critics by reason of certain passages in *The Scholemaster* (1570), he is best known as the teacher of the young Elizabeth and as her private tutor when she became queen in 1558. He was also for a while Latin Secretary to Mary I, notwithstanding that he was a Protestant. His *Toxophilus* (1545) is ostensibly on archery but it also offers observations on the value of physical education and contains such enchanting passages of prose as the description of 'the great snow that fell four years ago'.[2] *The Scholemaster* has the very great interest of first-hand references to Elizabeth and to Lady Jane Grey, of whom he gives a moving account in the words she used when telling him of her home life, praising her teacher,

> M. Elmer [John Aylmer, afterwards Bishop of London], who teacheth me so gentlie, so pleasantly, with soch faire allurements to learning that I thinke all the tyme nothing, whiles I am with him. And when I am called from him, I fall on weeping, because whatsoever I do else, but learning, is ful of grief, trouble, feare, and whole misliking unto me. . . .

---

[1] Most of the critical writings named in this section are included, either complete or in part, in *Elizabethan Critical Essays*, edited with an Introduction by G. Gregory Smith (2 vols. Oxford University Press, 1904).

[2] See *The Oxford Book of English Prose*, pp. 77–8.

The first edition of Francis Bacon's *Essays* was published during Elizabeth's reign, in 1597, but it contained only ten essays, while the final collection (1625) had fifty-eight. Bacon was an important and sinister historical figure in the later years of the Queen's life, but his literary work belongs almost entirely to the Jacobean period and is discussed in Vol. II of the present work.

Other Prose Writings

Occasional references have been made above to the importance of translations in shaping Elizabethan literature—poetry, prose, and (as will appear later) drama also. It is an important subject of which little more can usefully be said in brief terms. Two outstandingly influential books whose contemporary importance was as marked as is their lack of genuine interest now, were William Painter's *Palace of Pleasure* (1566–7) and (by George Pettie) *A Petite Pallace of Pettie his Pleasure* (1576), the latter having been regarded by some as the 'real creator of euphuism in its fullest development'. Lyly undoubtedly owed something to Pettie but the judgment here quoted is open to serious question, for (as has been said above) it is more probable that the impulse towards euphuism was in the air and had remoter and ultimately unidentifiable origins. Painter, for his 101 tales, went to numerous sources—Livy, Herodotus, Margaret of Navarre, Straparola, but mostly to Bandello and Boccaccio. In Painter's book these 'stories of blood and desire' fascinated the writers of his own and the next generation, particularly the playwrights, among whom Shakespeare probably annexed the plot of *Romeo and Juliet* from Painter, though he may have got it more directly from Fulke Greville's poem, *The Tragical Historye of Romeus and Juliet* (1562, i.e. several years earlier than Painter's version). Painter provided a rich mine for plot-hunters; Pettie's stories fascinated less, and what influence he exercised was more stylistic and gnomic in character, for his writing is not only euphuistic, it is also loaded with proverbs and wise saws: e.g.

> . . . it is to late to shut the stable dore when the steede is stolen, it booteth not to stop the breach when the towne is overflowen: it is to late to dislodge love out of ones breast, when it hath infected beefore every parte of the body. . . . For this virgin was

so vanquished by love, that shee neither forced her fathers faire wordes, neither feared his fierce threateninges, but told him plainly shee would not deny the love she bare *Admetus* . . .[1]

Shakespeare's debt to Painter was far less than that he owed to North's 1579 translation (from Amyot's French version) of Plutarch's *Lives of the Noble Greeks and Romans* for the plots of his classical tragedies and, in general, for much of his knowledge of Roman history. John Florio's 1603 edition of Montaigne's *Essays*; Philemon Holland's Livy (1600), Pliny (1601), Plutarch's *Morals* (1603), and Suetonius's *History of the Twelve Cæsars* (1606); William Adlington's *The Golden Asse* of Apuleius (1566): these are no more than a handful from the great outpouring of translations.

The chroniclers and antiquaries provided such masterpieces as Ralph Holinshed's *Chronicles of England, Scotlande, and Irelande* (1577), Shakespeare's source for his English historical plays and for *Macbeth, Lear,* and *Cymbeline*; John Stow's *Survey of London* (1598, 1603); Philemon Holland's English version (1610) of William Camden's *Britannia* (first published in Latin, 1586), an invaluable topographical, archæological, and historical compendium; and (something less than a masterpiece) John Foxe's *Actes and Monuments of these latter perilous times touching matters of the Church* (in Latin in 1559; in English 1563). As 'Foxe's Book of Martyrs', with horrifying pictures, this distressing Protestant work remained in active circulation for several centuries, and even as late as the end of the nineteenth century was piously foisted upon children as elevating Sunday reading.

A soberer and finer work is Richard Hooker's *Of the Laws of Ecclesiastical Polity* (1593 and later). Hooker (?1554–1600) rose from poverty to become a deputy professor of Hebrew at Oxford, and afterwards (1585) Master of the Temple in London. In the last years of his life he was rector of Bishopsbourne in Kent, and from the epitaph on his tomb there posterity knows him as 'the Judicious Hooker'. His monumental prose work is a defence of the Church of England against the Puritans, based at the outset upon fundamental principles of law. In subsequent

[1] 'Admetus and Alcest': *A Petite Pallace of Pettie his Pleasure*, edited by Herbert Hartman (Oxford University Press, New York and London, 1938).

parts Hooker examines the Puritan claim that the Bible is the
Christian's sole authority, and rebuts assertions that the Established Church was dominated by English practices. The fifth
book (the last published in the author's lifetime) upholds the
English Prayer Book, which was obnoxious to the Puritans.
Books 6 and 8 were published posthumously in 1648 and the
intermediate Book 7 in 1662, none of the three in an authentic
version. In an intolerant age Hooker was indeed judicious, cool
and balanced, and with more Christian charity in his nature
than was common. In an age of invective he preserved decency
and dignity in argument, and on topics which are often of
limited interest to those outside the circle of doctrinal controversy he nevertheless produced a prose masterpiece with a
perennial literary appeal. He also inspired one of Izaak Walton's
small masterpieces—the Life of Richard Hooker (in *Walton's
Lives*: see Vol. II of the present work).

While Richard Hakluyt (?1552–1616) was serving as chaplain to the English ambassador at Paris in the 1580s he was
seized of the conviction that his countrymen knew little and
cared less about the great maritime achievements of their
nation. He therefore set out to remedy this by collecting whatever documents he could acquire concerning the voyages of the
English seamen from Cabot onwards. He had already published
similar works relating to foreign navigators before his superb
Principall Navigations, Voiages, and Discoveries of the English Nation
came out in 1589 (enlarged edition 1598–1600). The Cabots,
Willoughby, Hawkins, Drake, Gilbert, Frobisher, Ralegh, are
among those whose exploits are recorded in one of the most
stirring of all English books.

CHAPTER VIII

TUDOR DRAMA

AMONG the less fortunate consequences of embedding literature in the scholastic curriculum rather than taking it first for enjoyment is that poetry and drama are too often treated as dead specimens fitter for dissection in a lecture-theatre than for acceptance as living and speaking creations. Ideally, poetry should be heard and drama should be done, seen, and heard before being read silently from the printed page. Although it is impracticable to have every play performed in front of every group of literature students, it should not always be impracticable at least to set the students to read aloud in the common hearing whatever plays they are to scrutinize analytically. Until the academic tendency to treat drama primarily as something in a book is superseded by a universal recognition of drama as *something done*, something to be acted on a stage in the presence of an audience, and brought into being for that purpose alone, a good deal of literary study will remain futile groping in a blind alley.

Before the modern type of theatre—completely roofed, artificially lit, and with the picture-frame stage and more or less realistic scenery—was established after the Restoration, a stronger link existed between playwrights and spectators. In the absence of scenery the audience would usually be required to make those imaginative leaps over time and place which Sidney thought so absurd (*see above*, p. 167), and occasionally the playwright provided verbal scene-painting, as in the famous passage (I, vi) sketching the exterior of Macbeth's castle, which the audience was required to see with the mind's eye alone. The drama is always dependent upon current stage conditions, and plays of any period can only be regarded intelligently when the contemporary circumstances of production—its facilities and its limitations—are appreciated. In the twentieth century lazy playwrights are relieved of much labour by the availability of telephones for stage use, and many plays are conditioned by this mechanical fact. In the sixteenth century the human fact that

no women players were allowed encouraged Shakespeare to put
several of his heroines into men's clothes. Though this was
a stage convenience he nevertheless employed it with such
exquisite skill that neither Viola nor Rosalind—nor, indeed,
Imogen—would even now seem so bewitchingly womanly if
they had not been created to be performed by young men acting
young women pretending to be young men. However charmed
we may be by the Violas and Rosalinds we see to-day, our view
of the Elizabethan drama is bound to be at least slightly out of
focus unless we restore it in imagination to its contemporary
setting, bearing in mind the various factors bearing upon the
playhouses, the players, and the audiences.

Conditions of Performance

The medieval drama (*see above*, pp. 48 ff.) progressed from
simple ritual ceremonies within the churches to large-scale
cyclical presentations of scriptural plays by the trade guilds in
public thoroughfares. These plays were genuine popular drama
inasmuch as the performances were attended by a large part of
the local community making holiday; the performers were guild
members; and the plays, religious in origin, became enlivened
by comic episodes, secular in character, often crude in humour,
and evidently of local derivation. Though the Miracle plays
controlled by the guilds declined after about the middle of the
fifteenth century, the parodied craftsman's play in *A Midsummer
Night's Dream* rings true enough to indicate that the impulse of
popular drama had lasted into Shakespeare's lifetime, even
though it may by then have become itself hardly more than an
absurd parody of the classical drama favoured by Renaissance
scholars, and probably aped by the unlearned when the familiar
scriptural stories lost ground to the little-comprehended lore of
antiquity.

While the Miracle plays of the guilds were at the height of
their popularity in the streets and market places, the more
intellectualized Morality plays with their personified virtues
and vices and allegorical themes developed in the later part of
the fourteenth century. These are in general much duller than
the scriptural plays; nevertheless they have more originality
and, however faintly, more of the essential dramatic element of
conflict: there is in them always the fundamental struggle

between Good and Evil to which all drama reduces in the last analysis. The weakness of the Moralities—the weakness which later playwrights had to cure before true drama could be born —was that in the conflict between pure Good and pure Evil the issue could never be in doubt and, consequently, there could be very little dramatic tension. Not until playwrights learned to put on to the stage characters in whom the elements were so mixed that their human likeness could not be questioned, and there could be no initial certainty that the balance of destiny would swing one way and not the other—not until then could the theatre carry out the function which made it unique among public institutions—the function of instructing and elevating through interest and entertainment: not dogmatizing, but showing in miniature Man's perpetual oscillation between well-doing and ill-doing. Morality plays, lacking this general interest of character, found their audience among the educated who were familiar with the intricacies and subtleties of medieval scholastic disputation. The Moralities therefore guided the acted drama into a wholly changed environment, away from the streets and into palaces and other great houses, into schools and colleges and inns of court. The vital factor in this change of location was not so much the shift from outdoors to indoors as the substitution of a fixed place of performance for the travelling stage (pageant) used by the guilds. Miracle plays were done in the closest proximity to the audiences, and no doubt with more than a little uninvited audience-participation, such as lingered in the Elizabethan popular theatres (*see* Beaumont and Fletcher's *The Knight of the Burning Pestle*), whereas the more sophisticated and more aristocratic audiences to whom the Moralities were presented by young scholars or others of their own class would be soberer in reception, and thus became the true ancestors of the modern theatre audience—i.e. spectators in the limited sense.

Relationship between audience and actors is a matter of importance in the development of drama, and the architecture of theatres is correspondingly important in so far as it affects this relationship. Two outstanding conventions in playwriting, the soliloquy and the aside, are far more difficult to accept in a modern-type theatre than in an Elizabethan one where the projecting (apron) stage, and the seating of some members of the audience on stools along the sides of the stage itself, produced a measure of intimacy between players and public and made possible a confidential relationship in which soliloquies and asides would not seem unnatural, even if any expectation of naturalness in the theatre had then existed. A few mid-twentieth-century playwrights have made tentative approaches to the restoration of direct address by actor to audience, but the post-Elizabethan picture-frame stage with its isolating pros-cenium arch and drop curtain fostered the make-believe that the players were unaware of the audience's presence and that the audience was seeing through a transparent wall and hearing through an accidental crevice. Modern 'naturalism' destroyed valuable freedoms enjoyed by Elizabethan playwrights and blocked channels of communication which, fully open to Shakespeare, made possible the subtle exploration of Hamlet's personality.

The Intermediate Drama [1]

Before the first theatre was built in Elizabethan London, several phases of development intervened between the rise of the Moralities and the full establishment of the professional drama. The Moralities were followed by the Interludes, of which Henry Medwall's *Fulgens and Lucrece* (*c.* 1495; first pub-lished 1926) and John Heywood's *The Four P.P.* (*c.* 1520) are representative. *Fulgens and Lucrece*, which came by a round-about route from a Latin treatise, was originally played in two parts at an entertainment punctuating a banquet given by Cardinal Morton (to whom Medwall was chaplain), probably at Lambeth Palace. The opening speech is made by a servant boy, called A, and his informal manner suggests that he was moving about among the guests and addressing them directly. The story of Lucretia (daughter of Fulgens, a Roman senator) and her two wooers, one a patrician, the other a plebeian, with the humorous underplot concerning her maid Joan, and the two male servants A and B, is unremarkable, but the play is important as the first known English example of a wholly secular tragi-comedy.

John Heywood (*c.* 1497–1580), a Court musician, married Sir Thomas More's niece, Elizabeth Rastell, whose brother William published her husband's plays, including *The Playe*

[1] See also above, p. 58.

¶Here is côteyned a godely interlude of Fulgens
Cenatoure of Rome. Lucres his doughter. Gapus
flaminius. ꝗ Publi9. Corneli9. of the disputacyon of
noblenes. ꝗ is deuyded in two ptyes/to be played at
ii.tymes. Côppled by mayster Henry medwall. late
chapelayne to þ ryght reuerent fader in god Johan
Morton cardynall ꝗ Archebysshop of Caūterbury.

Title-page of Fulgens and Lucrece

called the foure P.P. A newe and a very mery enterlude of A palmer,
A pardoner, A potecary, A pedler (performed, probably at Court, in,
it may be, 1520; published 1544). This is a debate between
the first three characters, with the pedlar as judge, to determine
which can tell the biggest lie. Though no more than a series of
narrative speeches it is surprisingly entertaining and lively, and
occasionally witty, in spite of some coarseness distasteful to us
but evidently inoffensive at the time, for the piece ends with
a religious address to the audience. Heywood's work showed
a definite advance in English drama, notwithstanding his almost
complete disregard of plot interest. His rhyming couplets are so
fresh, easy, and seemingly spontaneous that there is no difficulty
in accepting them as natural speech; and he breaks through
the confines of his circumscribed themes by his awareness of the
outer world and its people: in *The Four P.P.* he shows, indirectly,
a shrewd appreciation of the nature and ways of women.

By 1550 the Latin plays of Plautus (first century B.C.) and
Terence (*c.* 190–159 B.C.) in comedy and of Seneca (*c.* 4 B.C.–
A.D. 65) in tragedy seemed certain to impose a seal of barren
classical formalism on English drama. The Elizabethans knew
nothing of the Greek tragic dramatists' works at first hand,
and Seneca's treatment of stories used by Sophocles and Euripides robs them of most of their spiritual power and force of
character. Seneca adopted the five-act formula prescribed by
Horace and into that rigid mould he pressed the utmost extravagance of rhetoric and declamation and of reported (but
never acted) violence and horror. These excesses struck a
responsive chord in the Elizabethans and their immediate
successors, and the influence of Senecan blood and thunder is
plain in Kyd, Marlowe, Shakespeare (at its worst in *Titus
Andronicus,* but transformed in *Richard III*), Marston, Tourneur,
Webster, Ford, and others. Fortunately the uncontrolled violence of Elizabethan tragedy shattered the Senecan mould,
generating great poetry in place of booming rhetoric. The
Elizabethans outdid Seneca in their tragedies of horror, for
whereas he *described,* in plays which he intended only to be read
or recited, they *displayed* in the action of plays written for stage
performance.

The first-fruit of Senecan tragedy in English was *Gorboduc,*
by Thomas Norton (who wrote the first three acts) and Thomas

N

Sackville, first Earl of Dorset. Both were members of the Inner Temple, in the hall of which the play was performed in the presence of Queen Elizabeth at the beginning of 1562. The story, taken from Geoffrey of Monmouth's legendary history of the kings of Britain (*Historia Regum Britanniæ*, twelfth century), concerns the quarrel of Ferrex and Porrex, sons of King Gorboduc and Queen Videna, over the division of the kingdom. Porrex, having killed his brother, is slain by his mother, and the land is plunged into civil war when the Duke of Albany attempts to seize the Crown. Each act is preceded by a dumb show symbolizing the events and their consequences, but there is no action during the play proper; everything is reported, nothing done. Thus, unlike their successors, Norton and Sackville were true disciples of Seneca, and their near observance of classical principles earned Sidney's applause (*see above*, p. 166). *Gorboduc*, though a masterpiece of dullness, is important in literary history as the first *regular* English tragedy, and the first play in blank verse.

Some twelve years before *Gorboduc* introduced into England tragedy on the Latin model, Nicholas Udall (1505–56), headmaster of Eton and later of Westminster, wrote in doggerel verse for performance by schoolboys *Ralph Roister Doister*, the first regular [1] English comedy, written on the five-act classical pattern and owing a great deal to Plautus and Terence. Mathew Merygreeke incites Ralph Roister Doister to court Dame Christian Custance, a widow betrothed to Gawyn Goodluck, a merchant, who is away from home until the last act. Although Mathew and Ralph are based on stock characters of classical comedy, the humour is more native than imported and the play can claim to be an English product fitted into a classical framework. The schoolmaster in Udall appears in his use of the device of the letter (prepared by a scrivener) from Ralph to the widow, the meaning of which can be reversed according to the way in which the pauses are allowed to fall in reading. It is an ingenious lesson in punctuation, and it still retains some entertainment and instructional value.

The second important English comedy *Gammer Gurton's Needle*

---

[1] In the phraseology of literary historians the terms 'first regular English comedy' and 'first regular English tragedy' are used to distinguish the pioneer plays consciously following classical models (mainly in regard to construction and the use of character-types) from their less orderly English forerunners in the pre-Renaissance drama.

was performed at Christ's College, Cambridge, at an undetermined date, perhaps 1566 but possibly much earlier. The authorship also is uncertain. It is usually attributed to William Stevenson, a Fellow of Christ's College, but John Bridges was named as its author in two of the Marprelate tracts (*see above*, p. 150). Like *Ralph Roister Doister* it is in doggerel verse, and in structure derives from classical models; but in content and temper it is closer to the farcical kind of inelegant humour which appears in the medieval drama. The central theme of the mislaying of the Gammer's needle and its eventual rediscovery in the breeches of Hodge, her farm-labourer, is trivial, but the character drawing of Dame Chat, Doctor Rat the Curate, Diccon the wandering beggar, Cock the boy, Tib and Doll the maids, puts *Gammer Gurton's Needle* in the main stream of traditional English comedy, which abounds in rustic humour such as Shakespeare perfected and Hardy carried on three centuries later in his novels and *The Dynasts*.

The superiority of the earlier English comedies over the tragedies of the same period lies in the fact that this rustic humour was a pre-existing native comic element which almost immediately assimilated and transmuted the elements in classical comedy which would otherwise have given us more comic types than individual comic characters. The classical comic types are clearly distinguishable in early Elizabethan comedy, while in Ben Jonson, later, they almost take control; the English dislike of regimentation and temperamental unfitness for it has produced a strong sense of the ridiculous which foreigners often condemn as flippancy but which is in truth a rare sanity and instinct for proportion—a knocking of solemnity off its magisterial perch. The English comic sense is also common sense, with its own system of internal discipline.

There was no equivalent native tragic element ready to condition and control the imported Senecan mode. Shakespeare apart, English sixteenth- and seventeenth-century tragedies swing unsurely from dull monotony to unbridled horror, both monotony and horror often appearing together in one and the same play. Again leaving Shakespeare aside, the only saving grace of most English tragedies of the period is in the occasional passages of utterly magnificent poetry which impart a sensation of high tragedy in no way justified by either the basic plot or the conduct of the action. Apart from *Gorboduc* the only 'tragedy' of the 1560s and 1570s that need be given even passing mention is Thomas Preston's *Cambises* (*c*. 1570), notable not as tragedy but as one of those mixed plays—in this instance tragi-historio-comedy—which were so peculiarly fitted to the genius of the age that not all the protests of the learned purists could prevent their gaining favour.

Bearing a somewhat similar relation to comedy proper as Preston's *Cambises* did to tragedy, George Gascoigne's *Supposes* (1566) stands in the early part of the Elizabethan age as the first regular English comedy in prose. Gascoigne (?1525–77)—a Cambridge graduate, a member of Gray's Inn, and parliamentary representative for Bedfordshire—experimented as poet, playwright in prose and verse (his *Jocasta* was the second English blank-verse tragedy), novelist, satirist, and critic, and was a person of note in Elizabethan literary circles. *Supposes* was taken from an Italian play (*Gli Suppositi*, 1509) by Ariosto, who had planned it on classical lines. It contains a good deal of play on the word 'suppose', for the action depends upon the complications of the often used device of characters being mistaken for one another in the interests of light love: 'the master supposed for the servant, the servant for the master: the freeman for a slave, and the bond-slave for a freeman: the stranger for a well-known friend, and the familiar for a stranger'. But it is as a landmark—the first English prose comedy—that *Supposes* is important, for it ushered in a line of better plays in that medium.

John Lyly's spirit can hardly help considering it a misfortune that he wrote the *Euphues* romances and thus became almost exclusively associated in the mind of posterity with a peculiarly mannered style of writing. As the popularizer (we have already seen that he was hardly the inventor) of euphuism Lyly was a phenomenon if not a freak; as a playwright he was the author of comedies which can at least hold a candle to Shakespeare's. Shakespeare, indeed, if the metaphor be pursued, was no doubt conscious of lighting his own bright lamp from Lyly's candle, since the fairies of *A Midsummer Night's Dream* and certain characteristics of Falstaff may owe something to *Endimion*. In this and other plays by Lyly there are numerous euphuistic passages, but these are mostly free from the wilder conceits of

A lamentable tragedy

mixed ful of pleasant mirth, conteyning the life of
CAMBISES king of PERCIA, from the beginning
of his kingdome vnto his death, his one good deed of execution, after that many wicked deeds
and tirannous murders, committed by and
through him, and last of all, his odious
death by Gods Iustice appoin-
ted. Don in such order as
foloweth. By
Thomas Preston.

The diuision of the partes.

Councel. Huf. Praxaspes. Murder. Lob, the 3. Lord.	} For one man.	Prologue. Sifamnes. Diligence. Crueltie. Hob. Preparatiō the 1. Lord.	} For one man		
Lord. Ruf, Commons cry, Cōmōs cōplaint, Lord smirdis. Venus.	} For one man.	Ambidexter, Triall.	} For one man.		
Knight, Snuf. Small habilitie. Proof. Execution. Attendance. second Lord.	} For one man.	Meretrix. Shame. Otian. Mother. Lady. Queene.	} For one man.		
		Yung childe Cupid.	} For one man		
Cambises. Epilogus.	} For one man				

Title-page of Cambises

the style and only rarely go beyond the limit of easily speakable prose. The charm of Lyly's dialogue is in its elegance, luminous grace, and shapely artifice, admirably fitted to the mood of poetic fantasy in which he excels. It is a not daringly venturesome guess that at least *Campaspe* (1580–1) and *Endimion: The Man in the Moone* (1585) would be acceptable to modern audiences, and that both in story and in dialogue they would be lively in stage performance. In print they are apt to seem long-winded, for they belong to the type of play which was at length to develop into the Masque and to culminate in Jonson's masques and (in a more purely poetic and spiritual mode) Milton's *Comus*: the type, that is to say, which depended much upon visual and musical aids. During performance the physical presence of the entranced Endimion, and of Diogenes and his tub in *Campaspe*, would greatly assist the dialogue. In the printed text the lack of helpful stage-directions is hampering; nevertheless it is apparent that Lyly used the limited facilities of the contemporary stage with resource, moving the action smoothly from outer stage to inner stage and back again to ensure rapidity in performance. Moreover, although a fair amount of Lyly's humour is communicated through the words, much more must have been evident to Elizabethan audiences, if only through the well-tried medium of incongruity. Both *Campaspe* and *Endimion* were played in the presence of Queen Elizabeth, and both by the companies of boy actors (formed from the choir schools of the Chapels Royal and St. Paul's) who were of outstanding importance in the drama of the period. Known as the Children of the Chapel and the Children of Paul's, these companies originated in the sensible Renaissance practice of acting plays in schools as a fruitful part of education. Since they were also trained singers, the young actors at the leading choir-schools would be well qualified to give entertainments at Court, where they became so popular that in the later 1570s they acquired semi-professional rank at the Blackfriars Theatre, formed from part of the sequestrated buildings of the monastery of the Black Friars. This became the Children's Theatre from *c.* 1576 to *c.* 1584, to the considerable resentment of the adult companies who were just then establishing themselves professionally in the first public theatres that had been built in London, though outside the City walls.

To refer in this connection to Lyly's plays only, it is easy to
imagine the fun likely to arise in a performance of *Campaspe*
from the playing by young boys of the philosophers, among
them Diogenes, who was undoubtedly rendered as a richly
comic figure and made doubly comic by a saucy boy actor
cheeking a dignified boy actor playing Alexander, proud
conqueror of the world and perplexed lover of the unwilling
Theban captive virgin Campaspe. She falls in love with Apelles,
set to paint her portrait by Alexander, who at length magnani-
mously yields her to the artist. The remarkable skill with which
modern schoolboys have performed great masterpieces of drama
enables us to conceive the possibility that the Children may well
have challenged the highest professional standards of their time,
and that there may have been no great incongruity between
players and characters. Yet it is difficult to believe that Lyly's
tongue was not slyly in his cheek when he set 'her Majesties
Children and the Children of Paules' to play not only Alexander
and his warriors, and Campaspe and her friend Timoclea, but
also Plato, Aristotle, and five other philosophers besides
Diogenes. For Apelles Lyly wrote fine speeches and eloquent
soliloquies and also the best of his lyrics:

> Cupid and my Campaspe play'd
> At cards for kisses: Cupid pay'd.
> He stakes his quiver, bow, and arrows,
> His mothers doves and team of sparrows, . . .
> At last he set her both his eyes:
> She won, and Cupid blind did rise.
> O Love, has she done this to thee?
> What shall, alas, become of me!

Courtly compliments to the Queen abound in Lyly's plays,
but they are mostly woven with skill into the texture of the
dialogue and not fulsomely obtruded. This is particularly so in
Endimion, where the several addresses to Cynthia are appropriate to the play, however fully they may be charged with
praises of Elizabeth and allusions to her enemies. The attractive
treatment of the myth of Endimion, who is here caused to sleep
for forty years through the conspiracy of Tellus (victim of unrequited love) with Dipsas the enchantress, is probably bound
up with contemporary events and characters; but the possible
identification of Elizabeth with Cynthia—and Tellus with Mary

Queen of Scots, Leicester with Endymion, Eumenides with
Sir Philip Sidney, Semele with Lady Penelope Rich, and so on
—interests us less than the character of Sir Tophas 'a bragging
soldier', who descends from the stock-type braggart (the *miles
gloriosus*) of Latin classical comedy and, as comic boaster and
eccentric lover, points the way to Falstaff in both of his
Shakespearean aspects.

The Professional Stage

When Shakespeare was a thirteen-year-old schoolboy at Stratford there occurred in London an event that was to determine
his future. In the spring of 1576 James Burbage, an actor in the
Earl of Leicester's company, was granted a twenty-one-years'
lease of land and property outside the City wall on the north-
eastern side of London between Finsbury and Shoreditch, near
to the present Holywell Street. Burbage had begun as a joiner
before taking to the profession of a player, and his original
occupation must have been of practical service when, aided by
his father-in-law, he set about building a wooden playhouse on
the site they had bought for a thousand marks (about £660).
Named The Theatre, it opened in the autumn of 1576, the
admission charge being 1*d*., 2*d*., or 3*d*. according to the part of
the house the spectator preferred or could afford. Hitherto,
travelling companies of actors ('strolling players') had given
their public performances mainly in inn-yards where the usual
surrounding gallery provided convenient additional accommo-
dation for the audiences. No doubt for good reasons connected
with the keeping of public order, the corporation authorities in
the City of London at length ruled against the acting of plays in
open inn-yards, and that prohibition led Burbage to build his
theatre. Other permanent playhouses followed: The Curtain
(1577) in the same neighbourhood; The Rose (*c*. 1587) and The
Swan (*c*. 1594) at Bankside, the district bordering the Thames
at Southwark; The Blackfriars (*c*. 1597), adapted by Burbage
from the building formerly used for the Children of the Chapel;
The Globe (1599), built on Bankside by Cuthbert Burbage (son
of James) from material taken from The Theatre which after a
chequered career had been demolished; The Fortune (1600),
built at Cripplegate by Henslowe to rival Burbage's new house.
The Blackfriars, differing from the general pattern in being

completely roofed, was used by Burbage's company as a winter theatre; the others, open to the sky, were for the summer season.

The Globe became the most famous of the Elizabethan theatres and its structure was typical of others, though not necessarily identical with them. Circular on plan, it had at one side a timbered and gabled tiring house before which the stage projected well into the auditorium, the front portion being an uncovered and unenclosed platform, while the back portion formed a canopied inner stage with a gallery which could be used for musicians or for such purposes as Juliet's balcony. This inner stage was fitted with front curtains which could be drawn to close a scene and parted to begin a later scene—whence the familiar stage direction that a character is 'discovered' at the opening of a scene. Little or no movable scenery was provided, but there was some attempt at dressing the plays and even some magnificence of costume, though there was little attempt at historical accuracy in the chronicle plays. The circular galleries extended to the stage structure on both sides, the top tier being roofed with thatch, while the main part of the auditorium was open to wind and rain and sun. On the floor of the house the spectators stood around three sides of the stage. In the balconies some seating was available, and favoured patrons sat on stools at the sides of the fore-stage, often to the inconvenience of the players. The behaviour of the audience was not always exemplary, and by modern standards would no doubt seem rowdy at best and often outrageously ill-mannered.

For long after these professional playhouses had become a permanent feature of London life, and one well supported by the public, the actors continued to be nominally under the patronage of some royal or noble personage. Those not so enrolled were classed as rogues and vagabonds and could perform only illicitly. The principal companies were Queen Elizabeth's Men; the Admiral's Men (later the King's Men); the Earl of Leicester's, the Earl of Pembroke's, and Lord Strange's men; and the Lord Chamberlain's Men, the company with which Shakespeare was chiefly connected.

The Burbages (James and his sons Cuthbert and Richard) led the Elizabethan and Jacobean theatre world in London, rivalled by Edward Alleyn (1566–1626)—he made a fortune and founded Dulwich College—and Alleyn's stepfather Philip

Henslowe (*d.* 1616), who managed theatres (the Rose, the Fortune, and the Hope) but did not act. Henslowe's diary (in the possession of Dulwich College) [1] is a valuable source of information about the organization and finance of the Elizabethan stage. Alleyn played in Marlowe's *Tamburlaine, Dr. Faustus,* and *The Jew of Malta*; Richard Burbage was the original Hamlet, King Lear, Othello, and Richard III, while he also took other Shakespearean parts and was seen in plays by (among others) Kyd, Ben Jonson, and Webster.

Marlowe and Kyd

But for the establishment of permanent theatres for the professional companies of actors, which created a demand for plays fitted to the public taste and therefore profitable to the players and their managers, Elizabethan drama would almost certainly have been confined to amateur occasional pieces suitable for instruction in schools and colleges and for entertainment at the Inns of Court and in the palaces and great houses of royalty and nobility. The popular drama would have been limited to the craftsmen's plays and to such crude material as strolling players, the rogues and vagabonds, could have contrived for the amusement of casually assembled tavern-yard audiences. In the twentieth century a remarkable school of Irish playwrights was called into being by the coming of the Abbey Theatre in Dublin as a centre for the performance of new plays; and simultaneously the repertory theatres in Manchester, Birmingham, and elsewhere stimulated English writers who might not have written plays at all if there had not been enterprising local theatres to stage their works. From the late 1570s, a new kind of career opened for writers in London. If the theatres were to flourish they required a continuous flow of new plays from which to form their repertory and they were therefore compelled to encourage writers to supply what the new theatre-going public wanted.

What *did* the public want? The question can only be answered by noting what the public got, i.e. what has come down to us through the contemporary popular favour which

---

[1] *Henslowe's Diary.* Edited by W. W. Greg (2 vols. Bullen, London, 1904, 1908). *Henslowe Papers: being documents supplementary to Henslowe's Diary.* Ed. Greg. (Bullen, 1907).

preserved the texts of certain plays while allowing many more to perish unprinted. We cannot, of course, be sure that the Elizabethan public did get what it wanted; it may only have preferred what it was given by some writers rather than by others. But it is reasonable to assume that it wanted action on the stage, for the plays provided by the most popular dramatists often abounded in violent action, even when written by scholarly authors whose tendency would have been to keep (as in *Gorboduc*) to the classical pattern which prescribed that action should be reported to the audience but not performed in their sight. Besides action the Elizabethan audience loved words. Even if it is an exaggeration to say that poetry was the Elizabethans' natural speech, there can be no doubt that they listened willingly and intently to poetry. The plays they most approved (e.g. *The Spanish Tragedy* of Kyd) are full of lengthy poetical speeches which often appear to register pure delight in words rather than any purpose of furthering the action. In pre-Shakespearean plays, and in not a few post-Shakespearean ones also, there is a marked lack of unity between poetry and action, and the ability (or even the attempt) to create convincing characters is very rare indeed.

Taking Elizabethan drama in general, there is an over-balance on the side of poetry, while (except in Shakespeare) action is imposed upon the characters instead of action being the inevitable outcome of character or of the interplay between circumstance and character.

The Renaissance progress away from medieval concepts and forms in drama has already been seen in the Tudor plays discussed above; but, however hackneyed the excerpt may have become, the short Prologue to Marlowe's *Tamburlaine* (1587) remains the manifesto of the new drama of Elizabethan England ·

> From jigging veins of rhyming mother-wits,
> And such conceits as clownage keeps in pay,
> We'll lead you to the stately tent of war,
> Where you shall hear the Scythian Tamburlaine
> Threatening the world with high astounding terms,
> And scourging kingdoms with his conquering sword.
> View but his picture in this tragic glass,
> And then applaud his fortunes as you please.

The homespun rhyming verse and knockabout clowning of the old plays were indeed, through Marlowe's genius, to be displaced by 'high astounding' poetry and the monstrous deeds of stage figures whose excesses fall outside the limits of human judgment. As Tamburlaine's lust for power carries him through treachery, cruelty, and wholesale murder which does not stop

Tamburlaine the Great

short of the slaughter of his own young son, the audience has the sensation of looking into the pit of hell and witnessing the torments of the damned. Tamburlaine is as much a personification as any character in the Morality plays, and he is no more individualized as a human creature than if he were called Power. But this great work infinitely surpasses all the Morality plays by being itself charged with power through the majesty of its poetry, which alone redeems it from intolerable horror. Not even the poetry can save Tamburlaine from being incredible, however, nor endow him with interest in terms of human character. He is a monster; his love for Zenocrate and hers for him add to his beastliness, not redeem it; and what dramatic interest might have been given to his end is dissipated by our being denied the spectacle of his downfall by a reversal of

fortune—he merely dies from natural causes. That this abominable conqueror of the world should have been given great
poetry to declaim, in blank verse which only Shakespeare surpassed—'Marlowe's mighty line' Ben Jonson was to call it—
may be a psychological misfortune, but it is none the less
a literary fact which has to be accepted. His invocation to
Zenocrate (Pt. I. I, ii): 'Zenocrate, lovelier than the love of
Jove, . . .'), his monologues in her death scene (Pt. II. II, iv),
and the address to the defeated kings ('Now crouch, ye Kings
of greatest Asia, . . .' Pt. II. IV, iii), are but gems of a larger
size amid many that give a glowing sombre brilliance to the
whole.

Christopher Marlowe (1564–93) was in essence the typical
Renaissance man, and some part of the interest of his plays lies
in his own interior relationship to them. Tamburlaine's lust for
power, Dr. Faustus's lust for knowledge, the Jew of Malta's lust
for riches, were all comprehended, however dimly and frustratedly, in Marlowe himself. A Canterbury shoemaker's son,
he felt the same impulses as Tamburlaine the Scythian
shepherd's son:

> Nature, that fram'd us of four elements
> Warring within our breasts for regiment,
> Doth teach us all to have aspiring minds:
> Our souls, whose faculties can comprehend
> The wondrous architecture of the world,
> And measure every wandering planet's course,
> Still climbing after knowledge infinite,
> And always moving as the restless spheres,
> Will us to wear ourselves, and never rest, . . .

Marlowe went to Corpus Christi College, Cambridge, after
leaving the King's School, Canterbury. His friends included
most of the well-known writers and he appears to have had
some experience as an actor. The words he put into Tamburlaine's mouth in the last scene:

> Come, let us march against the powers of heaven,
> And set black streamers in the firmament,
> To signify the slaughter of the gods

were in all probability an echo of his own undisguised atheism,
which brought him into disfavour with the authorities. Shortly

before his thirtieth birthday he was killed in a quarrel at a
Deptford tavern. This was for a long time thought to have been
the consequence of a drunken brawl, but it may in fact have
been a planned political murder, for Marlowe appears to have
been a secret agent in government pay.

The Tragical History of Dr. Faustus (performed ?1588) was
based by Marlowe upon a recent English translation of the
German medieval legend. This story of a man who sold his
soul to the devil in exchange for benefits on earth has since
been made universally familiar by Goethe, but Marlowe was
early if not first in the field with a dramatized version. It is
untidier than *Tamburlaine*, and has some of the clownish conceits derided in the prologue to that play. Greater dramatic
interest could have been created if Faustus had made less
trifling use of the powers conferred upon him by Mephistophilis,
for the doomed man's original purpose had been to encompass
'learning's golden gifts'. As in the earlier play there is fine
poetry (of which the great rhapsody on Helen is most famous:
'Was this the face that launched a thousand ships, And burnt
the topless towers of Ilium?'), while Faustus's last soliloquy
before the devils carry him off has genuine dramatic power,
culminating in his final words:

> O soul, be chang'd into little water-drops,
> And fall into the ocean, ne'er be found.

The Jew of Malta (performed *c.* 1592) is another blood bath,
occasioned by the Jew's determination to be revenged for the
confiscation of his wealth and home. In this purpose he is at
last betrayed, and perishes by having one of his own stratagems
turned against him. Of little importance in itself, the main
interest of the piece (apart from the possibility that Barabas the
Jew foreshadowed Shylock) turns upon the change which is
seen to have come over Marlowe's blank verse in the five years
or so since *Tamburlaine*. There are few magnificent passages of
poetry in *The Jew of Malta*, and notwithstanding the revenge
motive and the wholesale slaughter (most of it out of sight of
the audience, however) the play is much quieter in tone than
Tamburlaine. Marlowe's blank verse was in process of becoming
a more flexible and more effective instrument for drama, and

if he had lived another ten years he might have ended by being as great a playwright as he was at first a poet.

That Marlowe was on the threshold of that additional greatness is more than promised by his *Edward II* (written *c.* 1593), which covers the last phase of the King's life after the return of his minion, Piers Gaveston, from the exile into which he had been forced by the lords. They now take arms against Edward and Gaveston and kill the latter and his successor as favourite, the younger Spenser. Edward is arrested and murdered in Berkeley Castle. The whole play, though it lacks the penetration and active movement of Shakespeare's histories, is a notable dramatic achievement. Edward represents a considerable development in Marlowe's treatment of character, for this portrait of the king does pierce the outer surface of personality and reveal something of Edward's inward nature. The king's speeches in prison are impressive and moving and the play at those moments comes near to genuine tragedy.

Of Marlowe's minor plays, *The Massacre at Paris* and *The Tragedy of Dido, Queen of Carthage*, nothing need be said. He wrote a few non-dramatic pieces, chiefly the long narrative poem *Hero and Leander* (completed by George Chapman; published 1598) and the well-known lyric, 'Come live with me and be my love'.

Thomas Kyd (?1557–?1595) has some claim to be regarded as the author of the most popular and most influential (in its day) of all Elizabethan plays, for *The Spanish Tragedy* (acted *c.* 1590) was frequently revived, and additional scenes were provided by Ben Jonson. Little is known about Kyd himself, except that he went to the Merchant Taylors' School, worked as a scrivener, wrote or had some hand in other plays, and was much thought of by contemporaries as a tragic poet. There is a persistent belief that he wrote a lost play on the *Hamlet* theme, and that Shakespeare was indebted to it. *The Spanish Tragedy* itself contains features akin to some in *Hamlet*: e.g. a Ghost urging revenge (though it appears to the father of a murdered son, the reversal of the *Hamlet* situation), a distracted heroine, a character named Horatio. The numerous murders and suicides were undoubtedly to the Elizabethan taste; contemporary audiences would have found the play less tiresomely protracted and involved than it appears now; and the frequent comings and goings of Hieronimo, the Marshal of Spain, rhetorically lamenting the murder of his son Horatio, would have seemed less extravagantly melodramatic. After 350 years it still retains impressive elements of tragedy and has undeservedly been singled out as the type-example of undisciplined Elizabethan plays of revenge and blood. The emotions in *The Spanish Tragedy* are often over-emphatically expressed, but they are also often genuinely expressed emotions as the particular characters would have felt them in the sixteenth century, which was less afraid of feeling than we are.

Yet, when all else has been said, it is the verse that interests most nowadays in *The Spanish Tragedy*. Kyd's blank verse is competent but intermittent, as though he wrote rhymed verse almost instinctively and with enjoyment but blank verse only by conscious effort and because it was the new mode which it behoved him to follow. He could not refrain from playing delightedly with words even when he was observing the formalities of blank verse; and when restraining himself from rhyme he would seek compensation by using the same head-word repeatedly in a succession of lines, or by a run of lines with balanced echoing phrases—e.g. Hieronimo before the body of his son:

> Here lay my hope, and here my hope hath end;
> Here lay my heart, and here my heart was slain;
> Here lay my treasure, here my treasure lost;
> Here lay my bliss, and here my bliss bereft;
> But hope, heart, treasure, joy, and bliss,
> All fled, fail'd, died, yea, all decay'd with this.

Robert Greene's *Friar Bacon and Friar Bungay* (*c.* 1589) has the curious interest of conjoining a Faust-like theme with a kind of historical-pastoral one. The calling up of the devil is not associated with any tragic issue, however, but only with giving speech to a head of brass which the two friars have made. Though the play is thematically a patchwork, it has merit and some eloquent verse-passages (mainly in Prince Edward's speeches to and about Margaret of Fressingfield, the keeper's daughter) which would achieve real beauty if the language were more restrained:

Edward or none shall conquer Margaret.
In frigates bottom'd with rich Sethin planks,
Topt with the lofty firs of Lebanon,
Stemm'd and encas'd with burnish'd ivory,
And overlaid with plates of Persian wealth,
Like Thetis shalt thou wanton on the waves,
And draw the dolphins to thy lovely eyes,
And dance lavoltas in the purple streams;
Sirens, with harps and silver psalteries,
Shall wait with music at thy frigate's stem,
And entertain fair Margaret with their lays.

Greene's numerous plays include also: *A Looking-Glass for London and England* (1592) set in Nineveh and introducing, besides an assortment of local kings, the prophet Jonas (Jonah) who at the opening of one scene (IV: ii) is 'cast out of the Whale's belly upon the stage'; it also has those bits of magic to which Greene was addicted. *George-a-Greene, The Pinner of Wakefield* (?1593), in which Robin Hood and Maid Marian appear, besides Edward King of England and James King of Scotland. *James the Fourth* (?1594) which has been called 'the finest Elizabethan historical play outside of Shakespeare'.

The Old Wives' Tale (*c.* 1590) by George Peele is described by one of its editors not very explicitly or illuminatingly as a satire on the contemporary romantic drama. It might as justly be called a crazy pantomime. Amid its rustic humours is interpolated an episode of particular note, concerning two brothers in search of their sister who is held in durance by an enchanter. This resembles the theme of *Comus*, though little credence is given to the suggestion that Milton got it from Peele.

The anonymous *Arden of Feversham* (*c.* 1592) is that rare thing in Elizabethan drama, a domestic tragedy dealing with people of the middle classes and based on an actual murder case (of the 1550s). The workings of conscience in Alice Arden and her lover Mosbie, who contrive the murder of her husband, provide scenes of genuine power which alternate with crude melodrama. Equally unusual for the time is Thomas Dekker's comedy of the working classes, *The Shoemakers' Holiday* (1599). It centres on Simon Eyre, the Lord Mayor's shoemaker, among whose workmen is a supposed Dutchman, Hans, really Lacy (nephew

o

of the Earl of Lincoln) who adopts this disguise in order to be
near Rose, the Lord Mayor's daughter, whom Lacy's uncle has
forbidden him to wed. The love romance (which ends in the
marriage of Lacy and Rose) is secondary to the author's real
intention, namely, to present 'A pleasant Comedy of the Gentle
Craft' of shoemaking (Dekker adapted his play from Thomas
Deloney's novel *The Gentle Craft*). The robust fun wears well

The murder of Arden of Feversham

and Simon Eyre, who rises to become Lord Mayor of London,
is an invigorating eccentric who introduces himself as 'the mad
shoemaker of Tower Street' and has a genuine pride in his
business. Much of the effectiveness of the play comes from the
impression that Dekker was thoroughly at home with his subject
and on familiar terms with the class he was celebrating.

CHAPTER IX

SHAKESPEARE

IDOLATRY of Shakespeare was for the most part a nineteenth-century cult, fostered by the publication of 'family' editions of his plays and by lecturers and other popularizers, among whom was Keats's early friend, Cowden Clarke. His wife, Mary Cowden Clarke, managed to combine extravagant sentimentality about Shakespeare with valuable industry in compiling her Shakespeare Concordance, to which later concordances have been much indebted. Whereas the nineteenth century bowdlerized the plays and explained away whatever offended the current moral sense, earlier hands 'improved' Shakespeare in a succession of adaptations which refurbished the plays as milliners refurbish out-of-fashion hats, while 'acting-versions' were prepared by and for popular players whose chief aim was to exploit their own personal talents.[1] Such acting-versions were also in vogue in the nineteenth century; and even in the present century, when actors' respect for Shakespeare's text is stronger than before, rearranged and garbled stage versions are still not unknown. But though the nineteenth century might, in the interests of propriety or histrionic glory, maul with impunity what Shakespeare wrote, it clung to the fiction that Shakespeare was somehow above criticism both as man and as playwright. He was accounted the supreme genius-saint of all time, and that least sanguine of men, Matthew Arnold, could so far lose his head as to write in his sonnet on Shakespeare:

> Others abide our question. Thou art free.
> We ask and ask: Thou smilest and art still,
> Out-topping knowledge.

Fortunately there has been no widespread violent reaction from these absurdities of bardolatry; no epidemic of denigra-

---

[1] The foundations of later Shakespeare scholarship were laid, however imperfectly or incompletely, in the eighteenth-century editions undertaken by Rowe (1709), Pope (1725), Theobald (1734), Hanmer (1743), Warburton (1747), Johnson (1765), Capell (1768), Steevens (1773), and Malone (1790). See Vol. II of the present work.

tion; only a steady progress towards critical understanding and acceptance of Shakespeare and his writings as like in kind, however superior in degree, to other playwrights and their works. The chief hindrance to this progress comes from what has been called 'the Shakespeare industry', run by that increasing army of commentators who erupt upon him a monstrous fungus of interpretative and metaphysical mumbo-jumbo which obstructs a clear view of the plays. While we can never be certain either that Shakespeare did or did not embed in his work the abstruse ideas which investigators have discovered there, it is certain that Elizabethan audiences enjoyed and were impressed by *Hamlet, King Lear,* and the rest for simpler reasons. If we could transport ourselves back among the spectators in Shakespeare's theatre we should no doubt find that 'the problem of *Hamlet*' had no existence then, and that the play was accepted at its face value, meaning no more than is said in the words and seen in action on the stage. Nothing can be so salutary and illuminating for an understanding of Shakespeare as to take more notice first and last of *what Shakespeare wrote* than of what others say he meant.

And just as it is well to approach Shakespeare with a not too awesome intellectual respect, so is it well to consider him also as one playwright among many playwrights then active. He soared above his fellows, yet he could not have soared so high but for his fellows. He became what he did become not solely by the possession of innate genius, but by the interaction of genius and circumstance, and by the instruction he absorbed from the works of Marlowe and others. Though he greatly bettered the instruction, the instruction was nevertheless vital. There could not have been a Shakespeare *in vacuo.*

William Shakespeare was born at Stratford-on-Avon, in April 1564, traditionally on the 23rd but there is no record of the actual day. He was christened on 26 April.[1] His father, John

---

[1] There is no space or occasion here to discuss conjectural or circumstantial detail concerning the life, personality, or works of Shakespeare. Much is in dispute on all points and the literature of the subject is vast. For the sake of clarity this section is based on Sir Edmund Chambers's *William Shakespeare: A Study of Facts and Problems* (2 vols., 1930). An abridgement of this by Charles Williams was issued as *A Short Life of Shakespeare, with the Sources* (1933); and Chambers himself presented an outline statement of the facts of Shakespeare's personal life in *Sources for a Biography of Shakespeare* (1946). (All Clarendon Press.)

Shakespeare, a glover or wool-dealer or both, was a man of
some substance and position in the town, though he apparently
suffered monetary reverses long before he died in 1601. It is
assumed, without documentary proof, that William was educated at Stratford Grammar School; while there is a possibility
that he was apprenticed to (and ran away from) a local butcher.
He married Anne Hathwey or Hathaway at the end of November 1582 when he was eighteen, and their recorded children
were Susanna (born in May 1583) and Hamnet and Judith,
twins (January 1585). Hamnet died in 1596. Shakespeare may
have left Stratford in consequence of a deer-stealing escapade
on the property of Sir Thomas Lucy of Charlecote; and he may
have become a provincial actor, first in a travelling company
associated with a Lancashire patron, and afterwards as one of
Lord Strange's Men, also a travelling company before they
settled in the metropolis.

By 1592 Shakespeare was working for the London stage. In
that year Part I of *Henry VI* was performed, and it was evidently
in connection with *Henry VI* that Robert Greene's attack on
Shakespeare was made (*see above*, p. 152). As Greene's allusion
relates to a line in Part III of that play, *Henry VI* must have
been completed (or botched from an earlier work) before
September 1592, when Greene died. Since Shakespeare can
hardly have leapt immediately into the position of script
writer, it is reasonable to suppose that he reached London long
enough before 1592 to have served the theatres first in some
minor capacity. The story (in a document of *c.* 1748) attributed
to Sir William Davenant that Shakespeare began in London by
looking after horses left outside the playhouse by gentlemen
spectators has persisted, and if Davenant (1606–68)—the Restoration dramatist, adapter of Shakespeare, opera librettist,
and Poet Laureate—was in fact Shakespeare's illegitimate son,
the statement may have some foundation. There is also a legend
that Shakespeare was employed as call-boy.

The first accredited evidences of Shakespeare's authorship
are the registration in the Stationers' Hall records of his *Venus
and Adonis* on 18 April 1593 and of *Lucrece* on 9 May 1594. From
Francis Meres's *Palladis Tamia* (*see above*, p. 168) it is known that
by 1598 Shakespeare had achieved eminence in both tragedy
and comedy with at least a dozen plays. *Henry VI* does not

appear in Meres's list, and its absence supports the view that
Shakespeare had only a minor hand in that trilogy. Meres also
refers to *Venus and Adonis* and *Lucrece*, while from him we know
too that Shakespeare's Sonnets were circulating privately in
manuscript by 1598, though they were not printed until 1609.[1]

Legal documents show that Shakespeare lived in Bishopsgate
in 1595, in Southwark in 1599, and in Cripplegate about 1604.
He bought a house in Blackfriars in 1613, but evidently did not
occupy it himself. In 1597, four years before his father died, he
began to buy property in Stratford, and he retired to his native
town about 1610, when he was forty-six, and some twenty years
after he arrived in London. In those twenty years, therefore, he
had accumulated at least a competence sufficient for his com-
fort. He was a shareholder, as we should say—or a 'sharer', or
'housekeeper', in Elizabethan terms—in the Globe and Blackfriars theatres and his money was no doubt mainly from that
source. Whether he received payment as playwright and
occasional actor in the years of success, in addition to his share
of the profits, we cannot know. He died at Stratford on 23 April
1616, and was buried in the church there. Apart from half-a-
dozen signatures in varying forms on legal papers there are no
authenticated specimens of Shakespeare's handwriting, though
a strong and to some minds convincing case has been made for
the opinion that three pages in the manuscript of *Sir Thomas
More*, an anonymous play in the British Museum, are additions
in Shakespeare's hand.

The poet's disposition of property in his will, like the period
of only six months between his marriage and the birth of his
daughter, have been put forward as indications that Shakespeare and his wife were unsatisfactorily mated. But the indications are feeble. That the child was conceived out of wedlock is
no proof that Shakespeare was forced to marry Anne by a
morally outraged family and that he therefore disliked his wife.
Nor is any reflection made upon Anne by his devising to her in
his will only their second best bed. She would of right, and
without need for the fact to be referred to in the will, receive
the legally prescribed widow's portion, a life interest in one-
third of his estate. The truth is that we know nothing of

---

[1] For transcripts of some thirty contemporary references and allusions to
Shakespeare *see* Chambers and Williams, *op. cit.*, Appendix II.

Shakespeare's relationship with his wife; but if speculative evidence of any kind is to be proffered, the traditional statements that he spent part of each year at Stratford and that his wife desired to be buried in the same grave as her husband are as deserving of note as any. Moreover, at the age of about forty-six he elected to spend his years of relatively prosperous retirement in his home at Stratford. That he had love affairs during the London period is probable, if only as a deduction from the Sonnets, but even loving husbands are vulnerable to passing fancies which sometimes produce living consequences.

The chronology of Shakespeare's plays cannot be determined with certainty and no order of dating is universally accepted. For the present purpose Chambers's dating (according to theatre seasons, not calendar years) will serve and is given without qualification. Those who desire to examine the complex problem further will need to turn to a number of bibliographical and critical sources involving a course of comparative study.

It is generally accepted that at the outset of Shakespeare's working life in the theatre he followed admiringly in the footsteps of Marlowe, whose non-dramatic poem *Hero and Leander* had already served in some measure as a pattern for *Venus and Adonis*. Marlowe's influence on the early plays was exercised mainly in directing Shakespeare's attention to the possibilities of blank verse as an infinitely variable dramatic instrument. *Henry VI* (1590–2), however much or little of it is by Shakespeare, is at best no more than apprentice work and the first play to show the new genius working on material such as Marlowe might have handled is *Richard III* (1592–3), in which the Marlowean splendour of poetic rhetoric is refined of much extravagance by the skill Shakespeare was already developing in the presentation of human character. Such attempts at characterization as may be detected in Marlowe's plays (with the possible exception of *Edward II*) are external, like a sculptor's chiselling of inert material. On the stage a Marlowe character is brought to life only when the personality of a player is imposed upon the lines given to him to deliver. The majority of Shakespeare's characters, on the contrary, are already alive in the lines, for the delivery of which the player need be no more than a sensitive and intelligent instrument.

Actors fail in Shakespeare when, instead of attuning themselves to the speeches in honest endeavour to objectify the characters as the playwright appeared to intend—i.e. *finding the characters in the play*—they preconceive the characters in the dim light of personal idiosyncrasy or current fashion. So, although *Richard III* may offer in part the pre-Shakespearean (though also post-Shakespearean) stage monster of iniquity, Richard —unlike Tamburlaine—is far from being all monster. We get inside Richard's skin, we perceive his point of view, we can feel the vile yet inescapable charm he exercises over Anne :

> Within so small a time, my Womans heart
> Grossely grew captive to his honey words, . . .[1]

The memorable dramatic effectiveness of the opening words of the play, spoken by Richard himself solitary on the stage, has placed them among the best-known of Shakespeare's lines:

> Now is the Winter of our Discontent,
> Made glorious Summer by this Son of Yorke: . . .

Probably in the same season (1592-3), but perhaps earlier, came Shakespeare's first comic piece *The Comedy of Errors*, adapted either directly or through a previous English version from the Latin *Menæchmi* and (in one scene, III, i) the *Amphitryo* of Plautus. In performance it is an amusing romp on the mistaken identity theme, with hilarious confusions arising from the cross-contacts of twin brothers served by twin attendants.

Titus Andronicus (1593-4) reverts to the older type of blood and horror tragedy. *The Taming of the Shrew* (1593-4) has been much looked down upon as either a rehash from an old play or as Shakespeare at his worst. It has nevertheless retained a certain popularity, for the rough horseplay and the exhibition of a boorish manly man softening a termagant into a docile womanly woman please the uncritical; but it is poor stuff, the characters are puppets, and it would no doubt be classed with a hugger-mugger of minor Elizabethan comedies if Shakespeare's name were detached from it.

Apart from some youthful grace and eloquence *The Two Gentlemen of Verona* (1594-5) is unremarkable except for Launce

---

[1] The Shakespeare quotations follow the text of the First Folio of 1623 (unless otherwise indicated).

the clownish servant—whose scene with his dog (IV, iv) is perhaps the first true sign of the mastery that Shakespeare was to develop in handling this type of character—and for the beautiful lyric 'Who is Silvia?' (IV, ii). *Love's Labour's Lost* (1594–5) has received less than its deserts from posterity. While it is a mannered piece with a profusion of artificial word-play and bantering wit, much of it is exquisite in the best sense. Though when listening to the 'courtly' dialogue between the King and his lords and the Princess and her ladies one may sometimes lose the thread of the discourse without feeling that the loss is serious, the verse is delicately musical and at moments enchanting. The comedy scenes with the curate, the pedant, the constable, the clown, and the page represent another step forward by Shakespeare towards Dogberry and Verges, Shallow and Slender, and his still greater comic characters.

If the present chronology is reliable, the first of Shakespeare's supreme masterpieces was *Romeo and Juliet* (1594–5) which has driven so deeply into the emotional consciousness of the civilized world that there is little need for comment. Nowhere else has the stripped ecstasy of unified love and passion been set down with such perfection of poetry, or so purified of sentimental dross in word and feeling. This is pure love: love without taint of either prudery or prurience, for Juliet takes no contagion from the earthy bawdry of the Nurse; love compounded, as love is, of pain and joy, and escaping time's destructive hand only through death. The play is misnamed if the word 'tragedy' in the title is read in the common way, for the death of Romeo and Juliet was their one inevitable way of escape from tragedy; it was the perpetuating culmination of their ecstasy and the apotheosis to which all lovers aspire in the moment of complete union. Of the lesser characters and the dramatic machinery in *Romeo and Juliet* there can be little to say, for the sole function of these is fulfilled in providing the setting for the two. Except, possibly, for the Nurse, these surrounding characters have little individuality. Indeed, Romeo himself shines only with reflected light from Juliet; the amorous shallow youth is stabilized, dignified, and glorified only by becoming the object of Juliet's love. Mercutio's immortality in his brief transit through the play has been achieved mainly through the Queen Mab speech. The tragedy, if tragedy must be found, is not in the primary fact of death for the lovers, which was inevitable in the nature of their own passion, but in the secondary aspect of that death as a sacrifice required for the healing of the feud between their families.

With *Richard II* (1595–6) Shakespeare reached the peak of his achievement in English historical tragedy. The play has been most remembered and dismembered on account of the 'patriotic passages (II, i), which are still undimmed in beauty after excessive repetition. Richard himself is the first of those Shakespeare characters whose tragedy consists in their own excess of poetic sensibility, which Shakespeare seemed to regard —out of what self-knowledge we cannot guess—as a mainspring of tragedy. Such excess disables Macbeth for evil and Hamlet for the rough justice of revenge; while it immobilizes Richard and disables him for kingship:

> For Gods sake let us sit upon the ground,
> And tell sad stories of the death of Kings:
> How some have been depos'd, some slaine in warre,
> Some haunted by the Ghosts they have depos'd,
> Some poyson'd by their Wives, some sleeping kill'd,
> All murther'd. For within the hollow Crowne
> That rounds the mortall Temples of a King,
> Keepes Death his Court, and there the Antique sits
> Scoffing his State, and grinning at his Pompe,
> Allowing him a breath, a little Scene,
> To Monarchize, be fear'd, and kill with lookes,
> Infusing him with selfe and vaine conceit,
> As if this Flesh, which walls about our Life,
> Were Brasse impregnable: and humor'd thus,
> Comes at the last, and with a little Pinne
> Bores through his Castle Walls, and farwell King.[1]

In contrast with Richard, Bolingbroke is the calculating man of action whose will is under self-command as he moves towards his determined goal, using whatever human or other instrument comes serviceably to hand. Shakespeare's *Richard II* became involved in the political troubles of Elizabeth's reign. The abdication scene was excised before the First Quarto appeared;

[1] III, ii. In the first line of this passage 'Gods' from the First Quarto (1597) is preferred to the Folio's 'Heavens'. In line 8 modern editors print 'antick' or 'antic' in place of 'Antique'.

and the Lord Chamberlain's Men were commissioned by some of the Earl of Essex's adherents to put on *Richard II* two days before the abortive plot to capture the Queen and her ministers of state was launched on 8 February 1601. Though no penalty seems to have fallen upon Shakespeare or the actors, Elizabeth was incensed by the popularity of this play and thought herself signified in the character of Richard.

A Midsummer Night's Dream (1595–6) may be said to have rounded off Shakespeare's first phase, for it proved that his power in comedy and romance was as great as he had shown it to be in tragedy and history. *A Midsummer Night's Dream* is also a masterpiece of construction, the themes involving the several sets of characters (Theseus and Hippolyta; Hermia and Lysander, Helena and Demetrius; Oberon and Titania; Bottom and the Craftsmen; with Puck as intermediary between the world and fairyland) being interwoven with exceptional skill and complete success. The craftsmen's play is both honest fun and glorious parody of the current passion for classical material in drama; and the nearly tiresome lovers never become entirely so, since their languishings are always held in check so far as the audience is concerned by the interventions and mischief of Puck. In spite of its fictional location in Athens and a wood near it, *A Midsummer Night's Dream* was the most English thing Shakespeare had done up to that time; the country scenes and the rustic characters are pure Warwickshire. The fairy scenes are perfectly imagined and perfectly executed, simple enough for the very young and sensible enough for the mature, never coy or mawkish. The greatest triumph of all, perhaps, is the complete control of the play and its atmosphere by the poetry, at the heart of which is the finest compliment ever paid to the Queen (II, i):

> Flying betweene the cold Moone and the earth,
> *Cupid* all arm'd; a certaine aime he tooke
> At a faire Vestall, throned by the West,
> And loos'd his love-shaft smartly from his bow,
> As it should pierce a hundred thousand hearts,
> But I might see young Cupids fiery shaft
> Quencht in the chaste beames of the watry Moone;
> And the imperial Votresse passed on,
> In maiden meditation fancy free.

Despite the high praise it received from some nineteenth-century writers *King John* (1596–7) does not reach the level of the historical plays which preceded and followed it, and it can be passed by here. Yet Shakespeare was then almost at the height of his powers, *The Merchant of Venice* (1596–7) containing, besides some most memorable passages of poetry, one of his greatest characters in Shylock. We interpret Shylock sympathetically, but he was probably less so to Elizabethan audiences, though Shakespeare drew him with objective understanding and without glossing over the contemptibility of the Gentiles who baited him. Portia is among the best of Shakespeare's women characters, yet it cannot be overlooked that the judgment she obtains against Shylock in court is based upon a legal quibble as preposterous as the terms of the contract which Shylock sought to establish.

The two parts of *Henry IV* (1597–8) are dominated—in certain respects over-dominated, in modern opinion—by Falstaff, who is unsurpassed among the comic characters in English literature and perhaps the supreme instance of a character who becomes greater than his creator intended. The first full-length critical study of him, Maurice Morgann's *Essay on the Dramatic Character of Sir John Falstaff* (1777), described him as 'a robber, a glutton, a cheat, a drunkard, and a liar; lascivious, vain, insolent, profligate, and profane . . .', yet with his counterbalancing qualities and the interaction of all the elements in the other characters he appears as a man of 'perfect good-nature, pleasantry, mellowness, and hilarity of mind'. Many harsh comments have been made upon Prince Hal, who roistered with Falstaff as his boon companion, only to reject him at once on becoming Henry V:

> I know thee not, old man: Fall to thy Prayers:
> How ill white haires become a Foole, and Jester.
> I have long dream'd of such a kinde of man,
> So surfeit-swell'd, so old, and so prophane:
> But being awake, I do despise my dreame. . . .[1]

Soon after, Falstaff is committed to the Fleet Prison. This personal treachery, as it seems, of Henry is dramatically the extension to a comic hero of the familiar Elizabethan tragic device of the sudden catastrophic turn of Fortune's wheel. It

---

[1] *Henry IV*, Part II (V, v).

might also be read as Shakespeare's own revenge upon a character self-grown beyond the stature originally intended for him. In fairness to Henry V, if the charge of treachery has to be met, it must be said that rejection of Falstaff was inescapable. He was an impossible figure to be in the entourage of a king, and he would have been most unlikely to absent himself voluntarily from Court. Shakespeare so far relented as to make his death scene in *Henry V* intensely moving and poetic, even though the event is only reported.

A supportable claim could be made for *Much Ado About Nothing* (1598-9) as the most brilliantly and buoyantly witty of Shakespeare's plays, though it is curiously and not altogether congruously shadowed by near-tragedy in the church scene (IV, i) where the misled Claudio lays his baseless charge of unchastity against Hero. Compared with *As You Like It* and *Twelfth Night*, the play lacks freshness and innocence. However delightful they may be in their intellectual adroitness, Beatrice and Benedick are more 'knowing' than is altogether comfortable for an audience: theirs is wry humour with an aftertaste. The low-comedy scenes introducing Dogberry and Verges are deliciously nonsensical.

The old view that *Henry V* (1598-9) is a straightforward historical play charged with stirring patriotic sentiment, exciting battle scenes, fine rhetorical speeches, rich comedy, and an impressive full-length character-portrait of an extrovert king, has to some extent been replaced by endeavours to read into it philosophical and psychological significances which might have surprised Shakespeare. It has in Pistol one of his most gloriously comic swashbucklers.

The first of Shakespeare's Roman plays, *Julius Cæsar* (1599-1600), is in characterization and construction the most satisfying of the group. It is less heavily sombre than *Coriolanus* and more closely knit than *Antony and Cleopatra* (both plays of later date), and though *Julius Cæsar* comes far short of the latter in poetic splendour, Mark Antony's public speech over the body of Cæsar is among the most effective pieces of mob oratory ever written, and has considerably more subtlety than most mob orators have wit enough to use. From a cast of over thirty named characters only three are really outstanding—Brutus, Cassius, and Antony—yet these three focus the whole play and prevent any such dispersion of interest as shatters *Antony and Cleopatra* from the standpoint of dramatic coherence.

In *As You Like It* (1599–1600) the conventional Renaissance pastoral play is transfigured into true human comedy in a natural country setting. Rosalind shares with Viola in *Twelfth Night* (1599–1600) the first place among Shakespeare's non-tragic girl heroines. Both are entirely lovable: Rosalind the more sunnily witty and lighthearted; Viola more poetic in spirit and with a fuller capacity for deep feeling. To Rosalind are given some of Shakespeare's most enchantingly carefree lines, as in her answers to Orlando's question "What were his markes?' after she has said that her uncle taught her to know a man in love:

> A leane cheeke, which you have not: a blew eie and sunken, which you have not: an unquestionable spirit, which you have not: a beard neglected, which you have not: (but I pardon you for that, for simply your having in beard is a yonger brothers revennew) then your hose should be ungarter'd, your bonnet unbanded, your sleeve unbutton'd, your shoo unti'de, and everie thing about you, demonstrating a carelesse desolation: but you are no such man; you are rather point device in your accoustrements, as loving your selfe, then [than] seeming the Lover of any other.

When in *Twelfth Night* the Duke asks Viola (masquerading as the young man Cesario) the history of her father's daughter (actually herself) who, as she tells him, loved a man, she answers, speaking obliquely of her own love for the Duke:

> . . . she never told her love,
> But let concealment like a worme i'th budde
> Feede on her damaske cheeke: she pin'd in thought,
> And with a greene and yellow melancholly,
> She sate like Patience on a Monument,
> Smiling at greefe. Was not this love indeede?
> We men may say more, sweare more but indeed
> Our shewes are more then [than] will: for still we prove
> Much in our vowes, but little in our love.

The difference in tone between these passages marks precisely the difference between Rosalind's character and temperament and Viola's. In other respects also the two comedies are in clear contrast. The melancholy of Jaques in *As You Like It* is hardly more than a pose, but throughout *Twelfth Night* there is a poignant undertone of sadness. The two plays contain, again in contrast, Shakespeare's two principal Fools, Touchstone and Feste. The latter's foolery is never entirely carefree, and his final song 'When that I was and a little tiny boy' is a coda with 'a dying fall,' as the Duke says of the music with which *Twelfth Night* opens.

'We get nowhere in our appreciation of *Hamlet* if we allow ourselves for one moment to forget that, however wonderful and profound a "study in human nature" Shakespeare's genius and insight made of it, the play of *Hamlet* is, in its essence, a superb melodrama of revenge, a play for the Elizabethan stage.'[1] In other words, we get nowhere if we lose sight of the story in *Hamlet* (1600-1) and concentrate lopsidedly on theories concerning the personality of Hamlet himself.

Hamlet, prince of Denmark, suspects that his father has been murdered by Claudius, his uncle, who has mounted the throne and speedily married the dead king's wife. The appearance to him of his father's ghost at the castle of Elsinore confirms Hamlet's suspicion and he undertakes to revenge the murder. Although at the ghost's revelation Hamlet is all haste to 'sweep to my revenge', he falls into a persistent mood of thinking too precisely upon the event. His melancholy demeanour sows fears in Claudius's guilty conscience, and to quieten this obvious alarm Hamlet feigns madness, which is taken to be an emotional disturbance due to his passion for Ophelia, daughter of the sententious old court chamberlain Polonius. When a company of strolling players visits the castle Hamlet has a play acted before Claudius in which the events match the circumstances of the late king's murder. Claudius, having by his manner betrayed his guilt to the watching Hamlet, plots to send him on a mission to England in the company of two courtiers, Rosencrantz and Guildenstern, who are to bear a warrant for Hamlet's assassination. Immediately after the play scene Hamlet is summoned by his mother to her chamber, where Polonius conceals himself behind the hangings. When she tells her son that he has offended the king, Hamlet in a passion of bitter torment and disgust reveals Claudius's crime and faces

---

[1] M. R. Ridley: Preface to 'The New Temple Shakespeare' edition of *Hamlet* (London, Dent, 1934). See also J. Dover Wilson: *What Happens in Hamlet* (Cambridge University Press, 2nd edn. 1951).

her with her own lust. When she calls for help, Hamlet, thinking it is Claudius that is in hiding, runs his sword through the arras and kills Polonius. In the later part of the scene the Ghost reappears to urge him again to his 'almost blunted purpose' of revenge. Hamlet departs for England, but on the ship he discovers the warrant for his death, substitutes another which will ensure the execution of Rosencrantz and Guilderstern when they reach England, and during a fight with pirates next day is captured by them and sent back to Denmark. Hamlet's strange behaviour had meanwhile unhinged Ophelia, and in her madness she falls into a stream while reaching for flowers and is drowned. Laertes, her brother, having come back from abroad to avenge his father finds that his sister also is dead. The returned Hamlet, while walking with his friend Horatio in a churchyard, meets the funeral procession and thus learns of Ophelia's end. Seeing the grief-stricken Laertes leap into the open grave to take a last farewell of his sister, Hamlet follows him and they struggle together before the attendants part them. Claudius, persuading Laertes that his father was wilfully murdered by Hamlet, arranges a fencing match between the two young men, in which Laertes' rapier will be poisoned. Laertes wounds Hamlet but drops his sword, which Hamlet then exchanges for his own, and Laertes too is struck with the poisoned weapon. The queen has in the meantime drunk to Hamlet's success from a poisoned cup intended for Hamlet if he should escape unwounded in the contest. Laertes reveals the stratagem of the fatal rapier to Hamlet and the queen realizes that she has drunk poison. Hamlet then stabs Claudius and forces the remainder of the poisoned drink into his mouth. The queen dies, Claudius dies, Laertes dies, Hamlet dies. Fortinbras, prince of Norway (whom the dying Hamlet has nominated for the succession) enters with English ambassadors. He gives orders for Hamlet's body to be borne off with military ceremonial—*and life goes on*. These final moments in *Hamlet* are of extreme importance, for they represent the continuance of life in the world beyond the corpse-strewn hall of the castle.

This bare telling of the plot of *Hamlet* shows how good a plot it is, Shakespeare's best, however much of it he may have drawn from the Norse legend in the twelfth-century Danish history by Saxo Grammaticus and from an earlier Hamlet play (perhaps by Thomas Kyd) which is known to have existed, though no copy survives. Modern attention has been much concentrated upon Hamlet's four great soliloquies beginning 'O that this too too sullied flesh would melt' (I, ii), 'O, what a rogue and peasant slave am I' (II, ii), 'To be, or not to be' (III, i), 'How all occasions do inform against me' (IV, iv), since these accord with the metaphysical temper of our time and serve as windows opening into the mind of Hamlet, showing his disgust with a world in which women are frail and incestuous and a king may be no better than a satyr; his contempt of himself who for a murdered father can summon less passion than the First Player does for an imagined crime; his 'dread of something after death' which closes the way to suicide; his consciousness of being unstirred to action even by the 'excitements of my reason and my blood' which 'a father kill'd, a mother stain'd' should provide, whereas those in the army of Fortinbras (which he had just watched pass by)

> . . . fortune, death and danger dare,
> Even for an egg-shell. Rightly to be great
> Is not to stir without great argument,
> But greatly to find quarrel in a straw
> When honour's at the stake.[1]

That Samuel Johnson should have written that 'the pretended madness of Hamlet causes much mirth' warns us that the eighteenth century did not see *Hamlet* as we see it and that Elizabethans would have seen it still more differently. The Ghost is little but a piece of stage machinery to us; to them it would more likely appear a genuinely impressive portent of the supernatural. While to us the play has become increasingly an intellectual exercise, to them it would be at once a thrilling entertainment and a spectacle heavy with the slowly creeping doom which the text holds and performance should intensify.

Hardly anyone can have thought the better of Queen Elizabeth for commanding (if she did) that Shakespeare should write a play showing Falstaff in love. *The Merry Wives of Windsor* (1600–1) is a pleasant affair, but Falstaff's reputation is not enhanced by his antics in it. *Troilus and Cressida* (1601–2) is

[1] This soliloquy appears in Quartos 2–4, but is omitted from the First Folio. The passage quoted here is from the modern Oxford edition.

unclassifiable among the kinds of drama: it is not tragedy nor comedy nor tragi-comedy. It is cynical and bitter as gall. Cressida is wanton, but not alluring as a stage-character; Thersites spits venom; Pandarus is a lubricious go-between. No other treatment of the Greek story is in greater contrast with Chaucer's *Troilus and Criseyde*, which has sunny beauty and tenderness, whereas Shakespeare's play tears away every shred of illusion. *All's Well that Ends Well* (1602–3) is as rarely performed as *Troilus and Cressida*, for, though its tone is less harsh, it has an unconvincing plot (of a girl-wife who by strategem imposes herself maritally upon a young husband who forswore her after an unwilling marriage), and no such excellence of characterization as might compensate. The theme of chastity and wantonness was much in Shakespeare's mind at this period and in *Measure for Measure* (1604–5) it is presented in sombre tones which belie the description of the play as a comedy. The text appears to have been subjected to a good deal of unskilful tinkering, and although attempts have been made to establish this among Shakespeare's greater works on the plea that it has subtleties and profundities undetected by earlier critics, it receives only limited approval, except for the one great though painful scene (III, i) in prison, where Claudio endeavours to save his life at the price of his sister Isabella's degradation. Some of Shakespeare's finest lines are given to Claudio and Isabella:

> CLAUDIO: If I must die,
> I will encounter darknesse as a bride,
> And hugge it in mine armes
>
> .   .   .   .   .
>
> CLAUDIO: Death is a fearefull thing
>
> ISABELLA: And shamed life, a hatefull.
>
> CLAUDIO: I [Ay], but to die, and go we know not where
> To lie in cold obstruction, and to rot,
> This sensible warme motion, to become
> A kneaded clod; And the delighted spirit
> To bath in fierie floods, or to recide
> In thrilling Region of thicke-ribbed Ice,
> To be imprison'd in the viewlesse windes
> And blowne with restlesse violence round about
> The pendant world: . . .

Following *Measure for Measure* came in succession the great
tragedies: *Othello* (1604–5), *King Lear* (1605–6), *Macbeth* (1605–6),
Antony and Cleopatra (1606–7), *Coriolanus* (1607–8). *Othello* differs
from all the rest of Shakespeare's tragedies in having as its chief
figure a man who has no inherent fatal flaw in his nature, but
is fatally vulnerable through the unblemished nobility which
disables him from conceiving the existence of pure evil as in
Iago. The villainy of Iago which is glaringly patent to us
because we see him from a variety of angles is hidden from
Othello who sees him from a single angle only. We may feel
that Othello suspected Desdemona's fidelity on ludicrously
flimsy evidence, but again it must be appreciated that his love
for her was his most delicately sensitive spot, that jealousy is the
most illogical and most consuming of passions, and that he was
incapable of supposing that anyone would bring such a charge
unless there were genuine grounds for it. If, as seems the case,
Shakespeare held excess of any kind to be a fault with tragic
potentialities, Othello's fault was excess of nobility. Shakespeare's greatest achievement in the play is Iago: the deathly
evil of his character is bottomless and in his own kind he has
no equal in all literature.

'*King Lear* seems to me Shakespeare's greatest achievement,
but it seems to me not his best play.'[1] This sentence expresses
what many have felt about this supreme work. As poetic drama
it is unequalled; as a stage play it has to be pressed into a mould
—and the precise truth about *King Lear* is that its greatness
consists in its having shattered every mould before it left its
creator's mind. The stage can only dwarf it, and when dwarfed
it ceases to be the *Lear* that Shakespeare intended, the *Lear* in
which the whole universe is split into its primal elements and
chaos is come again. It is faulty in its very greatness, inasmuch
as it suffers from *excess* of greatness and in that way itself offends
against the Shakespearean principle.

Macbeth links on to *Richard II* through the excessive poetic
sensibility of the chief character. Macbeth is immobilized by
words again and again: and to be immobilized by words means,
at root, excess of imagination. Macbeth and Lady Macbeth are
Shakespeare's most human villains; they excite sympathy because they are caught so inescapably in the toils of their own

[1] A. C. Bradley: *Shakespearean Tragedy* (Macmillan, London, 1904).

nature, so that here fate and personal character become virtually identical.

In a particular sense *Antony and Cleopatra* and *Romeo and Juliet* are complementary, the earlier play being lit by the white fire of youthful passion which is free from commitments to the world, whereas the love of Antony and Cleopatra is the flickering sultry fire of passion which licks destructively beyond the two to the world in which they figure on a larger than personal stage. *Antony and Cleopatra* is one of the most difficult plays to hold in a single coherent vision: its many changes of scene produce a semblance of disunity and fragmentation and almost cinematic movement. The famous passages of poetry are perhaps too evident as jewels, wonderful though they are; and the characters are realized poetically rather than dramatically. But Shakespeare rarely excelled the lengthy final scene culminating in Cleopatra's self-sought death.

Among Shakespeare's greater plays *Coriolanus* is the only one that can be said to be interesting rather than compelling. Though it has more variety of character and incident than is sometimes remembered, as a play it is curiously colourless. But the characteristic Roman quality of *gravitas* is more marked here than in any other of Shakespeare's Roman plays, and Volumnia is a Roman mother of titanic impressiveness.

Timon of Athens (1607-8) is more touched by detestation of the world and the people in it than appears directly anywhere else in Shakespeare. *Pericles, Prince of Tyre* (1608-9), is unimportant. *Cymbeline* (1609-10) is irradiated by the lovely character of the wronged Imogen, Cymbeline's daughter and wife of Posthumous, who is led to doubt Imogen's honesty by Iachimo, a pale shadow of Iago. It also contains the two lovely songs 'Hark, hark! the lark at heaven's gate sings' and 'Fear no more the heat o' the sun.' The jealousy of Leontes in *The Winter's Tale* (1610-11) is incomparably more motiveless than that of Othello, and by being so it robs the play of serious interest and throws us back for compensation upon the attractions of the country scenes and the pleasant curiosity provided by the restoration scene in which the supposed dead Hermione is given back to her once jealous but long repentant husband as a living statue after sixteen years. *The Tempest* (1611-12) concluded Shakespeare's work for the theatre (except for whatever

part he may have had in the writing of *Henry VIII*) and in it
he incorporated the speech (V, i) delivered by the retiring
magician Prospero, the end of which is traditionally taken as
Shakespeare's own farewell to the stage:

> Graves at my command
> Have wak'd their sleepers, op'd, and let 'em forth
> By my so potent Art. But this rough Magicke
> I heere abjure: and when I have requir'd
> Some heavenly Musicke (which even now I do)
> To worke mine end upon their Sences, that
> This Ayrie-charme is for, I'le break my staffe,
> Bury it certaine fadomes in the earth,
> And deeper then did ever Plummet sound
> Ile drowne my booke.

No final conclusion has been reached in regard to the authorship of *Henry VIII* (1612–13), but the weight of opinion assigns
it in part to Shakespeare (I, i–ii; II, iii–iv; III, ii in part; V, i)
and the remainder to John Fletcher. This gives Katherine's
trial scene and the best of Wolsey's speeches to Shakespeare,
but not Buckingham's farewell (II, i) which Hazlitt and others
have thought good enough for Shakespeare at his best.

This uncertainty about *Henry VIII* brings up the whole matter
of publication of the plays. *Henry VIII* first appeared in print
in the First Folio, 1623, seven years after Shakespeare's death.
The volume contained thirty-six plays, eighteen of which had
not been published before. *Pericles* (first issued in Quarto, 1609)
was omitted, but included in a later folio edition. The First
Folio was printed for publication by Isaac Jaggard and Ed.
Blount and edited by John Heminges (or Heming) and Henry
Condell, who had been actors in Shakespeare's company,
Heminges being possibly the first to play Falstaff. In their
prefatory note to the First Folio the editors amplify the claim
on the title page that the plays are 'according to the True
Originall Copies' by the statement that readers had previously
been given only stolen and surreptitious copies, maimed and
deformed by the frauds of injurious impostors. This refers to
the eighteen separate plays published in quarto size during
Shakespeare's lifetime. It is certain, then, that none of the plays
was prepared for publication by the author himself. From this

it is reasonable to deduce that he took no interest in having his plays printed[1] and set no value upon them as 'literature': their life for him was confined to performance on the stage. From what source, then, did the publishers of the Quartos obtain their manuscript copies for the printers' use? Some of the texts in these editions are so bungled and corrupt that they must have been written out, at least in part, from memory—either by a spectator or by some employee in the theatre. No system of shorthand adequate for verbatim reporting existed at the time, and since both reliable and unreliable passages sometimes exist in one and the same Quarto, the material was most probably supplied by an actor who had memorized (or had access to prompt copies of) certain speeches and relied on faulty recollection for the remainder. It has to be added that not all the Quarto editions are bad, and that the First Folio follows a number of the more reliable ones, or uses an identical text. In certain instances the versions used by Heminges and Condell are inferior to previously published ones, no doubt because the particular 'authentic' text upon which they relied was one that had been cut or amended somewhat clumsily for acting: for example, while the First Quarto (1603) of *Hamlet* is extremely bad, the Second (1604), Third (1611), and Fourth (undated) Quartos are better than the Folio, which gives only a 'cut' acting-version.

Much has been written about the sources upon which Shakespeare drew for the plot-material of his plays, since he exercised his imagination by transmuting rather than by inventing, though when he did invent—as he appears to have done largely in *A Midsummer Night's Dream*—the result was exceptionally happy. For the English historical plays, and in some degree for *King Lear*, *Macbeth*, and *Cymbeline*, he made use of Holinshed's *Chronicles*; for the Roman plays the chief source was North's translation of Plutarch's *Lives*. Boccaccio, Bandello, and other Italian writers whose works were popular in translation provided Shakespeare no less than other Elizabethans

---

[1] It should be remembered in this connection that the rights in acted plays were the property of the theatre managements, who understandably discouraged the printing of 'authorized' texts which might be utilized by rival companies.

with subjects; Ovid in translation also saturated the Elizabethan mind; while contemporary events (such as voyages of discovery in relation to *The Tempest*) and currents of political thought have to be considered as overt and covert influences on the literature of the age. The modern popular notion that it is shabby and rather shameful for a writer not to invent his own plots, ignores major considerations: first, that plots are not infinite in number—there are few indeed; second, that great writers deal with great themes, all of which are in essence familiar. No one thinks the less of the Greek tragic dramatists because they used stories then known to everyone. If they had not done so—if they had not illuminated afresh the vital age-old concerns of men and gods—they would have been accounted not 'original' but impious. In two instances when Shakespeare chose to build upon contemporary works his transforming power was brilliantly displayed. The charming but at bottom insipid pastoral romance *Rosalynde*, by Thomas Lodge, became *As You Like It*; and the tedious novel *Pandosto*, by Robert Greene, became *The Winter's Tale*, with characters (including Autolycus) added by Shakespeare himself. (Greene, however, does at least make Leontes' jealousy comprehensible.)

If Shakespeare had written nothing but his *Sonnets* he would still have a secure place among the great poets. Much ingenious cudgelling of brains has been given to attempts to identify the 'Mr. W. H.' to whom the first edition (1609) was dedicated by the publisher (not by the author) and the woman (the so-called 'dark lady') referred to in one group of the sonnets by the repeated application of the word 'black'. The chief candidate for Mr. W. H. remains Henry Wriothesley, Earl of Southampton[1] (the reversal of initials in Elizabethan dedications and other printed references was a common ruse), and Mary Fitton, one of the Queen's maids of honour, is as good a guess as any for the woman. The intensity of emotion in the *Sonnets* leaves no room for doubt in most readers' minds that they relate to Shakespeare's personal experiences, and are not conventional poetic exercises. But what those experiences were is no more

[1] Unless, as Sir Sidney Lee (*Life of Shakespeare*, 1898; 1925) declared, Mr. W. H. was only the surreptitious procurer of the manuscript of the *Sonnets* for the pirate-publisher Thomas Thorpe.

than allusively hinted, and it may well be that Shakespeare desired only to transmit the sensation of the experiences, not to give a riddling transcript of actual relationships or episodes. Individually, almost any one of his 154 sonnets equals the best of the sonnets written by other English poets; taken entire the sequence is the matchless lyric achievement of English poetry in its greatest age.

DESCRIPTIVE NOTES
TO THE ILLUSTRATIONS

These are grouped into two categories: a. Plates; b. Illustrations in the text.

1 (cf. text p. 2)

The so-called '*Caedmon*' Manuscript. Bodleian Library MS. Junius XI, f. 81. English, *c.* 1000. 12¾ × 7½ *in.*

This manuscript consists of a verse paraphrase of Genesis, Exodus, Daniel, and other poems. It was probably produced at Christ Church, Canterbury, but is assigned by some critics to Winchester.

The scenes here illustrate Genesis xv. 8–12. *Above*, Nimrod sending out his princes, who carry mallets for building, from Babylon to enlarge his boundaries. *Below*, 'Nimrod a mighty hunter before the Lord'.

These illustrations are by the second hand of the manuscript, whose work seems to run from f. 75 to f. 88.

2 and 3 (cf. text p. 7)

Brut, B.M. MS. Egerton 3028, ff. 25 and 30. English, mid XIVth century.

2, approximately three-fifths actual size; 3, approximately three-quarters actual size (British Museum copyright photographs).

This manuscript is an abridgement in French verse of Wace's verse chronicle of English History, but continues up to the beginning of the Hundred Years War (1338). The author's knowledge of this period is obviously very scanty as there are many incorrect statements.

The red and white dragons, representing the Saxons and the Britons, were discovered as Merlin had prophesied, fighting beneath Vortigern's tower. Vortigern was King of the Britons at the time of the arrival of the Saxons under Hengist and Horsa in the fifth century.

The drawing of Stonehenge, built (we are told) with the help of Merlin, is perhaps the earliest attempt to depict that famous monument.

4 (cf. text p. 7)

Geoffrey of Monmouth. *Prophetia Anglicana Merlini Ambrosii Britanni.* B.M. MS. Cott. Claudius B. VII, f. 224. English, *c.* 1250–1270. Approximately two-thirds actual size (British Museum copyright photograph).

The *Prophetia Merlini* was translated into rhymed Latin couplets from the Welsh at the request of Alexander, Bishop of Lincoln. It was probably produced separately before Geoffrey's *Historia Regum Britanniæ* was finished.

This illustration again shows the two dragons under Vortigern's tower, while Merlin, standing on a cloud, shows his prophecy to Vortigern. (See 2.)

5 (cf. text p. 11)

Gawayne and the Grene Knight. B.M. MS. Cott. Nero A. x, f. 90v. English, late XIVth or early XVth century. $6\frac{1}{2} \times 4\frac{5}{8}$ *in.*

King Arthur and Queen Guinevere at high table; on the left we seem to have Gawaine after he has obtained the boon from the King, and the subsequent holding out of the severed head by the Green Knight is shown below. The Queen, affrighted, clings to King Arthur. The figure on the right may be Agravayn a la Dure Main and the objects on the table are possibly salts.

6 (cf. text p. 11)

Pearl. B.M. MS. Cott. Nero A. x, f. 38. English, late XIVth or early XVth century. $6\frac{1}{2} \times 4\frac{5}{8}$ *in.*

The four illustrations to *Pearl* show the main scenes. Here the dead child Pearl appears in his vision to the Poet (lines 193–228). Her costume, which does not tally with the detailed description given in the poem, is of the time of Richard II and Henry IV.

The illustrations to *Pearl, Cleanness, Patience* and *Gawaine and the Grene Knight,* twelve in all, are of very poor quality.

7 (cf. text p. 14)

William Langland, *Piers Plowman.* Corpus Christi College, Oxford. MS. 201, f. 1. English, last third of the XIVth century. Approximately actual size.

The illumination shows Piers Plowman sleeping on the Malvern Hills by a stream

'And as I lay and lened and loked in the wateres,
    I slombred in a slepyng'.

The text is of the second version.

8 (cf. text p. 14)

William Langland, *Piers Plowman.* Trinity College, Cambridge. MS. B 15.17. English, last third of XIVth century. Approximately half actual size.

This manuscript which is decorated with slightly ornate initials is in a clear book hand. The lines shown are the opening of passus I, the *Vision of Holy Church.* The manuscript is one of the best two texts of the second version.

9, 10 and 11 (cf. text p. 26)

Geoffrey Chaucer, *The Canterbury Tales,* The Huntington Library, San Marino, California, MS. El 26 C 12, ff. 127v., 76 and 80v. English, early XVth century. 9 and 10 approximately three-fifths actual size, 11 approximately two-fifths actual size.

This manuscript, known as the Ellesmere Chaucer since it has been in the Ellesmere family since the XVIIth century, is one of the most attractive manuscripts of *The Canterbury Tales.* For the beginning of each tale there is an elaborate border and the figure of the pilgrim. There is also the figure of Chaucer at the beginning of the Tale of Melibeus.

12 (cf. text p. 17)
Thomas Hoccleve, *De Regimine Principum*. B.M. MS. Harley 4866, f. 88.
English, early XVth century. 10½ × 7 *in.* (British Museum copyright
photograph.)
This is the earliest surviving portrait of Chaucer, and is probably the
source of the other known portraits. It was painted from memory after
Chaucer's death to illustrate Hoccleve's lines on him. For a full discus-
sion of this and other so-called portraits of Chaucer, see M. H. Spielmann,
The Portraits of Geoffrey Chaucer (Chaucer Society, 1900).

13 (cf. text p. 23)
Geoffrey Chaucer, *Troilus and Criseyde*, Corpus Christi College, Cam-
bridge, MS. 61, Frontispiece, English, *c.* 1400. 9¼ × 4⅜ *in.* (British
Museum copyright photograph).
One of the finest existing English miniatures of the period. It represents
Chaucer addressing a noble company, which includes a prince in a
golden robe. In the group by the castle is a queen and her attendants.
There is a wide decorative border round the central illustration. The
manuscript of which this is the frontispiece is one of the best texts of
the poem.

14 (cf. text p. 28)
The Equatorie of the Planetis, Cambridge, Peterhouse MS. 75 (1), f. 74,
1392. 14½ × 11 *in.* Reproduced by permission of the Syndics of the
Cambridge University Press from a photograph in their possession.
Chaucer's interest in astronomy is well known, particularly on account
of his *Treatise on the Astrolabe*. The manuscript volume from which the
present illustration is taken was written in 1392 and may conceivably
be another treatise by Chaucer. If this were so, we should have, for the
first time, an example of Chaucer's handwriting as the manuscript is
clearly an author's heavily corrected holograph draft. This might lead
to the identification of further manuscripts by Chaucer and would also
be of great help in textual criticism as it would give an uncorrupted
specimen of his language and spelling.
In any case it is an extremely interesting example of early technical
writing in English.
Like the *Astrolabe* the treatise appears to be drawn from some Arabic
or Persian source. The *equatorie* was an instrument for determining the
position of the planets with respect to the circle of the Zodiac. The
page illustrated shows the *epicycle* alone and the complete Equatorie,
set in position for determining the position of the Moon. (For a fuller
description of the MS. see *The Times Literary Supplement* for 29 February
and 7 March 1952, 'The Equatorie of the Planetis', by Dr. Derek Price.)

15 (cf. text p. 33)
John Gower, *Confessio Amantis*, B.M. MS. Egerton 1991, f. 7v. English,
early XVth century. 3⅛ × 3⅛ *in.*
This scene illustrates lines 200–202 in Book I.

> The selve Prest, which as sche wolde
> was redy there and sette him doun
> to hiere my confessioun.

The text of the manuscript is an imperfect one of the earlier version of the poem, which is dedicated to Richard II.

16 (cf. text p. 33)

John Gower, *Vox Clamantis*, B.M. MS. Cott. Tiberius A. iv, f. 9*v*. English, mid XVth century. 9 × 6¼ *in*. (British Museum copyright photograph).

This illumination comes at the end of the index giving the subject matter of each chapter. It illustrates a quatrain, in which the author warns evildoers to beware of his shafts though the innocent have no need to fear his words. The divisions into which the world is divided may represent the four elements: water below and above, air and fire on the left and earth on the right.

17 (cf. text p. 33)

Detail of John Gower's monument in Southwark Cathedral. (Photograph by the National Buildings Record.)

The effigy of the poet, which is life size, shows his head resting on his three great books, and lies under a three-arched canopy. He wears a crown of roses and ivy and a collar with Henry IV's badge of a swan. The original paintings of Charity, Mercy, and Pity in the three arches, and the inscription: *Hic jacet J. Gower, arm. Angl. poeta celeberrimus ac huic sacro edificio benefac. insignis. Vixit temporibus Ed. III et Ric. II* have disappeared, but are known from the description of the tomb in Berthelet's edition (1532) of the *Confessio Amantis*.

18 (cf. text p. 35)

John Lydgate, *Troy Book*, B.M. MS. Cott. Augustus iv, f. 98*v*. English, early XVth century. 3¼ × 3¾ *in*.

This is one of the chief manuscripts of the work written by Lydgate between 1412 and 1420. It is a translation into heroic verse of the prose *Historia Trojana* of Guido delle Colonne. The text corresponds with the edition printed by Pynson in 1513.

The six miniatures come at the beginning of the prologue and five books into which the work is divided. The one illustrated, that to book four, shows Agamemnon in his tent outside the walls of Troy, conferring with his leaders after the death of Hector. The figure in bed is that of Achilles who 'in his tente ylade w^t his woundes mortall'. The figure on the left, inside Troy, may be Priam, who came to beg from Achilles the body of his son, Hector, for burial.

19 (cf. text p. 35)

John Lydgate, B.M. MS. Harley 4826, f. 1. English, mid XVth century. 7¼ × 7⅞ *in*.

This lovely drawing, which has been inserted at the beginning of a Lydgate manuscript, shows Lydgate as a monk in Benedictine habit. He presents a pilgrim who offers *The Pilgrimage of the Life of Man* to Thomas Montacute, Earl of Salisbury. The drawing was certainly done in England, possibly by a Flemish artist, but Mr. E. G. Millar believes him to have been English. Some drawings in the Chaundler MS. at Trinity College, Cambridge, are probably by the same hand.

20 (cf. text p. 50)

Shrewsbury School. MS. Mus. iii. 42, ff. 38 and 40. English, *c.* 1400. 8⅛ × 5¾ *in.* (each sheet). Reproduced by permission of the Governing Body of Shrewsbury School.

This fragment is the earliest known manuscript of a Mystery in English. It contains the parts played by a single actor in three different plays, the words, necessary cues, and the Latin words of the Liturgy with which the plays are associated.

The parts are those of the third Shepherd in the *Officium Pastorum*, the third Mary in the *Officium Resurrecciones* and Cleophas in the *Officium Peregrinorum*.

This is the only extant example of a play in English acted during the service in a church (possibly in the Diocese of Lichfield).

F. 38 shows the beginning of the *Officium Pastorum*; after the Latin words of the Gospel come the first speeches in English. The player is given a short cue, on the right, before each of his speeches. F. 40 shows one of the sung Latin pieces, with music, which formed a part of the performance.

This type of liturgical drama was a direct development of troping. During the eighth or ninth centuries the habit arose of adding florid melodies to suitable parts of the mass—such as the Alleluia. Singers found these melodies hard to remember and eventually it was discovered that if a text was added, memorization was simplified. These tropes never formed part of the official liturgy, and occupied a secondary position outside the main body of Gregorian plainsong. Antiphonal singing lent itself to dialogue, and dramatic action was latent in the ceremonies of certain ecclesiastical rites.

(For a fuller discussion of tropes and liturgical drama, see G. Reese, *Music in the Middle Ages*, J. M. Dent & Sons, 1941, pp. 185–97.)

21 (cf. text p. 52)

Plan drawn by Renward Cysat, in the Municipal Library, Lucerne. Swiss, 1583. Approximately one-third actual size.

This is one of a pair of drawings showing the sites at which the various scenes of the Passion Play were performed. At the east end the market place is closed by the 'Haus zur sonne', against which the main platform of Heaven is built. On this is the Father Eternal with the seven angels. In front are Mount Sinai, Paradise and the Tree of Knowledge, and the garden of the Magdalene. At the west end, also on a platform, is the Christmas manger, and in the corner Hell, while scattered over the middle of the market place are small platforms for the Sacrifice of Abraham, for the Cain and Abel scene, for the tree of Zacchæus, and so on. On the second day, Sinai becomes the Mount of Olives, and the tree of Zacchæus turns into that on which Judas hangs himself.

22 (cf. text p. 52)

Hubert Cailleau, The Passion Play of Valenciennes. Paris, Bibliothèque Nationale, MS. franc. 12,536. French, 1547. 8¼ × 16½ *in.*

In this case the play was performed on a stage, but again the different scenes take place in their set positions. The stage is divided into bays by projecting buildings marked Paradise, The Temple, The Palace and Limbo and Hell, while the bays represent Nazareth, Jerusalem, The Bishops' House and the Golden Gates. Other illuminations in the manuscript show several of the scenes in progress.

23 (cf. text p. 66)

Wiclif, translation of the Bible from the Book of Proverbs to the Apocalypse inclusive, two volumes. B.M. MS. Egerton 618, f. 74. English, XIVth century. $17\frac{1}{2} \times 11\frac{3}{4}$ *in.* (British Museum copyright photograph).

This is the earlier version of the translation.

On the first leaf are blazoned the arms of Thomas of Woodstock, Duke of Gloucester, murdered in 1397. It has been suggested that these might be the 'bible en Englys en ii grantz livres covrez de rouge cuyr' in the list of objects seized by the Escheator of the counties of Hereford and Essex at Pleshey Castle and delivered to the Exchequer on 14 December 1397.

24, 25 and 26 (cf. text p. 67)

Mandeville's Travels. B.M. MS. Royal 17. C. xxxviii, ff. 28, 54 and 57. English, early XVth century. All slightly smaller than actual size.

These are three of a numerous series of illustrations in the lower margins of the manuscript. The text is an abridgement of a defective version.

27 (cf. text p. 75)

Chertsey tile in the British Museum, *c.* 1270. $9\frac{1}{2}$ *in.* diameter (reproduced from a tracing).

This is one of a series of pictorial tiles, many of them showing scenes from the Romance of Tristram, which formed part of the pavement of Chertsey Abbey. Other tiles from the same stamps have been found at the Premonstratensian Abbey of Halesowen near Birmingham. They are of red earthenware about an inch thick and the design is in cream slip. These round tiles were made to fit into a squared tile frame on which the inscriptions were written.

The scene here illustrated is the moment when Tristram, having recovered his patrimony in Brittany, goes to Tintagel and finds the nobles lamenting over their sons, of whom sixty were to be selected by lot to be sent as 'truage' to the King of Ireland.

28 (cf. text p. 75)

Morte Arthur. BM. Add. MS. 10294, f. 65*v.* French, early XIVth century. Actual size.

The *Morte Arthur* here forms the third part of *Lancelot du Lac.* The author's name is given as 'mes sites robers de borron, qui ceste estoire translata de latin en franchois'. The text of the MS. substantially agrees with the Paris edition of 1513. The scene illustrated shows the dead maid, Elaine, carried in a boat to Camelot.

This MS. and the tile (27) are two of a great variety of medieval illustrations of the Arthur legend.

29, 30, 31 and 32 (cf. text p. 81)

Hartmann Schopper *Panoplia Omnium Artium*, Frankfurt, 1568. Wood-cuts, each 3⅛ × 2⅜ *in*. From a copy in the British Museum.

This book contains descriptions in Latin and illustrations of some hundred and thirty occupations, varying from Pope and King to pedlar. These include many interesting scenes of craftsmen at work.

33 (cf. text p. 83)

Caxton presenting his *Recuyell of the Historyes of Troye* to Margaret of York, Duchess of Burgundy. Anonymous engraving, *c.* 1475. 7 × 4¾ *in*. From the Huntington Library, San Marino, California.

This is the only known copy of the engraving, which has been inserted at the beginning of a copy of the *Recuyell*. We know from the foreword that the translation was completed at the 'dredefull comandement' of Margaret of York and that the MS. was presented to her and well rewarded. The engraving may have been specially done for insertion in Margaret's own copy of the book for this copy is known to have belonged to the wife of Margaret's brother, Edward IV.

The *Recuyell* was printed in Flanders and the engraving is undoubtedly Flemish.

34 (cf. text p. 87)

Hans Holbein the younger, *Sir Thomas More and his Family*. Pen, 1526. 15⅛ × 20½ *in*. In the Basle Museum of Fine Arts.

This drawing is a careful sketch for a painting (probably ordered to com-memorate More's fiftieth birthday) which originally decorated a room in More's house in Chelsea but was destroyed, probably by fire in 1752. The annotations, which give the names and ages of the sitters, are in the hand of Nicholas Kratzer, tutor to More's children, and were probably added when the drawing was sent as a gift to Erasmus.

A copy of the painting, by Richard Locky (1530), is in the possession of Lord St. Oswald at Nostell Priory, and the drawings, by Holbein, for six of the heads are in the Royal collection at Windsor.

35 (cf. text p. 88)

Sir Thomas More, *Utopia*, Basle, Nov. 1518, p. 25. Woodcut, 2½ × 4⅛ *in*. By Ambrosius Holbein. From a copy in the British Museum.

This woodcut represents the scene in the garden of Peter Giles (to whom the preface is written) in Antwerp, in which Raphael Hythloday, the traveller, describes to the host and Sir Thomas More his ad-ventures in Utopia.

Ambrosius Holbein was the elder brother of Hans Holbein the younger and died, probably in 1518, at the age of about twenty-four. It is not always easy to distinguish the work of the two brothers.

36 (cf. text p. 97)

John Skelton, *A ryght delectable tratyse upon a goodly Garlande of Laurell*. 4°. London, 3 October 1523, back of title page. Woodcut. 4⅞ × 3 *in*. From a copy in the British Museum.

This is presumably an idealized portrait of John Skelton, shown as a young courtier holding a laurel branch in one hand and a posy of flowers in the other.

37 (cf. text p. 96)

Title page of the *Great Bible* (1539), School of Holbein. Woodcut. 13¾ × 9⅛ *in.* From a copy in the British Museum.

This title-page to *Cranmer's Bible* has been ascribed to Holbein, but is probably by one of his followers. It shows above, Henry VIII distributing *Verbum Dei*, the Bible, to the clergy and nobles; below, they in turn pass it on to the ordinary people. At the bottom the preacher reads the text from I Timothy II, v. 1. 'I exhort, therefore that, first of all, supplications, prayers intercessions and giving of thanks, be made for all men; for kings, etc.', while the people cry 'God Save the King.'

38 (cf. text p. 95)

The New Testament translated by William Tindale, assisted by William Roy, 1525. Woodcut, 5¾ × 2⅝ *in.* From the copy in the British Museum.

This is the only known fragment of the uncompleted edition of which, according to Cochlaeus, three thousand copies of the first ten sheets had been secretly printed at Cologne, when the editors were obliged to flee to Worms and there begin the work afresh. The fragment containing eight of the ten sheets gives the text of Matthew I. v. 22. It is the earliest edition of the New Testament in English.

39 (cf. text p. 95)

William Tindale, by an unknown artist, inscribed GUGLIELMUS TYNDALUS MARTYR OLIM EX AULA MAGD. Oil, 41 × 30½ *in.* From the painting at Hertford College, Oxford. (Photograph by F. R. Newens.)

40 (cf. text p. 120)

Edmund Spenser, *The Faerie Queene* (1590), p. 184. Woodcut, slightly enlarged. From a copy in the British Museum.

This woodcut is from the first edition. The publisher, William Ponsonby, procured a licence for the publication of 'The fayre Queene dysposed into xij bookes' on 1 December 1589, only a few weeks after Spenser's return to London from Ireland, and the first three books were published in the next year.

41 (cf. text p. 142)

Francis Quarles, *Emblemes*. London, 1635, p. 188. Engraving by W. Simpson. 3¼ × 2⅛ *in.* From a copy in the British Museum.

The illustration accompanies three verses, a quotation from S. Augustine and the following Epigram:

> Pilgrim trudge on: What makes thy Soule complaine,
> Crownes thy complaint: The way to rest is paine:
> The Road to Resolution lies by doubt:
> The next way Home's the farthest way about.

42 (cf. text p. 142)

Henry Peacham, *Minerva Britanna* (1612), p. 32. Woodcut, 8⅞ × 6 *in.* (page size). From a copy in the British Museum.

This poem and its illustration are dedicated *To the worthie Ladie the L:E:W* who was obviously worried by the wild behaviour of her son.

43 (cf. text p. 120)

Hans Eworth, *Queen Elizabeth Confounding Juno, Minerva and Venus.* Signed and dated 1569 H.E. Oil on Wood, 25 × 33 *in.* From Hampton Court. Reproduced by gracious permission of Her Majesty the Queen.

This is a visual representation of the type of court flattery found in *The Faerie Queene.* The picture is a *Judgement of Paris* brought up to date, with the Orb for the apple, and Queen Elizabeth for Paris, who surprises the goddesses by awarding the prize to herself. On the frame, which is the original one, are two Latin couplets which, translated, read: 'Juno is mighty with the sceptre, Pallas with wit, and beauty blooms on the rosy features of Venus. Elizabeth came and Juno fled stricken, Pallas was amazed and Venus blushed.'

Windsor Castle is seen in the background.

44 (cf. text p. 136)

Sir Philip Sidney, attributed to Federigo Zucchero inscribed ANᵒ DNI 1577 AETATIS SUAE 22. Oil, 45½ × 35½ *in.*

From the painting at Penshurst Place, by permission of The Lord De L'Isle and Dudley. This is one of several versions of the portrait; another is at Woburn.

Federigo Zucchero was an Italian painter who visited England in 1574 and painted many portraits of court personages, including Queen Elizabeth herself.

45 (cf. text p. 158)

Scene from the *Arcadia*, by Emanuel de Critz. Oil, 18½ × 72 *in.* Mid XVIIth century. Reproduced by permission of the Earl of Pembroke.

This is one of twenty-seven panels which were painted by Emanuel de Critz, an English painter of Flemish descent, for the fourth Earl of Pembroke, son of the Countess of Pembroke for whom the Arcadia was written.

The panels form a decorative frieze round the Cube room at Wilton, under the dado. These paintings are the first representations from English literature in decorative painting.

(This information was kindly supplied by Mr. E. Croft-Murray from his book on decorative painting in England to be published by *Country Life.*)

46 (cf. text p. 138)

Michaell Drayton, *Poly-Olbion.* London, 1612. Title-page engraved by William Hole. 8⅞ × 6¼ *in.* From a copy in the British Museum.

Q

The figure of Great Britain is dressed in a robe of maps with rivers, hills and towns, and carries a cornucopia of fruit and flowers. On one side are Brutus and a Saxon, on the other Cæsar and a Norman. Swags of shells, coral and crabs, decorate the arch. John Morris, an early owner of the book has written his name on the title-page.

47 (cf. text p. 133)

Sir Walter Ralegh after Marc Gheeraedts, inscribed *Sr Walter Ralegh Knight, Lord Warden of the Stanneries Governour of the Isle of Jersey and her Majesty's Lieutenant General of the Countyes of Devonshire and Cornwall* and dated *1602*. Oil, 36 × 28 *in*. From the painting at Knole, by permission of Lord Sackville.

This portrait is a contemporary copy of part of a full-length portrait of Ralegh and his son which was painted for the Carews of Beddington, the family of Lady Ralegh.

He is wearing a very elaborate white satin vest embroidered with pearls and partly covered by a brown velvet doublet. In his hat is a large ruby and pearl brooch. His portraits show him as a handsome man, six feet tall or more. Gheeraedts was a Flemish painter who settled in England during the religious wars and became painter to Queen Elizabeth. He died there before 1604.

48 (cf. text p. 134)

Sir Walter Ralegh, *History of the World*, London, 1614. Title page engraved by Renold Elstrack. 12 × 7 *in*. From a copy in the British Museum.

The world is supported by Magistra Vitæ who treads on Death and Oblivion. It is flanked by Good Reputation and Bad Reputation and below by Experience and Truth, and is watched over by the eye of Providence.

49 (cf. text p. 134)

Map of the Nile Delta. Sir Walter Ralegh's Commonplace Book. 9½ × 6¾ *in*. Reproduced by permission of Mr. W. F. Oakeshott.

This is a page from the Commonplace Book compiled by Ralegh for his *History of the World*, during his years (1603–1616) in the Tower. In addition the MS. contains a set of verses, in which his mind goes back to Cynthia, and what is presumably a list of the library he had with him. This includes atlases, travel books, Biblical commentaries, and so on, from which he drew material for his book.

The manuscript was identified in 1952 when the British Museum arranged an exhibition to celebrate the fourth centenary of the births of Ralegh and Hakluyt.

50 (cf. text p. 175)

The pleasant and stately Morall, of the Three Lordes and Three Ladies of London. 1590. Title-page woodcut, 3¾ × 4½ *in*. From a copy in the British Museum.

The scene shown is a stage, looking from the back across the actors to the audience, presumably at a private performance. The woodcut was not done for this book but is one of a set illustrating *The Trauayled Pylgrim* by Stephen Bateman, 1569, and is ultimately derived from the fifteenth-century illustrations to the *Chevalier Délibéré* of Olivier de Marche. Although it does not give an exact picture of an English performance of 1590 yet it was not considered inappropriate as a title-page to the play.

51 (cf. text p. 175)
An Enterlude for children to play named Jack Jugler both wittie and very plesant: probably after 1518–19. Title-page. Woodcut 2½ × 4¼ *in*. From the only complete copy of this, the third, edition in the Folger Shakespeare Library, Washington, D.C. A stage performance with dancers and musicians is in progress in the background of what is, clearly, a representation of the return of the prodigal son.

52 (cf. text p. 184)
Interior of the Swan Theatre, by Johannes de Witt, copied by Arend van Buchell. Pen, very slightly enlarged. MS. 842, f. 132, in the University Library, Utrecht.
This is a copy of the sketch made by the Dutchman de Witt on a visit to London in 1596, and is the only contemporary drawing of the interior of an Elizabethan theatre.
Van Buchell also recorded some of de Witt's observations in Latin. He describes the Swan as the most important and largest of the four London theatres, holding a seated audience of 3,000, built in stone, and with wooden columns which because of their marble-coloured paint, could deceive the most discerning.
It has been suggested that the scene on the stage is from *Twelfth Night*, where Malvolio appears, cross-gartered, before Maria and Olivia.

53 (cf. text p. 184)
A detail from the '*West part o(f) Southwarke toward Westminster*', by Wenceslaus Hollar. Pencil and pen, actual size. Reproduced by permission of Mr. I. A. Williams.
This is one of the sketches (done before he left England in 1644) from which Hollar etched his 'Long View of London', published in Amsterdam in 1647. In the 'Long View' the names of the Globe (on the left) and the Bear-garden are reversed and it seems probable that they were put in from memory at Antwerp. Most of the pencil lines have been inked over either by Hollar himself or by a later hand. This is probably the most reliable pre-Restoration picture of the Bankside theatres.

54 (cf. text p. 185)
Richard Burbage. Oil, 12 × 10¼ *in*. Dulwich College Picture Gallery. Reproduced by permission of the Governors.
Burbage, one of the best-known actors of his day, was closely associated

Q 2

with Shakespeare, taking principal parts in most tragedies and histories. He built both the Blackfriars and the Globe theatres. He was also known as a painter, though if this portrait is indeed by him, as is traditionally said, he was scarcely a good one.

55 (cf. text p. 185)
Edward Alleyn, artist unknown. Oil, 80 × 44¼ in. Dulwich College Picture Gallery. Reproduced by permission of the Governors.
Edward Alleyn, actor and theatre manager, was noted for his performances of tragic characters. Partly from the profits of a bear-garden, he accumulated a considerable fortune, which he used to establish The College of God's Gift in 1619. This developed into a public school (Dulwich College), Junior School, almshouses, etc. He also founded the Dulwich Picture Gallery, which houses (with other paintings) one of the most interesting collections of theatrical portraits in England.

56 (cf. text p. 195)
Shakespeare's portrait from *Mr. William Shakespeares Comedies, Histories and Tragedies*. London, 1623. Engraved by Martin Droeshout, 11½ × 6¼ in. From a copy in the National Portrait Gallery.
This portrait and the monument at Stratford are the most authoritative Shakespeare portraits, though both were done after Shakespeare's death.

57 (cf. text p. 195)
The Booke of Sir Thomas More. B.M. MS. Harley 7368, f.[9]. Half actual size. (British Museum copyright photograph.)
This manuscript is the damaged and much revised fair copy of an Elizabethan play bearing the title: *The Booke of Sir Thomas More.* Apart from that of the original scribe, five different hands occur in the seven inserted leaves. The play had also been censored by Edmund Tilney, Master of the Revels from 1579 to 1610. It appears to date from about 1600 and is supposed to be of joint authorship, one hand being most probably that of Shakespeare. The side illustrated is one of three by the fourth hand, which is believed to be his.
For a complete survey of the different theories see *Shakespeare Survey 2* (1949), 'The Booke of Sir Thomas More, and its problem,' by R. C. Bald.

58 (cf. text p. 195)
Shakespeare's signature from the deposition in the case of Belott *v.* Mountjoy, date 11 May 1612. P.R.O. Requests 4/3. Actual size. Reproduced by permission of the Public Record Office.
This is the earliest of the six undoubted signatures.

59 (cf. text p. 195)
Signature from Shakespeare's Will, dated 25 March 1616, at Somerset House. Actual size.
This signature, the last of the three on Shakespeare's will, was written shortly before his death.

60 (cf. text p. 214)

Raphael Holinshed *Chronicles*, Volume III. London, 1586, title page, 11 × 7 *in*. From a copy in the British Museum.

This is the second edition of the *Chronicles* first published in 1577 and is the edition believed to have been used by Shakespeare as the source for a number of his historical plays, for *Macbeth*, *Lear* and for part of *Cymbeline*.

61 (cf. text p. 211)

Matthew Paris, *Historia Maior*, Corpus Christi College, Cambridge. MS. 26, f. 11. XIIIth century.

Mathew Paris, a monk of St. Albans, who died in 1259, was one of the few great writers who also illustrated his own works. This lively drawing is from the first volume of his *Historia*, which goes from the Creation to the end of 1188; the second volume carries the narrative to 1233. The moment chosen is the test of love set by Lear to his three daughters. Cordelia's banner reads 'Tant as tant vouz te pris pere', which Shakespeare renders 'I love your Majesty according to my bond'. The inscriptions identifying Regan, Goneril and Cordelia are in a late XIVth-century hand.

There is considerable controversy on the subject of the sources of Shakespeare's *Lear*. The story was a popular one and first appears in Geoffrey of Monmouth's *Historia Regum Britanniæ* (*c.* 1153), professedly translated from a Welsh or Breton MS. It is also found in Wace, Layamon, and other sources before Matthew Paris.

Shakespeare certainly knew the version in Holinshed (who mentions both Geoffrey and Matthew Paris by name) and probably the version in John Higgins's enlarged editions of *A Mirrour for Magistrates* (1574, 1587), as well as the old play *King Leir* (? 1594), using some elements from each and possibly taking a hint also from Spenser's modified summary of Holinshed in *The Faerie Queene* (II, x, 27–32). The theme of Gloucester and his two sons is derived from Sir Philip Sidney's *Arcadia*.

62 (cf. text p. 200)

Illustration to Titus Andronicus, Act 1, Scene 1, line 130 (attributed to Henry Peacham, 1595). Pen and wash. Approximately three-quarters actual size. Reproduced by permission of The Most Hon. the Marquess of Bath, Longleat.

Probably the only contemporary drawing of a Shakespeare play it illustrates the moment (I, i) after Titus's refusal of Tamora's prayer, when his sons have carried away the doomed Alarbus. Tamara is accompanied by her two younger sons and Aaron her Moorish paramour, and Titus by two attendants.

There can be little doubt that this was drawn from an actual performance and it is of considerable interest that although the two attendants are apparently in 'modern dress', in the costume worn by the main characters every effort has been made to attain historical accuracy.

Below the drawing stand forty lines of text. These are taken from two different acts of the play and were probably added some twenty-five years later.

The attribution to Henry Peacham and the date 1595 are contemporary with the text but the drawing is very different from and superior to drawings known to be by Henry Peacham, author of *The Compleat Gentleman* (1622) who was only 18 or 19 in 1595.

For a fuller discussion of this drawing see *Shakespeare Survey I* (1948) p. 17: '*Titus Andronicus* on the Stage in 1594' by J. Dover Wilson.

Text illustration, p. 27

Geoffrey Chaucer *The Canterbury Tales* (? 1484). Woodcut, 4 × 4¾ *in.* From a copy in the British Museum.

This woodcut is one of a series from the second edition of *The Canterbury Tales* printed by William Caxton. The 1478 edition is unillustrated. The same woodcuts were used in the Wynkyn de Worde edition of 1498.

Text illustration, p. 57

Everyman, edited by Iohn Skot (n.d.). Title-page, woodcut, 4 × 3½ *in.* From the copy in the British Museum.

Here as in so many early English illustrations the woodcut is copied from Continental sources. The figure of Everyman is from a French edition of Terence, and Death carrying a coffin in a graveyard is from *Compost des Bergers* (1500), edited by Guy Marchant.

There are only four known surviving early copies of Everyman, each of a different edition. This gives some indication of the popularity of the work.

Text illustration, p. 67

The Voiage and Trauaile of Syr Iohn Maundeville Knight (1568), p. 185. Woodcut, 2½ × 3 *in.* From a copy in the British Museum.

From the fifth edition of *Mandeville's Travels*, this cut is a close copy of one in the second edition of 1499, printed by Wynkyn de Worde. The first edition, 1496, is unillustrated.

Text illustration, p. 78

Sir Thomas Malory, *Morte Darthur* (1498). Woodcut, 4 × 5⅛ *in.* From a copy in the John Rylands Library, Manchester.

This is from the first illustrated edition, the third, printed by Wynkyn de Worde.

Text illustration, p. 83

Jacobus de Cessolis, *The Game and Playe of the Chesse* (? 1483). Woodcut, 4 × 4¾ *in.* From a copy in the British Museum.

The earliest English illustrated books are *Paruus Cato*, by Dionysius Cato (? 1480), *The Myrrour of the Worlde*, by Bellavacensis Vicentius (? 1481), and this, the second, edition of *The Game and Playe of the Chesse*. As none of the books is dated, the order is uncertain. All three were printed by Caxton.

Text illustration, p. 90
Sir Thomas More, *Utopia*, Louvain, 1516. Woodcut 6½ × 4¾ *in.* From a copy in the British Museum.

Text illustration, p. 124
Edmund Spenser, *The Shepheardes Calender* (1579). Woodcut, 2⅞ × 4 *in.* From a copy in the British Museum.
This is the first edition and each month is illustrated by a charming woodcut of a pastoral scene. February shows the old shepherd Thenot and the herdsman's boy Cuddie; above is the sign of the Zodiac for February, Pisces.

Text illustration, p. 140
Thomas Campion, *Book of Ayres* (1613). Approximately two-thirds actual size. From a copy in the British Museum.
This three-part song is so printed that the one copy could be read by all three singers together, usually seated round a small table on which the music was laid flat.

Text illustration, p. 151
(?) John Lyly, *Pappe with an hatchet* (1589). Title-page, actual size. From a copy in the British Museum.

Text illustration, p. 176
Henry Medwall, *Fulgens and Lucrece* (n.d.). Title-page, actual size. From the only known perfect copy, in the Huntington Library, San Marino, California.
This is believed to be the earliest printed English play and was printed by John Rastell before Michaelmas 1519, probably not later than 1516.

Text illustration, p. 181
Thomas Preston, *Cambises* (*c.* 1569). Title-page, actual size. From a copy in the British Museum.
This title-page shows how the thirty-eight separate parts are divided among eight actors; one of them, perhaps a youth, takes most of the women's parts and another is obviously a child.

Text illustration, p. 188
Christopher Marlowe, *Tamburlaine the Great* (1593). Woodcut, actual size. From a copy in the British Museum.
This is from the second edition but the woodcut also appears in the first edition of 1590. Though Tamburlaine was an Oriental conqueror of the fourteenth century, he is depicted wearing sixteenth-century European armour.

Text illustration, p. 194
The Lamentable and true tragedy of Master Arden of Feversham in Kent (1633). Woodcut, 3 × 6 *in.* From a copy in the British Museum.

This illustration, from the third edition, shows the moment when the two murderers Blackwill and Shakbag attack Arden as he sits playing backgammon with Mosbie, his wife's lover. Backgammon is said to have been invented in the tenth century and a similar game was known to the Romans.

Text illustration, p. 216

Raphael Holinshed, *Chronicles* (1587). Woodcut, $1\frac{1}{2} \times 6\frac{1}{4}$ *in*. From a copy in the British Museum.

This charming decoration, from the second edition, comes at the head of the Life of Richard II.

INDEX

ABBEY Theatre, Dublin, 186
Achilles Tatius: *Clitophon and Leucippe*, 157
Actes and Monuments of these latter perilous times touching matters of the Church. See Foxe, John
Adlington, William: transl. Apuleius' *The Golden Asse*, 170
Admiral's Men (King's Men), 185
Ægidius: *De Regimine Principum* (Regiment of Princes), 34
Ælfric, 7, 64
Æschylus, 50
Æthelwold, 60
Æthiopica. See Heliodorus
After London. See Jefferies, Richard
Age of Discovery, 81, 89
Albion's England. See Warner, William
Alençon, Duke of, 119
Alexander VI, Pope, 132
Alfred, King, 6–7, 61
Alison, Richard, 141
All's Well that Ends Well, 210
Allegory, 16, 21, 35–6, 41–2, 102, 114–116, 120, 122, 124, 126
Alleyn, Edward, 185–6
Alliteration, 6, 10–13, 16, 55, 101, 121
Alliterative Revival, 10–13
Almond for a Parrat, An, 152
Amerigo Vespucci, 89
Amoretti. See Spenser
Amphitryo. See Plautus
Amyot, Jacques, 170
Ancient Mariner, The. See Coleridge
Ancren Riwle (The Anchoresses' Rule), 8 and n.2, 61
Anelida and Arcite. See Chaucer
Anglo-Saxon Chronicle, The (*The English Chronicle*), 7, 61
Anglo-Saxon dialects. See Dialects
Anglo-Saxon Poetry. See Bone, Gavin
Anglo-Saxon poetry. See Poetry, Early English
Anglo-Saxon versification, 5–6, 55
Anne of Bohemia, 22
Anthologies, Elizabethan, 106–7, 113, 128–9
Antony and Cleopatra, 205–6, 211–12
Apologie for Poetrie, An (*The Defence of Poesie*). See Sidney, Sir Philip
Apron stage, 174
Apuleius: *The Golden Asse*, 170
Arber, Edward, 'English Reprints' series, 165n.

Arcadia. See Sidney, Sir Philip
Arden of Feversham, 193
Ariosto, Ludovico, 123; *Orlando Furioso*, 123; *Gli Suppositi*, 180
Aristotle, 123, 165
Arnold, Matthew, 195
Arte of English Poesie, The. See Puttenham, George
Arte of Rhetorique. See Wilson, Thomas
Arthur, King, 8, 12, 77, 79, 123
Arthurian Legends, 9, 75, 77, 79, 123
Arundel, Countess of, 131
Arundel, Earl of, 83n.
As You Like It, 36, 128, 158, 205, 206–7, 215
Ascension of Christ, The. See Cynewulf
Ascham, Roger, 168; *The Scholemaster*, 168; *Toxophilus*, 168
Astrophel. See Spenser
Astrophel and Stella. See Sidney, Sir Philip
Atalanta in Calydon. See Swinburne
Augustine: St.: *De Civitate Dei*, 88
Authorized Version of the Bible. See Bible
Ayenbyte of Inwyt, The. See Michel of Northgate, Dan
Aylmer, John, 168

BACON, Sir Francis, xiii, 169; *The New Atlantis*, 92
Baldwin, William, 114
Bale, John: *King John*, 58
Ball, John, 17, 84
Ballads, 37, 43–4, 46–7
Bandello, Matteo, 169, 214
Barbour, John: *The Bruce*, 38–9
Barclay, Alexander, 102–3; *The Ship of Fools*, 102
Barnes, Barnabe, 128, 132; *A Divine Centurie of Spirituall Sonnets*, 132; *Parthenophil and Parthenophe*, 132; *The Divils Charter*, 132
Barnfield, Richard, 128–9, 132–3
Bartholomæus Anglicus: *De Proprietatibus Rerum*, 69
Beaufort, Joan, 39
Beaumont, Francis: *The Knight of the Burning Pestle*, 174
Bede: *History Ecclesiastica Gentis Anglorum* (Ecclesiastical History of England), 1, 6–7
Benvenuto Cellini, 86

Beowulf, 3–4, 9, 43
Beowulf MS., 2
Berkeley, Lord, 69
Berners, Lord (John Bourchier), 84–5; transl. Froissart's *Chronicles*, 84; transl. *Huon of Bordeaux*, 85
Bible, The: Cranmer's, 96; English (Coverdale), 96; Great (Coverdale), 96; Gutenberg, 82; translations of: Aelfric's, 7, 64; Authorized Version, 66, 95–6; Tindale's, 66, 95–6; Wiclif's, 64, 66, 95
Biography, 101*n*.
Black Death, 17
Blackfriars Theatre (Children's Theatre). See also Elizabethan Theatres, 182
Blake, William, 115
Blanche, Duchess, 20–21
Blank verse, 5, 107–8 and *n*. 2, 111, 122, 178, 180, 189–90, 192, 199
Blount, Ed., 213
Boccaccio, Giovanni, 21–2, 25–6, 70, 85, 169, 214; *Il Teseide*, 22; *Il Filostrato*, 22; *Decameron*, 25, 70, 85*n*.; *Olympia*, 85*n*.
Boethius: *Consolation of Philosophy*, 7, 31
Boke of Enydos, The. See Caxton
Boke of Margerie Kempe of Lynn, The. See Kempe, Margery
Boke of Phyllyp Sparowe, The. See Skelton, John
Boke of the Governour, The. See Elyot, Sir Thomas
Boleyn, Anne, 88, 110, 147
Bone, Gavin: *Anglo-Saxon Poetry*, 3*n*.
Book for Boys and Girls, A. See Bunyan
Book of the Duchesse, The. See Chaucer
Bookes of Ayres. See Campion, Thomas
Boswell, James, 75
Bourchier, John. See Berners, Lord
Bowge of Court, The. See Skelton, John
Boy actors, 182–3
Boyle, Elizabeth, 119, 126
Boyle, Sir Richard (Earl of Cork), 119
Bradley, A. C.: *Shakespearean Tragedy*, 211*n*.
Breton, Nicholas, 129; *A Mad World my Masters*, 129; *The Passionate Shepheard*, 129
Breton lays, 9
Bridges, Dr. John (Dean of Salisbury), 150, 179; *Defence of the Government established in the Church of England for Ecclesiastical Matters*, 150
Britannia. See Camden, William
Browne, Sir Thomas, xiv
Browning, Robert, 115
Bruce, The. See Barbour, John
Brut. See Layamon
Bryan, Sir Francis, 107

Bunyan, John, xii, xiv, 17, 80: *A Book for Boys and Girls*, 142–3; *The Pilgrim's Progress*, xii
Burbage, Cuthbert, 184–5
Burbage, James, 184–5
Burbage, Richard, 185–6
Burgundy, Duchess of, 83
Burns, Robert, 38
Burton, Robert: *Anatomy of Melancholy*, xv
Butler, Samuel: *Erewhon*, 92
Byrd, William, 139

Cabot, John, 171
Cabot, Sebastian, 171
Cade, Jack, 114
Cædmon: *Cædmon's Hymn*, 1–2, 5; Cædmon MS., 2
Cambyses. See Preston, Thomas
Camden, William: *Britannia*, 170
Campaspe. See Lyly, John
Campion, Thomas, 141–2; *Bookes of Ayres*, 141; *A New Way of Making Four Parts in Counterpoint*, 141; *Observations in the Art of English Poesie*, 141
Canterbury Tales, The. See Chaucer
Capell, Edward, 195*n*.
Carde of Fancie, The. See Greene, Robert
Carew, Thomas, 141
Carey, R., 123
Carols, 37, 43–4, 46–7
Case is Altered, The. See Jonson, Ben
Castel of Helth, The. See Elyot, Sir Thomas
Castiglione, Baldassare: *The Courtier*, 154
Cavendish, George: *Life of Wolsey*, 101*n*.
Caxton, William, 70, 75–9, 82–3 and *n*., 84, 97 and *n*.; *Morte Darthur*. See Malory, Sir Thomas; *The Boke of Enydos*, 97; *The Game and Playe of the Chesse*, 83; *The Golden Legend*, 70, 83; *The Recuyell of the Historyes of Troye*, 83
Chambers, Sir E. K.: *English Literature at the Close of the Middle Ages*, 77*n*.; *Sources for a Biography of Shakespeare*, 196*n*., 198*n*.; *William Shakespeare: A Study of Facts and Problems*, 196*n*., 198*n*., 199; ed. *The Oxford Book of Sixteenth Century Verse*, 106*n*.
Chambers, R. W., 59, 63, 92; *On the Continuity of English Prose*, 8 *n*.1, 59–60, 92
Characterization: in Chaucer, 18, 23, 30–31; in Elizabethan novels, 157, 160; in Elizabethan drama, 174, 187–8; in Shakespeare, 199–200, 204

Chaucer, Geoffrey, 3, 7, 9–10, 17–36, 38, 40–1, 44, 70, 83, 98, 110, 115–16, 126, 167; *A Complaint to His Purse*, 20; *A Complaint to His Lady*, 31; *A Treatise on the Astrolabe*, 28, 32; *Anelida and Arcite*, 22; *Le Roman de la Rose*, 10, 20, 31; *The Book of the Duchesse*, 20; *The Canterbury Tales*, 3, 19–20, 25–6, 31, 83; *Prologue*, 20, 25–6, 28–31; *The Knight's Tale*, 9, 22; *The Parson's Tale*, 61; *The Tale of Melibeus*, 28; *The Tale of Sir Topas*, 26–7, 55–6; *The Wife of Bath's Tale*, 26, 30, 48; *The Hous of Fame*, 21; *The Legend of Good Women*, 24–6; *The Parlement of Foules*, 21–2; *Troilus and Criseyde*, 22–3, 31–2, 210

Chaucer, John, 19

Chaucer, Philippa, 19

Chaucerian verse, 31, 35, 40–1, 101, 103

Chaucerians, 33, 36, 116; *English*, 32, 34–5; *Scottish*, 32, 38–41

Chester Plays, 51, 55–6

Chettle, Henry: *Kind-Harts Dreame*, 152

Children of the Chapel, The, 182–3

Children of St. Paul's, The, 182–3

Choice of Emblemes, A. See Whitney, Geoffrey

Chronicles of England, Scotlande, and Irelande. See Holinshed, Ralph

Churchyard, Thomas, 107

Civill Warres, The. See Daniel, Samuel

Clanvowe, Sir Thomas: *The Cuckoo and the Nightingale*, 36

Clarence, Lionel, Duke of, 19

Classical drama. *See* Drama

Classical metres. *See* Harvey, Gabriel

Cleanness (or *Purity*), 11–12

Clitophon and Leucippe. See Achilles Tatius

Cloud of Unknowing, 72

Cocktail Party, The. See Eliot, T. S.

Coleridge, Samuel Taylor: *The Ancient Mariner*, 121

Colet, John, 86–7

Colin Clout. See Skelton, John

Colin Clouts Come Home Again. See Spenser

Collection of Emblemes, A. See Wither, George

Colloquies. See Erasmus

Columbus, Christopher, 81, 89

Comedy of Errors, The, 168, 200

Complaint to his Purse, A. See Chaucer, Geoffrey

Complaint of the Black Knight, The. See Lydgate, John

'Complaynt of Henry, Duke of Buckingham.' *See* Sackville, Thomas

Condell, Henry, 213

Confessio Amantis. See Gower, John

Congreve, William, xiv

Consolation of Philosophy. See Boethius

Constable, Henry, 128, 132; *Diana*, 132; *In certaine sweete Sonnets*, 132; *The praises of his Mistress*, 132

Continuity of English Prose, On the. See Chambers, R. W.

Coriolanus, 205, 211–12

Courtier, The. See Castiglione, Baldassare

Courtly Love, 9–10

Coventry Plays, 51, 53

Coverdale, Miles, 96. *See also* Bible, The

Cowden Clarke, Charles, 195

Cowden Clarke, Mary: *Shakespeare Concordance*, 195

Cranmer, Thomas, 96. *See also* Bible, The, and English Prayer Book, The

Crystal Age, The. See Hudson, W. H.

Cuckoo and the Nightingale, The. See Clanvowe, Sir Thomas

Curtain, The. *See* Elizabethan Theatres

Cymbeline, story of, 8; *Cymbeline*, 170, 212, 214

Cynewulf, 2, 4; *The Ascension of Christ*, 4; *The Legend of St. Juliana*, 4; *Elene*, 4; *The Fates of the Apostles*, 4

Cynthia. See Ralegh, Sir Walter

Dance of the Sevin Deidly Synnis, The. See Dunbar, William

Daniel, Samuel, 130, 133, 137–8; *Delia*, 137; *The Civill Warres*, 137–8

Dante, 21–22, 85; *The Divine Comedy*, 31

Daphnis and Chloe. See Longus

Davenant, Sir William, 197

De Civitate Dei. See Augustine, St.

De Proprietatibus Rerum, 69

De Regimine Principum, 34

Decameron. See Boccaccio

Defence of Conny-Catching, The. See Greene, Robert

Defence of the Government established in the Church of England for Ecclesiastical Matters. See Bridges, Dr. John

Defoe, Daniel, 159–60; *The Shortest Way with the Dissenters*, 146

Dekker, Thomas, 128, 160; *The Shoemaker's Holiday*, 160, 193–4

Delia. See Daniel, Samuel

Deloney, Thomas, 154, 160–2; *Jacke of Newberie*, 154, 160–2 *and n.*; *The Gentle Craft*, 160, 194; *Thomas of Reading*, 160–1 *and n.*

Deor's Complaint, 3

Devotional writings, 61

Dial of Princes, The. See Guevara, Antonio de

Dialects, *Anglo-Saxon*: Northumbrian, 1–2, 5; West Saxon, 2, 5–6; *Middle English*: East Midland, 2, 18; Kentish, 61; South-East Midland, 68; Surrey, 10; West Midland, 11; Yorkshire, 63
Diana. See Constable, Henry
Dickens, Charles, xiv, 55
Dictionary of Syr T. Eliot, The. See Elyot, Sir Thomas
Discourse of English Poetrie, A. See Webbe, William
Disputation between a He Conny-Catcher and a She Conny-Catcher, A. See Greene, Robert
Divils Charter, The. See Barnes, Barnabe
Divine Centurie of Spirituall Sonnets, A. See Barnes, Barnabe
Divine Comedy, The. See Dante
Donet, The. See Pecock, Reginald
Donne, John, xiv–xv, 115, 141
Douglas, Gavin, 32, 41; *King Hart*, 41; *The Palice of Honour*, 41; transl. Virgil's *Æneid*, 41
Drake, Sir Francis, 171
Drama, 49–50: classical, 48–50, 102, 173, 177–9, 184; Elizabethan (Tudor), 100, 105, 128, 169, 172–94; Elizabethan comedies, 178–80; Elizabethan tragedies, 109, 177–80; Medieval, 49, 53–6, 173–4, 179; Religious (liturgical), 48, 50–1; Secular, 51, 58
Drayton, Michael, 129–30, 133, 138–9; *Idea*, 139; *Poly-Olbion*, 138; *The Shepheards Garland*, 138
Dream device, 10, 15, 20–1, 41–2
Dreme, The. See Lyndsay, Sir David
Dryden, John, 9, 115
Dunbar, William, 32, 41–2; *The Dance of the Sevin Deidly Synnis*, 42; *The Flyting of Dunbar and Kennedie*, 42; *The Goldin Terge*, 42; *The Lament for the Makaris*, 41–2; *The Thrissil and the Rose*, 42; *The Twa Maryit Women and the Wedo*, 42; *To the Merchantis of Edinburgh*, 42
Dynasts, The. See Hardy, Thomas

E.K., 126 *and n*.
Earl of Leicester's Men, 185
Earl of Pembroke's Men, 185
Early English Poetry. See Poetry
Education or Bringinge up of Children, The. See Elyot, Sir Thomas
Edward the Confessor, 7
Edward II. See Marlowe
Edward III, King, 19
Edward IV, King, 77, 114

Edward VI, King, 96
Elene. See Cynewulf
Eliot, T. S., 4, 108 *n*.2
Elizabeth I, Queen, 105, 107, 119, 123, 126, 133–4, 136, 147–8, 169, 178, 182–3, 203, 209
Elizabethan Age, The, 145, 163
Elizabethan chronicles, 105, 170
Elizabethan drama. See Drama
Elizabethan literary criticism, 162–9
Elizabethan novels, 105, 128, 153–62
Elizabethan pamphlets, 105, 146–53
Elizabethan poetry. See Poetry
Elizabethan prose. See Prose
Elizabethan theatres, 174–5, 182, 184–5; The Blackfriars, 184–5, 198; The Curtain, 184; The Fortune, 184, 186; The Globe, 184–5, 198; The Hope, 186; The Rose, 184, 186; The Swan, 184; The Theatre, 184
Elizabethan translations. See Translations
Elyot, Sir Thomas, 93–4; *The Boke of the Governour*, 94; *The Castel of Helth*, 93; *The Dictionary of Syr T. Eliot*, 94; *The Education or Bringinge up of Children*, 94; *The Rules of a Christian Lyfe*, 94
Emblem books, 142–3
Emblemes. See Quarles, Francis
Endimion: The Man in the Moone. See Lyly, John
England's Helicon, 128 *and n*., 129, 134
English Prayer Book, The, 96, 171
Epic, the, 4, 43, 47, 138
Epithalamion. See Spenser
Erasmus, Desiderius, 86–9, 93, 159; *The Praise of Folly*, 87; *Colloquies*, 87
Erewhon. See Butler, Samuel
Essay on the Dramatic Character of Sir John Falstaff. See Morgann, Maurice
Essex, Earl of, 203
Euphues and his England; *Euphues the Anatomy of Wit*. See Lyly, John
Euphuism, 154–5, 158, 164–5, 169, 180
Euripides, 177
Eve of St. Agnes. See Keats, John
Everyman, 58
Exeter Book, The, 2

Faerie Queene, The. See Spenser
Falls of Princes, The. See Lydgate, John
Fates of the Apostles, The. See Cynewulf
Ferrers, George, 114
First Blast of the Trumpet against the monstrous Regiment of Women, The. See Knox, John
Fish, Simon, 147–8; *A Supplicacyon for the Beggars*, 147–8

Fisher, John, 88
Fitton, Mary, 215
Fleming, Richard, 65
Fletcher, John, 213; *The Knight of the Burning Pestle*, 174; *The Two Noble Kinsmen*, 9
Florio, John: transl. Montaigne's *Essays*, 170
Flower and the Leaf, The, 36
Flyting of Dunbar and Kennedie, The. *See* Dunbar, William
Ford, John, 177
Form of Perfect Living. *See* Rolle, Richard
Fortescue, Sir John: *On the Governance of England*, 70–1
Fortune, The. *See* Elizabethan theatres
Four Elements, The. *See* Rastell, John
Four P.P., The. *See* Heywood, John
Foxe, John: *Actes and Monuments*, 170
Free verse, 5, 108 *and n.*2
Friar Bacon and Friar Bungay. *See* Greene, Robert
Frobisher, Sir Martin, 171
Froissart, Jean, 20, 83; *Chronicles: See* Berners, Lord
Fulgens and Lucrece. *See* Medwall, Henry

GALEN, 93
Game and Playe of the Chesse, The. *See* Caxton
Gammer Gurton's Needle, 178–9
Garland of Laurel, The. *See* Skelton, John
Gascoigne, George, 180; *Supposes*, 180; *Jocasta*, 180
Gentle Craft, The. *See* Deloney, Thomas
Geoffrey of Monmouth: *Historia Regum Britanniæ*, 7–8, 178
George-a-Greene, The Pinner of Wakefield. *See* Greene, Robert
Gesta Romanorum, 69–70
Geste des Bretons. *See* Wace
Gilbert, Sir Humphrey, 171
Gli Suppositi. *See* Ariosto
Globe, The. *See* Elizabethan theatres
Godwin, William: *Political Justice*, xv
Goethe, Johann Wolfgang, 190
Golden Asse, The. *See* Apuleius
Golden Legend, The (*Legenda Aurea*), 70, 83
Goldin Terge, The. *See* Dunbar, William
Gorboduc. *See* Norton, Thomas *and* Sackville, Thomas
Gorgious Galley of Gallant Inventions, A, 113
Gosson, Stephen: *The Schoole of Abuse*, 164–5, 167

Gower, John, 32–3, 70, 167; *Speculum Meditantis* (*Mirour de l'Omme*), 33; *Vox Clamantis*, 33; *Confessio Amantis*, 33–4 *and n.*, 83
Gray, Thomas, 115
Greek prose fiction, 157
Greek tragedy. *See* Drama, Classical
Greene, Robert, 86, 128, 152–3, 156–7, 192–3, 197; *A Disputation between a He Conny-Catcher and a She Conny-Catcher*, 153; *A Looking-Glass for London and England*, 193; *A Notable Discovery of Cozenage*, 153; *Friar Bacon and Friar Bungay*, 192–3; *George-a-Greene, The Pinner of Wakefield*, 193; *Greenes Groatsworth of Wit*, 152–3; *James the Fourth*, 193; *Menaphon*, 156–7; *Pandosto*, 156, 215; *The Carde of Fancie*, 156–7; *The Defence of Conny-Catching*, 153
Greville, Fulke: *The Tragical Historye of Romeus and Juliet*, 169
Grey, Lady Jane, 168
Grey de Wilton, Lord, 119
Grimald, Nicholas, 107
Groats-worth of Wit, Greenes. *See* Greene, Robert
Grocyn, William, 86–8
Guevara, Antonio de: *The Dial of Princes*, 154
Guild Cycles. *See* Chester, Coventry, Wakefield, and York Plays
Guilds, 51–3, 54*n.*, 173
Guillaume de Loris: *Le Roman de la Rose*, 9–10
Guillaume de Machault, 20, 31
Gutenberg, Johann Gensfleisch zum, 82

HAKLUYT, Richard, 171; *Principall Navigations, Voiages, and Discoveries of the English Nation*, 171
Hamlet, xiii, 101, 191, 196, 207 *and n.*, 208–9, 214
Hanmer, Sir Thomas, 195*n*.
Hardy, Thomas, 115; *The Dynasts*, 179
Harpsfield, Nicholas: *Life of Sir Thomas More*, 59, 101*n*.
Harrington, Sir John, 123
Harvey, Gabriel, xiii, 118–19, 124, 167
Hastings, Lord, 93
Hathwey (Hathaway), Anne, 197
Hawes, Stephen, 32, 35–6: *The Passtyme of Pleasure*, 36
Hawkins, Sir John, 171
Hazlitt, William, 211
Hekatompathia, The, or Passionate Centurie of Love. *See* Watson, Thomas
Heliodorus: *Æthiopica*, 157

Heminges (Heming), John, 213
Henry IV, King, 20
Henry IV, 168, 204
Henry V, King, 34, 77
Henry V, 150, 205
Henry VI, King, 114
Henry VI, 153, 197–9
Henry VII, King, 35
Henry VIII, King, 84, 86, 88, 94–7, 100, 102, 110, 147
Henry VIII, 101n., 213
Henry the Minstrel (Blind Harry), 32, 39; *Wallace*, 39
Henryson, Robert, 32, 40; *Orpheus and Eurydice*, 40; *The Testament of Crisseid*, 40
Henslowe, Philip, 186; *Henslowe Papers*, 186n.; *Henslowe's Diary*, 186n.
Herbert, George, 115, 143
Hero and Leander. See Marlowe
Herodotus, 169
Heroic couplets, 31, 36
Heywood, John, 107, 175, 177; *The Four P.P.*, 175, 177
Hieroglyphikes of the Life of Man. See Quarles, Francis
Higden, Ranulf: *Polychronicon*, 69
Hilton, Walter, 66, 72; *Scala Perfectionis*, 66
Historia Ecclesiastica Gentis Anglorum (Ecclesiastical History of England). *See* Bede
Historia Regum Britanniæ. See Geoffrey of Monmouth
History of the Twelve Cæsars. See Suetonius
History of the World. See Ralegh, Sir Walter
Hoby, Sir Thomas, 154
Hoccleve (Occleve), Thomas, 32, 34; *La Male Règle*, 34
Holbein, Hans, 88
Holinshed, Ralph: *Chronicles of England, Scotlande, and Irelande*, 170, 214
Holland, Philemon, 170
Homer, 43, 123
Hooker, Richard: *Of the Laws of Ecclesiastical Polity*, 170–1
Hope, The. *See* Elizabethan theatres
Horace, 177
Hous of Fame, The. See Chaucer
Howard, Henry. *See* Surrey, Earl of
Hudson, W. H.: *The Crystal Age*, 92
Humanism, 86 and n., 94
Humphrey, Duke of Buckingham, 76
Hundredth good pointes of husbandrie. See Tusser, Thomas
Huon of Bordeaux. See Berners, Lord
Huxley, Aldous, 31
Hythloday, Raphael, 89–91

Idea. See Drayton, Michael
Idylls. See Theocritus
Il Filostrato. See Boccaccio
Il Teseide. See Boccaccio
In certaine sweete Sonnets. See Constable, Henry
Interludes, 54, 58, 100, 103, 175
Ireland, Spenser in, 119–120, 122, 135

JAGGARD, Isaac, 213
James I, King, 105, 134
James I of Scotland, King, 31–2, 39–40; *The Kingis Quair*, 31, 40
James IV of Scotland, King, 42
James the Fourth. See Greene, Robert
James V of Scotland, King, 103
James, Henry, xiv, 155
Jean de Meung: *Le Roman de la Rose*, 9–10
Jean d'Outremeuse, 67; *Mandeville's Travels*, 67–9; *Miroir des Histoires*, 67
Jefferies, Richard: *After London*, 92
Jerusalem Delivered (Gerusalemme Liberata). See Tasso
Jew of Malta, The. See Marlowe
Jocasta. See Gascoigne, George
John, King, 147
John of Gaunt, 19–20
John of Guildford: *The Owl and the Nightingale*, 10 and n.
Johnson, Samuel, 139, 195n., 209
Jolly Rutterkin. See Skelton, John
Jones, Robert, 141
Jonson, Ben, 105, 128, 138, 141, 179, 186, 189, 191; *The Case is Altered*, 129
Joyce, James, 159
Juliana of Norwich, Dame, 71–3; *XVI Revelations of Divine Love*, 72
Julius Cæsar, 205

KEATS, John, 36, 115, 121, 195; *Eve of St. Agnes, The*, 121
Kempe of Lynn, Margery, 72–4; *The Boke of*, 73–4
Ker, W. P.: *Medieval English Literature*, 34n.
Kind-Harts Dreame. See Chettle, Henry
King Hart. See Douglas, Gavin
King John. See Bale, John
King John (Shakespeare), 168, 204
Kingis Quair, The. See James I of Scotland
Kirby, Margaret, 62
Kirk, Edward, 126
Knight of the Burning Pestle, The. See Beaumont, Francis, *and* Fletcher, John
Knox, John: *The First Blast of the Trumpet against the monstrous Regiment of Women*, 148–9

Kyd, Thomas, 177, 186, 191–2, 209;
    The Spanish Tragedy, 187, 191–2

La Belle Dame Sans Merci. See Ros, Sir
    Richard
La Male Règle. See Hoccleve, Thomas
Lament for the Makaris, The. See Dunbar,
    William
Langland, William, 14–19, 33, 86;
    Vision concerning Piers Plowman, The,
    13–16 and *n*., 17–18, 47, 81
Latimer, Hugh, 94–5;*On the Card*, 95;
    Of the Ploughers, 95
Latin classical comedy. See Drama,
    Classical
Layamon: *Brut*, 7–8
Lays, 43, 47
Lear, story of, 8, 70; *Lear, King*, 170,
    196, 211, 214
Lee, Sir Sidney: *Life of Shakespeare*,
    215*n*.
Legend of Good Women, The. See Chaucer
Legend of St. Juliana, The. See Cynewulf
Leicester, Earl of, 118–19, 136, 184
Leonardo da Vinci, 86
Linacre, Thomas, 86–8
Lionel, Duke of Clarence, 19
Lives of the Noble Greeks and Romans. See
    Plutarch
Livy, 169–70
Lodge, Thomas, 128, 154, 157–8, 160;
    A Defence of Poetrie, 167; *Rosalynde*:
    Euphues Golden Legacie, 128, 157–8,
    215
Lollards, 65–6, 70
Lombard, Peter, 63
London Lickpenny. See Lydgate, John
Longus: *Daphnis and Chloe*, 157
Looking-Glass for London and England, A.
    See Greene, Robert
Lord Chamberlain's Men, 185, 203
Lord Strange's Men, 185, 197
Lorens, Friar: *Somme des Vices et des
    Virtues*, 61
Love Labours Wonne, 168
*Lover Comforteth Himself with the Worthi-
    ness of his Love, The*. See Surrey, Earl
    of
Love's Labour's Lost, 112, 168, 201
Lucrece (Shakespeare), 197–8
Lucy, Sir Thomas, 197
Lullay, Lullay, Like a Child. See Skelton,
    John
Lydgate, John, 32, 34–6, 167; *London
    Lickpenny*, 35; *The Complaint of the
    Black Knight*, 35; *The Falls of Princes*,
    xv, 35, 114; *The Pilgrimage of the Life
    of Man*, 35; *The Story of Thebes*, 35;
    The Troy Book, 35

Lyly, John, 84, 128, 150, 152, 154–7,
    160, 164–5, 169, 180, 182–4; *Campaspe*
    182–3; *Endimion: The Man in the
    Moon*, 180, 182–4; *Euphues the
    Anatomy of Wit*; *Euphues and his Eng-
    land*, xv, 84, 146, 154–6, 164
Lyndsay, Sir David, 102–4 and *n*.;
    *Ane Publict Confessioun of the Kingis
    auld Hound callit Bagsche*, 103; *Ane
    Supplicatioun agains Syde Taillis*, 103;
    The Dreme, 103; *The Satire of the
    Three Estates (Ane Pleasant Satire of the
    Thrie Estaitis in Commendatioun of
    Vertew and Vituperatioun of Vyce)*, 97,
    103–4; *The Testament and Complaynt of
    our Soverane Lordis Papyngo*, 103
Lyric poetry. See Poetry
Lytell Geste of Robin Hood, A, 47

Macbeth, 109, 170, 211, 214
Macpherson, James: *Ossian*, xv
Mad World my Masters, A. See Breton,
    Nicholas
Madrigal verse, 141*n*.
Magnificence (Magnyfycence). See Skelton,
    John
Mallock, W. H.: *The New Republic*, 92
Malone, Edmond, 195*n*.
Malory, Sir Thomas, 75–80, 156: *Morte
    Darthur*, 75 and *n*., 76–9, 83; Win-
    chester manuscript of, 75, 77
Mandeville, Sir John, 67
Mandeville's Travels. See Jean D'Outre-
    meuse
Mannerly Margery Milk and Ale: See
    Skelton, John
Mare, Walter de la, xiv
Margaret of Navarre, 169
Margaret Tudor, 42
Marlowe, Christopher, 86, 105, 107,
    134, 152, 177, 186–91, 196, 199;
    Edward II, 191, 199; *Hero and Leander*,
    191, 199; *Tamburlaine*, 186–90; *The
    Jew of Malta*, 186, 189–90; *The
    Massacre at Paris*, 191; *The Tragedy of
    Dido, Queen of Carthage*, 191; *The
    Tragical History of Dr. Faustus*, 186,
    189–90
Marprelate Controversy, 149–52, 179
Marston, John, 177
Martin Marprelate. See Marprelate
    Controversy
Mary I, Queen, 95–6, 148–9, 168
Mary Magdalen, 56
Mary, Queen of Scots, 124, 130, 184
Masques, 141, 182
Massacre at Paris, The. See Marlowe
Matter of Britain, the, 9
Matter of France, the, 9

Matter of Rome the Great, the, 9, 18
Measure for Measure, 210–11
Medieval drama. *See* Drama
Medwall, Henry: *Fulgens and Lucrece*, 58, 175–6
Menæchmi. See Plautus
Menaphon. See Greene, Robert
Merchant of Venice, The, 70, 168, 204
Merchant Taylors' School, 117, 191
Meres, Francis: *Palladis Tamia*, 106, 168, 197–8
Merry Wives of Windsor, The, 30, 209
Metaphysical literature, 112
Metaphysical poetry. *See* Poetry
Michel of Northgate, Dan: *The Ayenbyte of Inwyt*, 61
Michelangelo, 86
Middle English poetry. *See* Poetry
Midsummer Night's Dream, A, 168, 173, 180, 203, 214
Milton, xiv, 107, 108 *n*.2, 115; *Paradise Lost*, 1; *Comus*, 182, 193
Minerva Britanna. See Peacham, Henry
Minstrelsy of the Scottish Border. See Scott, Sir Walter
Miracle plays, 48, 53–4, 56*n*., 58, 61, 173–4
Mirror for Magistrates, A, 114–15
Mr. W. H. *See* Shakespeare, *Sonnets*
Modern Utopia, A. See Wells, H. G.
Montaigne, Michel: *Essays*, 170
Morality plays, 53–4, 58, 100, 103, 173–5, 188
More, Sir Thomas, 58, 86–8 *and n.*, 89–93, 101*n.*, 106, 159, 175; *Utopia*, 87–88 *and n.*, 89–91 *and n.*, 92, 147; *The History of King Richard III*, 92–3; *The Supplication of Souls*, 147; *Life of Sir Thomas: See* Harpsfield, Nicholas
Morgann, Maurice: *Essay on the Dramatic Character of Sir John Falstaff*, 204
Morris, William, 3; *News from Nowhere*, 92
Morte Arthure, 77
Morte Darthur. See Malory, Sir Thomas
Morton, Cardinal, 88, 92–3, 175
Mountjoy, Lord, 87
Much Ado About Nothing, 205
Muiopotmos. See Spenser
Mulcaster, Richard, 117, 126*n*.
Munday, Anthony, 128–30
Mysteries. See Miracle Plays *and* Morality Plays

Narrenschiff. See Brandt, Sebastian
Nashe, Thomas, 86, 128, 150, 152, 154, 158–60; *The Unfortunate Traveller, or The Life of Jacke Wilton*, 153, 158–9 and *n.*, 160

Nennius, 8
New Atlantis, The. See Bacon
New Republic, The. See Mallock, W. H.
New Way of Making Four Parts in Counterpoint, A. See Campion, Thomas
News from Nowhere. See Morris, William
Nicholas of Guildford: *The Owl and the Nightingale*, 10 and *n.*
Nicholas of Hereford, 66
Nominalists, 64
Norman Conquest, 2, 7–8, 60
Norman-French language, 2, 59–61
North, Sir Thomas: transl. *Plutarch's Lives*, 170, 214; transl. *The Dial of Princes*, 154
Northumbria, 2, 6
Northumbrian centres of learning, 6
Norton, Thomas: *Gorboduc*, 114, 166–7, 177–8, 180, 187
Notable Discovery of Cozenage, A. See Greene, Robert
Nun's Rule, The. See Morton, James
Nut Brown Maid, The, 37

Observations in the Art of English Poesie. See Campion, Thomas
Of the Laws of Ecclesiastical Polity. See Hooker, Richard
Of the Ploughers. See Latimer, Hugh
Oh read over Dr. John Bridges, for it is a worthy worke (The Epistle), 150
Old Wives' Tale, The. See Peele, George
On the Card. See Latimer, Hugh
On the Governance of England. See Fortescue, Sir John
Orlando Furioso. See Ariosto
Orm (or Ormin): *Ormulum*, 8
Orpheus and Eurydice. See Henryson, Robert
Osborne, Dorothy, 71
Ossian. See Macpherson, James
Othello, 211
Ovid, 20, 215
Owl and the Nightingale, The, 10 and *n.*

PAGEANT (travelling stage), 52 and *n.*, 174
Painter, William, 169–70; *Palace of Pleasure*, 169
Palace of Pleasure. See Painter, William
Palice of Honour, The. See Douglas, Gavin
Palladis Tamia. See Meres, Francis
Pandosto. See Greene, Robert
Pappe with an Hatchet, 152
Paradise Lost. See Milton
Paradyse of Daynty Devises, The, 113
Parlement of Foules, The. See Chaucer

Parthenophil and Parthenophe. See Barnes, Barnabe

Passionate Pilgrim, The, 133

Passionate Shepheard, The. See Breton, Nicholas

Passtyme of Pleasure, The. See Hawes, Stephen

Paston Letters, The, 71

Pastoral convention in poetry and prose, 128

Pastoral poetry. *See* Poetry

Pastoral romance, 154, 157–8, 160

Patience, 11–12

Peacham, Henry: *Minerva Britanna,* 142–3

Pearl, 10 and n.2, 12, 18, 85n.

Peasants' Revolt, The, 17, 33, 65, 81, 84

Pecock, Reginald, 70–1; *The Repressor of overmuch blaming of the clergy,* 70; *The Donet,* 70

Peele, George, 128, 193; *The Old Wives' Tale,* 193

Pembroke, Countess of, 158

Percy, Thomas: *Reliques of Ancient English Poetry,* 47

Pericles, Prince of Tyre, 212–13

Peterborough Chronicle, The, 61

Petite Pallace of Pettie his Pleasure, A. See Pettie, George

Petrarch, 22, 85, 130

Petrarchan sonnet. *See* Sonnets

Pettie, George: *A Petite Pallace of Pettie his Pleasure,* 169–70 and n.

Piers Plowman: The Vision concerning. See Langland, William

Pilgrim's Progress, The. See Bunyan

Pilgrimage of the Life of Man, The. See Lydgate, John

Plato, 89, 117

Platonism, 117

Plautus, 49, 177–8: *Amphitryo,* 200; *Menæchmi,* 200

Pliny, 157, 165, 170

Plutarch: *Lives of the Noble Greeks and Romans,* 170, 214; *Morals,* 170

Poems Against Garnesche. See Skelton, John

Poetry: Early English, 1–3, 8–9; Elizabethan, 105–46, 162, 165–7, 169; Lyric, 37–8, 46, 108–9, 128, 142; Metaphysical, 132, 142–3; Middle English, 10–13; Pastoral, 124, 128–9, 134; Popular, 45–7; Renaissance, 106–7. *See also* Verse Forms

Political Justice. See Godwin, William

Poly-Olbion. See Drayton, Michael

Polychronicon. See Higden, Ranulf *and* Trevisa, John

Poor Preachers, the, 65

Pope, Alexander, 115, 195n.

Praise of Folly, The. See Erasmus

Praises of his Distress, The. See Constable, Henry

Preston, Thomas: *Cambises,* 180–1

Prick of Conscience. See Rolle, Richard

Principall Navigations, Voiages, and Discoveries of the English Nation. See Hakluyt, Richard

Printing, invention of, 81–2

Prose: Continuity of English, 59–61; Elizabethan, 84, 144–71; Didactic, 93

Prosopopoia (Mother Hubberds Tale). See Spenser

Prothalamion. See Spenser

Publict Confessioun of the Kingis auld Hound callit Bagsche, Ane. See Lyndsay, Sir David

Purcell, Henry, 139

Puritanism, 3, 117, 150, 163, 165

Puttenham, George: *The Arte of English Poesie,* 164

Quarles, Francis: *Emblemes,* 142; *Hieroglyphikes of the Life of Man,* 142

Queen Elizabeth's Men, 185

Quia Amore Langueo, 38 and n.

Rabelais, François, 159

Ralegh, Sir Walter, 106, 122–3, 126, 129, 133–6, 171; *Cynthia,* 136; *History of the World,* 134

Ralph Roister Doister. See Udall, Nicholas

Rastell, Elizabeth, 175

Rastell, John: *The Four Elements,* 58

Rastell, William, 175

Realists, 64

Recuyell of the Historyes of Troye, The. See Caxton, William

Reformation, The, 81, 86, 147

Religious (Liturgical) drama. *See* Drama

Reliques of Ancient English Poetry. See Percy, Thomas

Renaissance, 36, 81, 85–7, 96, 107, 120–2, 128, 160, 162, 187

Renaissance, the English, 86–7

Renaissance poetry. *See* Poetry

Repressor of overmuch blaming of the clergy, The. See Pecock, Reginald

Republic, The. See Plato

Restoration, the, 172

Revelations of Divine Love, XVI. See Juliana of Norwich

Revival of Learning, the, 81, 85, 87, 89, 93

Rhyme-Royal, 31, 34, 35, 40, 101–2, 114

Rhyming couplets, 31, 56, 101, 107–8, 111, 138, 177
Rich, Lady Penelope, 137, 184
Richard II, King, 19–20, 22, 33, 114
Richard II, 168, 202 and *n*., 203, 211
Richard III, King, 92
Richard III, The History of King. See More, Sir Thomas
Richard III, 168, 177, 199–200
Richardson, Samuel, 157
Robin Hood, 47
Robin Hood, A Lytell Geste of, 47
Robynson, Ralph: transl. *Utopia*, 87–9, 91*n*.
Roet, Sir Payne, 19
Rogers of Chester, Archdeacon, 52
Rolle, Richard, 62–4, 65, 72; *Prick of Conscience*, 62; *The Form of Perfect Living*, 62
Roman de la Rose, Le. See Chaucer
Romance literature, 7
Romeo and Juliet, 157, 168–9, 201–2, 212
Ronsard, Pierre de, 130
Roper, William, 88, 101*n*.
Ros, Sir Richard: *La Belle Dame Sans Merci*, 36
Rosalynde: Euphues Golden Legacie. See Lodge, Thomas
Rose, The. See Elizabethan theatres
Rowe, Nicholas, 195*n*.
Ruin, The, 2
Rules of a Christian lyfe, The. See Elyot, Sir Thomas

SACKVILLE, Thomas (Earl of Dorset), 114–15; *Gorboduc*, 114, 166–7, 177–8, 180, 187; *Induction to A Mirror for Magistrates*, 114–15; 'The Complaynt of Henry, Duke of Buckingham,' 114
Saint Peters Complaint. See Southwell, Robert
Salthowes, 73
Satire of the Three Estates, The. See Lyndsay, Sir David
Saxo Grammaticus, 208
Scala Perfectionis. See Hilton, Walter
Scholemaster, The. See Ascham, Roger
Schoole of Abuse, The. See Gosson, Stephen
Scott, Sir Walter, 38; *Minstrelsy of the Scottish Border*, 47
Seafarer, The, 2
Secular drama. See Drama
Seneca, 49, 177–9
Sermo Lupi ad Anglos. See Wulfstan
Seven Virgins, The, 48
Shakespeare, John, 197
Shakespeare, William, xii–xiv, 30, 32,

101*n*., 105, 107, 108 *n*.2, 115, 131*n*., 133, 139, 152, 166–70, 173, 175, 177, 179–80, 184, 189, 195–216; *All's Well that Ends Well*, 210; *Antony and Cleopatra*, 205–6, 211–12; *As You Like It*, 36, 128, 158, 205, 206–7, 215; *Comedy of Errors, The*, 168, 200; *Coriolanus*, 205, 211–12; *Cymbeline*, 170, 212, 214; *Hamlet*, xiii, 101, 191, 196, 207 and *n*., 208–9, 214; *Henry IV*, 168, 204; *Henry V*, 150, 205; *Henry VI*, 153, 197–9; *Henry VIII*, 101*n*., 213; *Julius Cæsar*, 205; *King John*, 168, 204; *King Lear*, 170, 196, 211, 214; *Love's Labour's Lost*, 112, 168, 201; *Lucrece*, 197–8; *Macbeth*, 109, 170, 211, 214; *Measure for Measure*, 210–11; *Merchant of Venice, The*, 70, 168, 204; *Merry Wives of Windsor, The*, 30, 209; *Midsummer Night's Dream, A*, 168, 173, 180, 203, 214; *Much Ado About Nothing*, 205; *Othello*, 211; *Pericles, Prince of Tyre*, 212–13; *Richard II*, 168, 202 and *n*., 203, 211; *Richard III*, 168, 177, 199–200; *Romeo and Juliet*, 157, 168–9, 201–2, 212; *Sonnets*, 107, 130, 168, 198, 215 and *n*., 216; *Taming of the Shrew, The*, 200; *Tempest, The*, 212, 215; *Timon of Athens*, 212; *Titus Andronicus*, 168, 177, 200; *Troilus and Cressida*, 209–10; *Twelfth Night*, 205–7; *Two Gentlemen of Verona, The*, 168, 200–1; *Venus and Adonis*, 131, 197–9; *Winter's Tale, The*, 128, 156, 212, 215
Shakespeare: First Folio, 200*n*., 209*n*., 213; Quartos, 214
Sheepheard Tonie. See Munday, Anthony
Shelley, Percy Bysshe, 115
Shepheardes Calender, The. See Spenser
Shepheards Garland, The. See Drayton, Michael
Ship of Fools, The. See Barclay, Alexander
Shoemaker's Holiday, The. See Dekker, Thomas
Shore, Jane, 92
Shortest Way with the Dissenters, The. See Defoe, Daniel
Sidney, Sir Henry, 136
Sidney, Sir Philip, 118–19, 126, 129, 135–7, 154, 158, 160, 165–7, 172, 184; *An Apologie for Poetrie (The Defence of Poesie)*, 165–7; *Arcadia*, 128, 158; *Astrophel and Stella*, 137
Sir Gawayne and the Grene Knight, 11–12
Sir Launfal, 9
Sir Orfeo (Orpheus), 9

Sir Thomas More, 198
Skeat, W. W., 31
Skelton, John, 97–101 and n., 102, 167; Jolly Rutterkin, 99; Lullay Lullay, Like a Child, 99 ; Magnyfycence, 100–101 and n.; Mannerly Margery Milk and Ale, 99; Poems Against Garnesche, 102; Speak Parrot, 99; Colin Clout, 99; The Boke of Phyllyp Sparowe, 98–9, 102; The Bowge of Court, 99; The Garland of Laurel, 99; The Tunning of Elinor Rumming, 98; Why Come Ye Not to Court, 99; Woefully Arrayed, 99
Skeltonics, 98, 101
Somerset, Edward, Duke of, 107
Somerset, Lady Elizabeth, 127
Somerset, Lady Katherine, 127
Somme des Vices et des Virtues. See Lorens, Friar
Song Books, Elizabethan, 139–42
Song of Roland, The, 9
Sonnets: Petrarchan, 85, 107–8, 111; Elizabethan, 107–8, 111, 122, 130, 132–3, 137, 139, 145
Sonnets, Shakespeare's, 107, 130, 168, 198, 215 and n., 216
Sophocles, 50, 177
Southampton, Earl of (Henry Wriothesley), 215
Southwell, Robert, 128, 130–2; Saint Peters Complaint, 131
Speak Parrot. See Skelton, John
Speculum Meditantis (Mirour de l'Omme). See Gower, John
Spencer, Sir John, 116
Spenser, Edmund, xiii–xiv, 35–6, 41, 98, 115–27, 135, 137, 168; Amoretti, 126; An Hymne of Heavenly Beautie,117; Astrophel, 126; Colin Clouts Come Home Again, 116, 126, 135, 137; Epithalamion, 41, 119, 127; Muiopotmos, 116; Prosopoia (Mother Hubberds Tale), 116, 119, 126; Prothalamion, 116, 127; The Faerie Queene, xiii, 36, 116, 119–124; The Shepheardes Calender, 115, 118, 124–6, 167; The Teares of the Muses, 116; View of the Present State of Ireland, A, 119
Spenser, John, 116
Spenserians, 116
Spenserian stanza, 122, 145
Steevens, George, 195n.
Stevenson, William, 179
Stichomythia, 102
Story of Thebes, The. See Lydgate, John
Stow, John: Survey of London, 170
Straparola, 169
Stratford-on-Avon, 196–9
Straw, Jack, 84
Strode, Ralph, 33

Strolling players, 184
Suetonius: History of the Twelve Cæsars, 170
Sumer is icumen in, 37
Supplicacyon for the Beggers, A. See Fish, Simon
Supplication of Souls, The. See More, Sir Thomas
Supplicatioun: againis Syde Taillis, Ane. See Lyndsay, Sir David
Supposes. See Gascoigne, George
Surrey, Earl of (Henry Howard), 107, 110–13, 159; The Lover Comforteth Himself with the Worthiness of his love, 112–13; transl. Virgil's Æneid, 110–11
Survey of London. See Stow, John
Swan, The. See Elizabethan theatres
'Sweet Themmes runne softly, till I end my Song,' 127
Swift, Jonathan, 30, 159
Swinburne, Algernon Charles, 6, 81
Symbolism, 142

Tamburlaine. See Marlowe
Taming of the Shrew, The, 200
Tasso: Jerusalem Delivered (Gerusalemme Liberata), 123
Teares of Fancie, The. See Watson, Thomas
Teares of the Muses, The. See Spenser
Tempest, The, 212, 215
Tennyson, Alfred, Lord, xiv, 115
Terence, 49, 177–8
Terza rima, 31
Testament and Complaynt of our Soverane Lordis Papyngo. See Lyndsay, Sir David
Testament of Crisseid, The. See Henryson, Robert
Theatre, The. See Elizabethan theatres
Theobald, Lewis, 195n.
Theocritus, 130; Idylls, 128
Thomas of Reading. See Deloney, Thomas
Thorpe, Thomas, 215n.
Thrissil and the Rose, The. See Dunbar, William
Throckmorton, Elizabeth, 133
Timon of Athens, 212
Tindale, William, 95, 146–7; Translation of the Bible, 66, 95–6
Titus Andronicus, 168, 177, 200
To the Merchantis of Edinburgh. See Dunbar, William
Tottel, Richard: Tottel's Miscellany, 107, 113
Tourneur, Cyril, 177
Towneley Plays. See Wakefield Plays

Toxophilus. See Ascham, Roger
Tragedy of Dido, Queen of Carthage, The. See Marlowe
Tragical History of Dr. Faustus, The. See Marlowe
Tragical Historye of Romeus and Juliet, The. See Greville, Fulke
Translations, 69, 81–5; Elizabethan, 105, 169–70; of the Bible: *See* Bible
Treatise on the Astrolabe, A. See Chaucer
Trevisa, John: transl. *De Proprietatibus Rerum*, 69; *Polychronicon*, 69
Troilus and Cressida, 209–10
Troilus and Criseyde. See Chaucer
Troy Book, The. See Lydgate, John
Tunning of Elinor Rumming, The. See Skelton, John
Tusser, Thomas: *Hundredth good pointes of husbandrie*, 113
Twa Maryit Women and the Wedo, The. See Dunbar, William
Twelfth Night, 205–7
Two Gentlemen of Verona, The, 168, 200–1
Two Noble Kinsmen, The. See Fletcher, John
Tyler, Wat, 17, 84

UDALL, Nicholas: *Ralph Roister Doister*, 178–9
Unfortunate Traveller, The. See Nashe, Thomas
University wits, 112
Utopia. See More, Sir Thomas

VAUX, Thomas, Lord, 107
Venus and Adonis (Shakespeare), 131, 197–9
Vercelli Book, the, 2
Verse forms: Anglo-Saxon, 5; Alliterative, 10, 12–13, 16; Chaucerian, 31, 35, 40–1, 101, 103; in Medieval drama, 56. *See also* Blank Verse, Free Verse, Heroic Couplets, Rhyming Couplets, Rhyme-Royal, Skeltonics, Sonnets, Spenserian Stanza, Terza Rima
Villon, 41

Virgil, 85, 123, 130; *Æneid*, 41, 97*n.*, 110–11
Vox Clamantis. See Gower, John

WACE: *Geste des Bretons*, 7
Wakefield (Towneley) Plays, 51, 55
Waldegrave, Robert, 150
Wallace. See Henry the Minstrel
Walsingham, Sir Francis, 136
Walton, Izaak, 171
Wanderer, The, 2
Warburton, William, 195*n.*
Warner, William, 128; *Albion's England*, 130
Watson, Thomas, *The Hekatompathia, or Passionate Centurie of Love*, 130; *The Teares of Fancie, or Love Disdained*, 130
Webbe, William: *A Discourse of English Poetrie*, 130, 167–8
Webster, John, 177, 186
Wells, H. G.: *A Modern Utopia*, 92
Wesley, John, 86
Whitman, Walt, 5, 108 *n.*2
Whitney, Geoffrey: *A Choice of Emblemes*, 142
Why Come Ye Not to Court. See Skelton, John
Wiclif, John, 61, 63–6, 80, 86; Translation of the Bible, 64, 66; Wicliffites, 64–5
Widsith, 2
William of Ockham, 64
William the Conqueror, 59
Williams, Sir Roger, 150
Willoughby, Sir Hugh, 171
Wilson, Thomas, 163–4; *Arte of Rhetorique*, 163–4, 166
Winter's Tale, The, 128, 156, 212, 215
Wither, George: *A Collection of Emblemes*, 142
Woefully Arrayed. See Skelton, John
Wolsey, Cardinal, 97, 99–101 and *n.*, 147
Wolsey, Life of. See Cavendish, George
Wordsworth, William, 28, 115
Wulfstan: *Sermo Lupi ad Anglos*, 7
Wyatt, Sir Thomas, 107–111
Wynkyn de Worde, 47, 72

YORK plays, 51 and *n.*, 53, 54*n.*, 55